IMAGES
of America

LOST BAY CITY

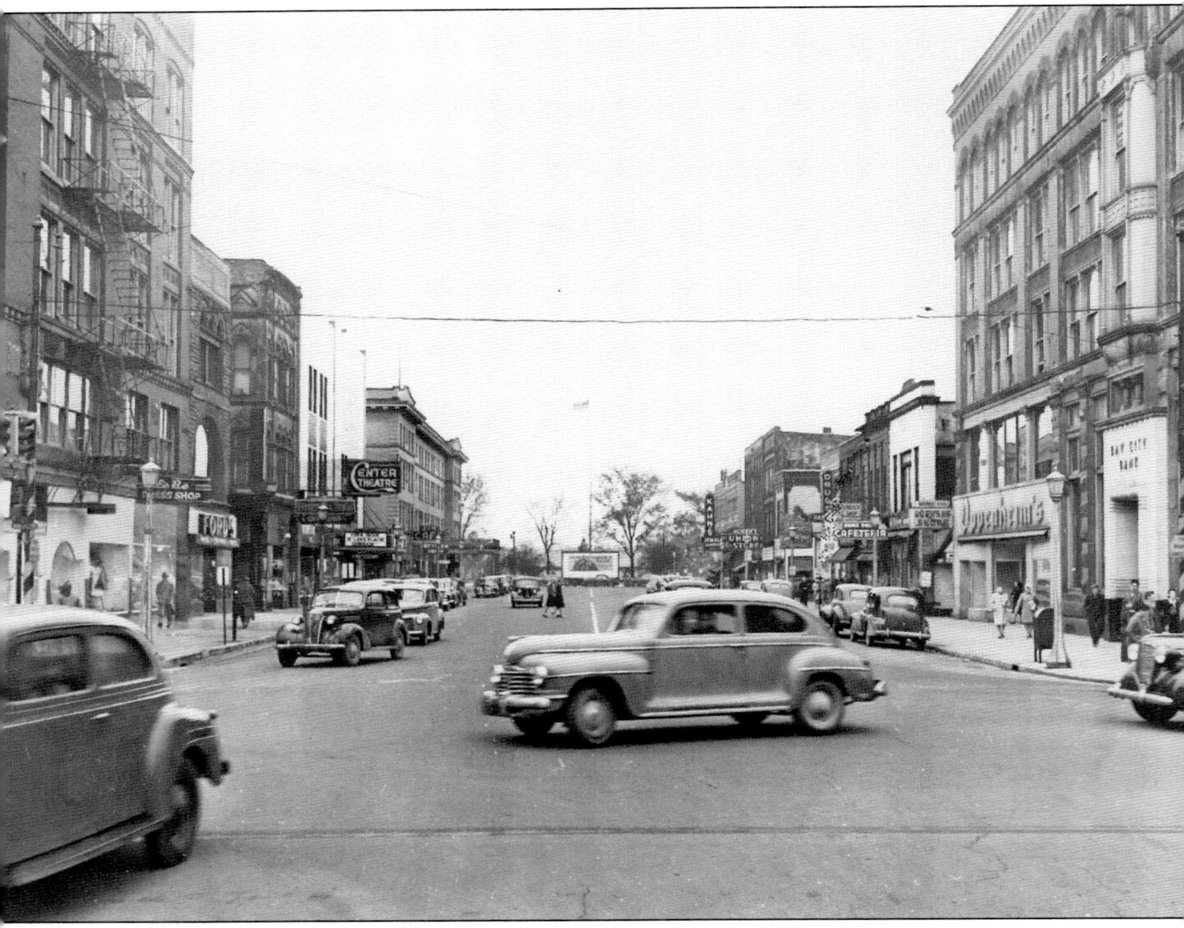

In 1944, Bay Citians were still in the grips of World War II when this photograph of Center Avenue looking west from Washington Avenue was taken. *Lake Placid Serenade* was playing at the Center Theater, and pre-war era cars line the street in front of the Wenonah Hotel. Popular stores like Oppenheims's and Ford's await patrons on a busy downtown day. An American flag flies over the city from Wenonah Park. (Courtesy of the Bay County Historical Society.)

On the Cover: The Independent Order of Odd Fellows (IOOF) was a society that gained popularity during the mid-to-late 19th century. It still exists today, though in smaller numbers than when this photograph was taken on Washington Avenue around 1895. Their motto is "We seek to elevate and improve the character of man." Their members are asked to visit the sick, relieve the distressed, bury the dead, and educate the orphan. (Courtesy of the Bay County Historical Society.)

IMAGES
of America

LOST BAY CITY

Ron Bloomfield

ARCADIA
PUBLISHING

ISBN 978-1-4671-1413-4

Published by Arcadia Publishing
Charleston, South Carolina

Printed in the United States of America

Library of Congress Control Number: 2014958539

For all general information, please contact Arcadia Publishing:
Telephone 843-853-2070
Fax 843-853-0044
E-mail sales@arcadiapublishing.com
For customer service and orders:
Toll-Free 1-888-313-2665

Visit us on the Internet at www.arcadiapublishing.com

To my parents, Marilyn and Wayne, for encouraging me to follow my passion for history and writing, and teaching me the value of a good book.

Contents

ACKNOWLEDGMENTS

The majority of the images in this work are from the extensive collections of the Bay County Historical Society. In addition to their general image files, several distinct collections of photographs were also used, namely a collection of images taken from the glass plates of T.E. Webster and images from the voluminous photo album collection of Capt. Benjamin Boutell. I am indebted to Richard VanNostrand for his work scanning the Thomas E. Webster images prior to donating his entire collection. I am also indebted to volunteer and former society president Leon Katzinger for his many years of work scanning images for the digital archive currently being assembled.

In addition, I would like to thank the following individuals for their help with and support of this project: Terry Kelly, Roy Torres, and Don Grischke for their help with the images and support material for Summer Celebration; Stephen Kent, for his forethought to document remnants of Mural City and willingness to loan me his images; Gary "Dr. J" Johnson for his insight; staff at the Historical Museum of Bay County for their help with a few image identifications; the volunteers in the Butterfield Memorial Research Library for their help sorting out a few conundrums; and Jacel Egan and Jesse Darland at Arcadia Publishing for their help getting this book off the ground and keeping me on track during the process.

All images not otherwise credited appear courtesy of the Bay County Historical Society.

INTRODUCTION

Many kids in the early 1980s wanted to be archaeologists because of Indiana Jones, the fedora-clad whip-carrying archaeologist portrayed by Harrison Ford in *Raiders of the Lost Ark*. Not because of riches or fame, but for the thrill of finding that which has been lost. Dr. Jones, this bigger-than-life movie hero, seemed to truly care about finding these pieces of lost human existence and returning them to the public realm.

Think of this book as an archival archeology dig. We are uncovering remnants of Bay City's past just like the slow, meticulous methods used by archaeologists uncovering artifacts that are then pieced back together to create a snapshot of a civilization at a particular time and place. Just like the archaeological dig, this city has layers, and our dig is the entire city, with a focus on certain areas where more documentation has been saved. Instead of three-dimensional artifacts, we are uncovering a very powerful tool, the photograph. The camera lens allows the subject to remain frozen in time, an exceptional way to preserve that which has been lost. Some of these featured places are snapshots in time, while for others we can use multiple images to see change throughout the years, some changing hands multiple times before finally succumbing to disaster, the wrecking ball, neglect, or transformation.

Our subject, Bay City, sits at the exact place where the "thumb" of Michigan meets the "mitten." It is an easily identifiable point, even on satellite images taken from space. The earliest inhabitants used the abundant resources of the area for food and subsistence. The area was visited early during the fur trade due to the easy access from Saginaw Bay to the entirety of the Great Lakes watershed and the trade routes that developed on the waterways therein. Few traders actually settled here until the early 1800s, when they started to take an interest in the resources. Permanent settlement started around the 1830s, and soon settlements started cropping up on both sides of the Saginaw River, which now runs through the center of the city. Five principal villages formed: Lower Saginaw (later Bay City) and Portsmouth on the east side, and Banks (1853), Wenona (1864), and Salzburg (1862) on the west side. In the latter half of the 19th century, those on the east side became Bay City in 1865, and the others combined to form West Bay City in 1877. In 1905, both sides of the river consolidated into one town, dubbed Greater Bay City at the time. The primary industry for most of the last half of the 19th century was lumber, a huge industry that encompassed the woods, mills, rivers, and other ancillary industries that supported and moved it forward. When the trees became scarce, the industry packed up and moved west. Bay City found it a necessity to diversify, and a host of other industries, many of which you will encounter on this tour, tried to fill the void. Through all of this, a city developed with its own distinct culture, heritage, and trappings, some unique to Bay City and others part of the larger collective heritage. Many of these manmade pieces of the day-to-day living, business, and entertainment were temporary, discarded in what was dubbed progress.

Bay City is now known for its commitment to historic preservation, evidenced by the many historic markers, historic structures, and three nationally registered historic districts. However, this preservation ethic only dates back to the 1970s, with the near-demolition of our historic city hall, which was halted by preservationists. Today, that 1897 monument is a shining homage to Bay City's prosperous heritage. Unfortunately, many other buildings succumbed to progress in the preceding years and were torn down to be replaced by other structures or simply made into parking lots. Some of this destruction was due to necessity, while others were removed unnecessarily. Many images exist that help fill in the patchwork puzzle of modern-day Bay City and show the progression of a community that was once the king of lumber in the Midwest, later devastated by the loss of that industry, and has spent over a century trying to piece together a community that would again prosper one day.

The word lost can have several different meanings. Something that is lost may truly be gone from existence, or it may be hiding in plain sight. Additionally, something that is lost may be a tangible building or work of art, or it may be the intangible, as in a way of life or an organizational collective based on common goals, likes, or dislikes. The stories in this volume do not exist in a vacuum. Many things that have been lost have parallels or links to other such items or places, and many have been lost on several levels, both intangible and tangible.

We have limited space and limited resources with which to make this journey. We are limited by the surviving photographs, the available research, the rights to publish certain photographs, and the existing stories. In addition, we only have so many words and photographs that can be used. There are many more things that have been lost to time than we have room to fill, so judgments were made based on a number of factors. Over 1,000 photographs were initially selected and had to be whittled down to a manageable amount for this book. If something you remember does not appear in this book, please keep all of this in mind. In addition, there have been many good books written on particular topics, some of which can be found in the bibliography at the end of this book. We also have a limited number of chapters within which to tell the story, and while we may have devoted more space to one topic than another, it does not mean that they are not each as important as the other. The Wenonah Hotel gets a full chapter by virtue of the story and the material available. J.A. Sparr has a single caption, though you probably will remember him when you throw away your next broken umbrella.

It is truly interesting how old has become new again in Bay City. Murals once again grace our downtown. Uptown has built large buildings where equally imposing buildings once stood. The World's Most Unusual Store was torn down only to see homage paid to its name and distinctive red letters. The restored Shearer Building, the only one left of three, now houses condos where shops and offices once thrived. A group seeks to restore and preserve the Masonic temple. New streetscapes take on a historical flair that recalls our rich history while catering to modern needs. A mural is discovered under siding, another piece of Lost Bay City revealed.

One

A CHANGING COMMUNITY

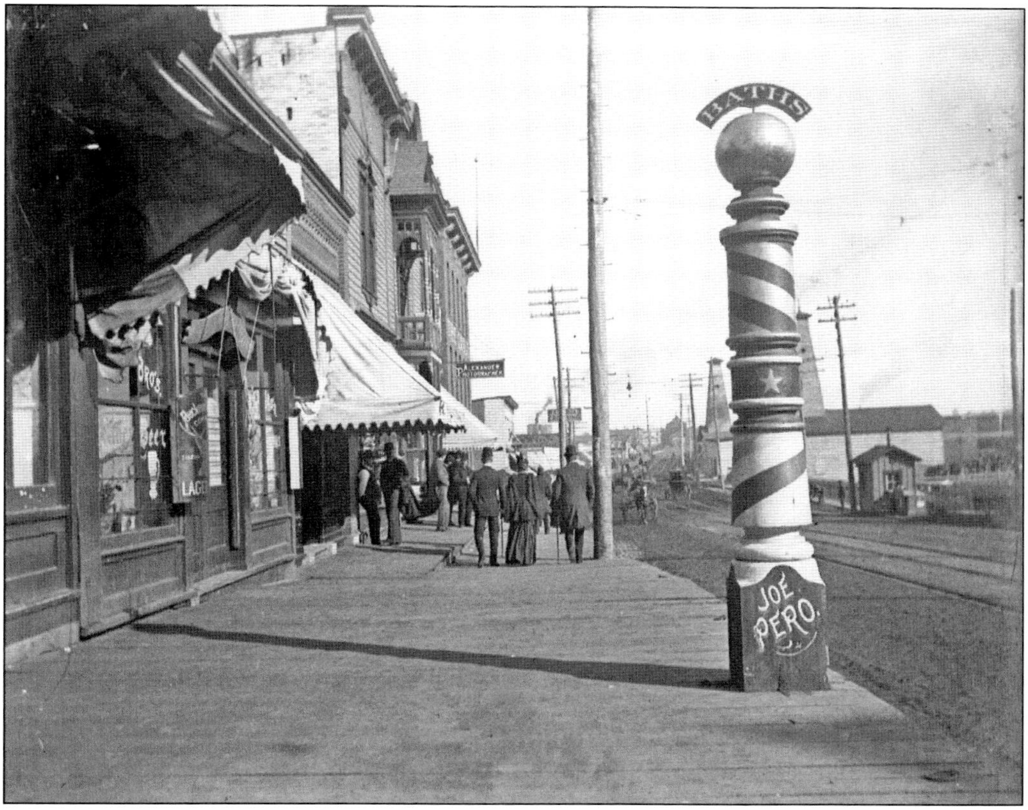

This Thomas Webster photograph of the 800 block of Midland Street (between North Walnut and Litchfield Streets) dates from around 1883. It captures a scene that has not been seen in (West) Bay City since the end of the lumbering era. On the right, salt derricks from the adjacent lumberyard are part of the same landscape as Joe Pero's Barbershop (805 East Midland Street), Hayes Brothers' Saloon (807 East Midland Street), Dominic Francoer's Saloon (811 East Midland Street), and Alexander Photographer (815 East Midland Street).

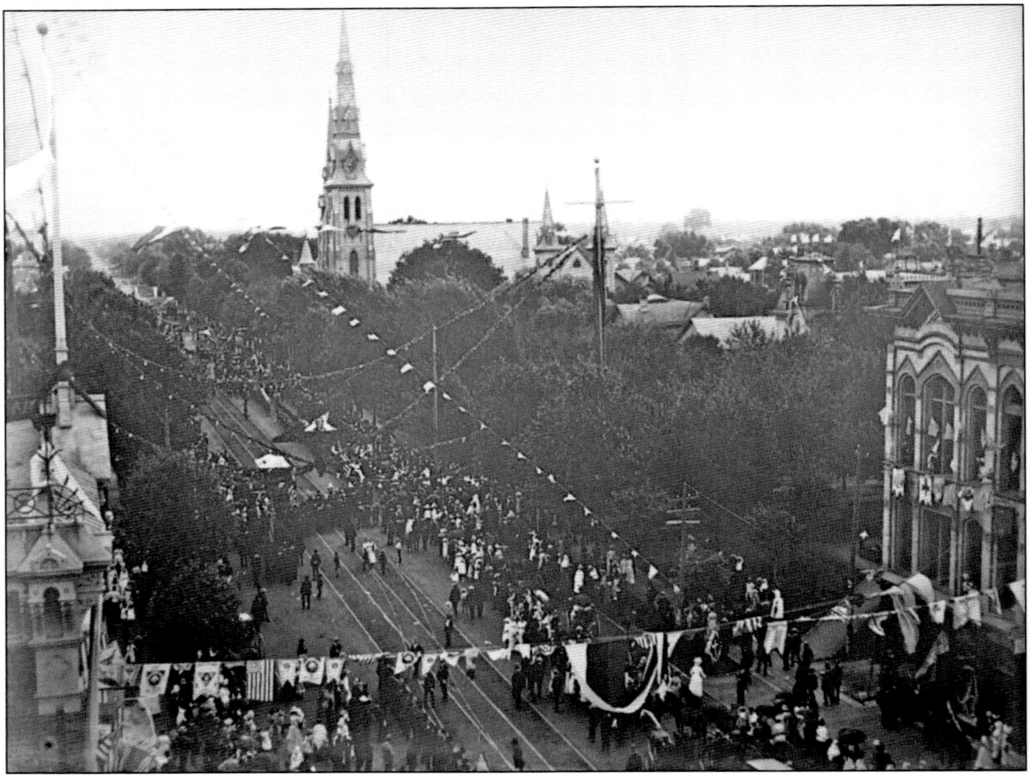

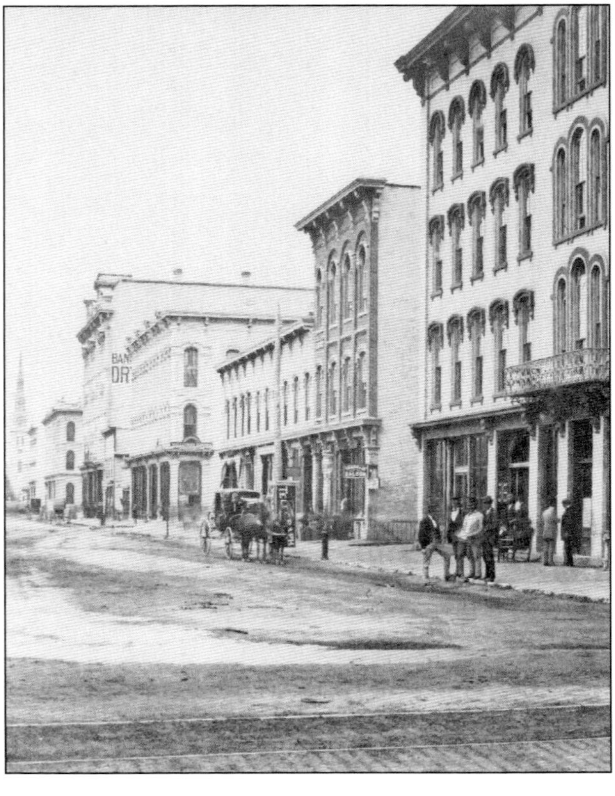

Look east down Center Avenue today, and the vista is quite different from this Thomas Webster photograph taken on July 4, 1877. The lush trees are gone. The spires of the First Baptist Church gave way years ago to a parking lot on the southeast corner of Madison and Center Avenues. The trolley tracks that dominate the streetscape also gave way to other types of transportation.

Another view, of the south side of Center Avenue looking east from Water Street, shows one of the main hubs of Bay City during the early 1880s. The Fraser House dominates the right side of the photograph. The Munger Block sits next to the Westover Opera House, which dwarfs all other buildings at the corner of Washington Avenue, with the distinctive steeples of the First Baptist Church visible in the distance.

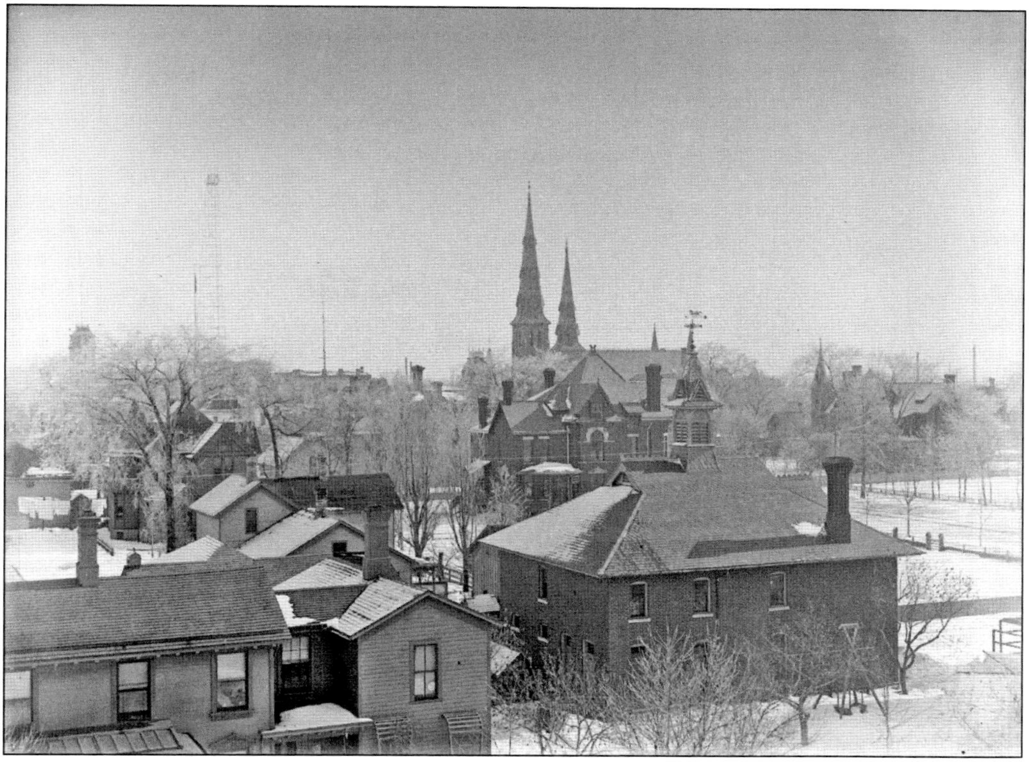

Looking north with Madison Avenue to the right, the First Baptist Church is in the center background. The small tower of the original Bay County courthouse can be seen on the left. The houses and trees in the middle have given way in recent years to the Alice and Jack Wirt Library. Thomas Webster took this photograph around 1880.

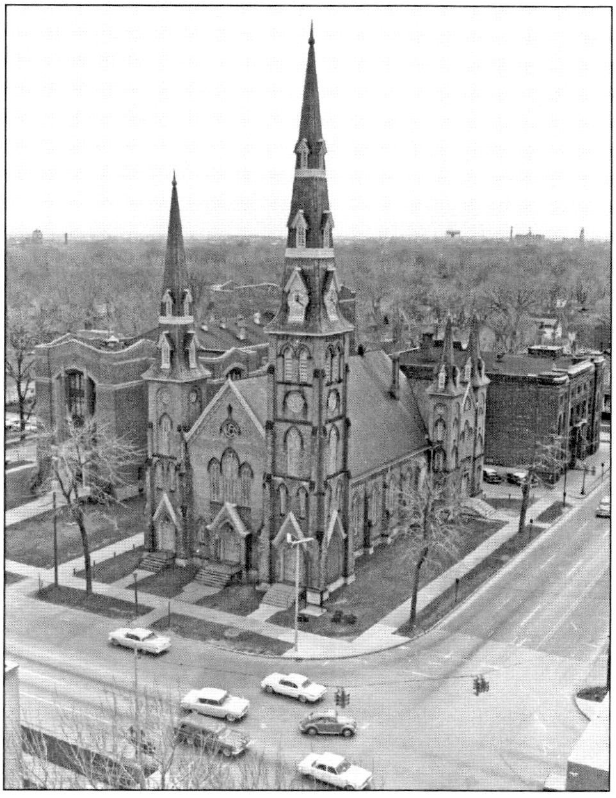

By the 1960s, the area around the First Baptist Church had changed dramatically. The block now contained two large Masonic buildings, the original Masonic temple built in 1893 and the Scottish Rite Cathedral (Consistory) built in 1926. Many trees were lost to improvements at Center and Madison Avenues necessitated by increased automobile and truck traffic from the M-25 corridor. The church, constructed in 1872, was eventually torn down in the 1970s.

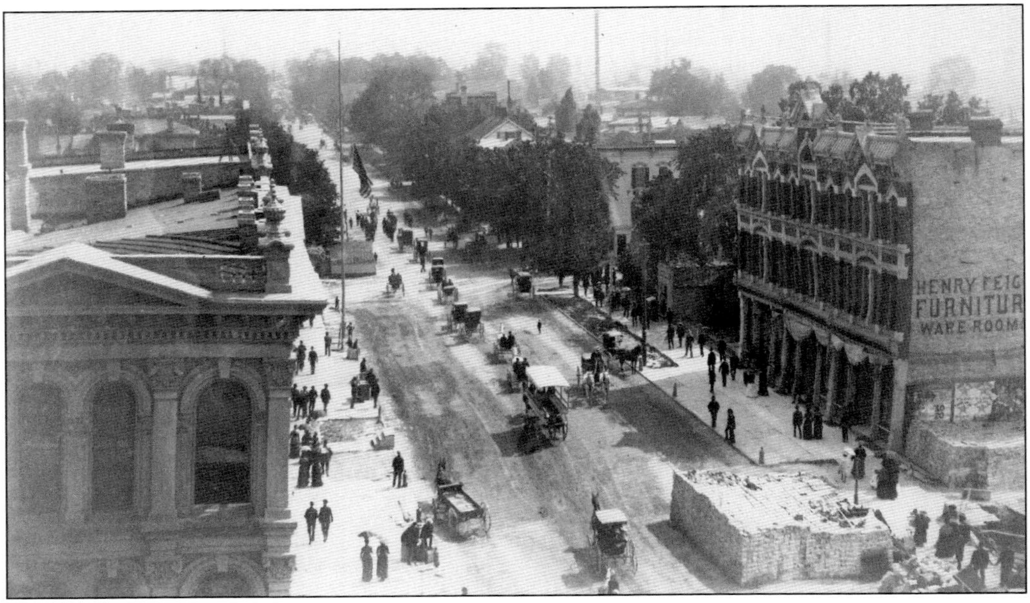

Washington Avenue, shown looking south from Center Avenue in 1886, became Bay City's primary corridor of business and commerce. When the Westover Opera House burned in 1886, it left a major void in the landscape that was quickly filled by the construction of the Phoenix Building, as evidenced by the lumber at lower right.

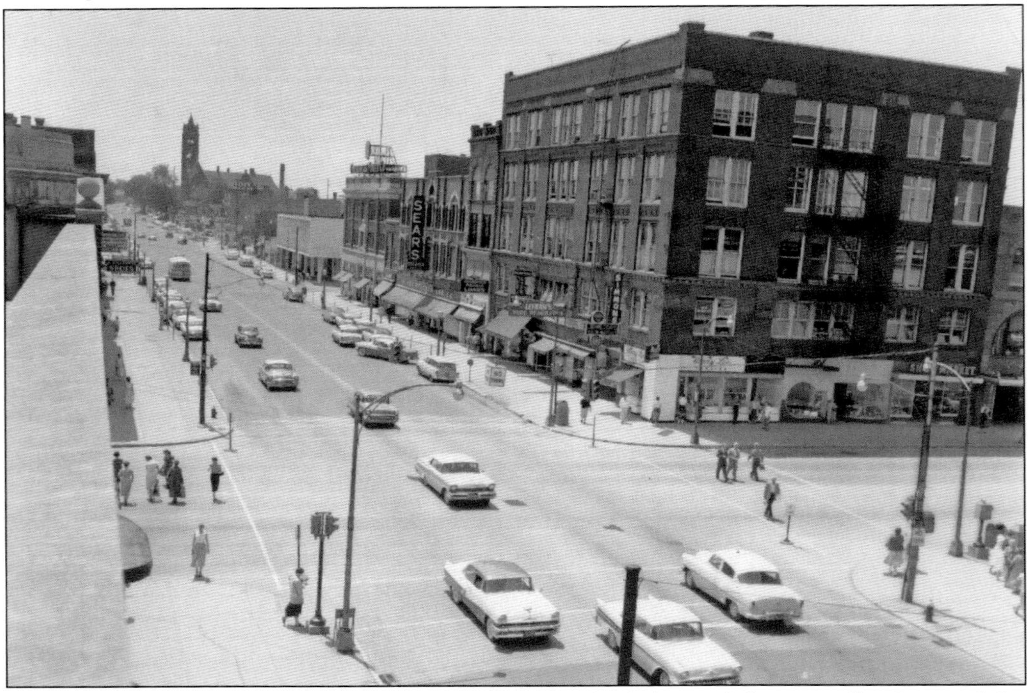

By the 1950s, the landscape of Washington Avenue had changed dramatically. Some of the buildings were still present, but modern makeovers had begun. The features and ornamentation of the previous century had given way to modern metal façades with clean lines and sleek looks. In this view, the Phoenix Building appears to dominate the landscape; however, the 1897 city hall in the distance would become the most recognizable landmark in this view.

Bay City took on a notorious reputation during the lumbering era of the 1870s–1890s as the place to go for a good time as a result of the large number of bars, brothels, and other places of vice located within the several-block area surrounding Third and Water Streets. This view, looking north along Water Street from Center Avenue around 1880, shows the entrance to this area of Hell's Half Mile.

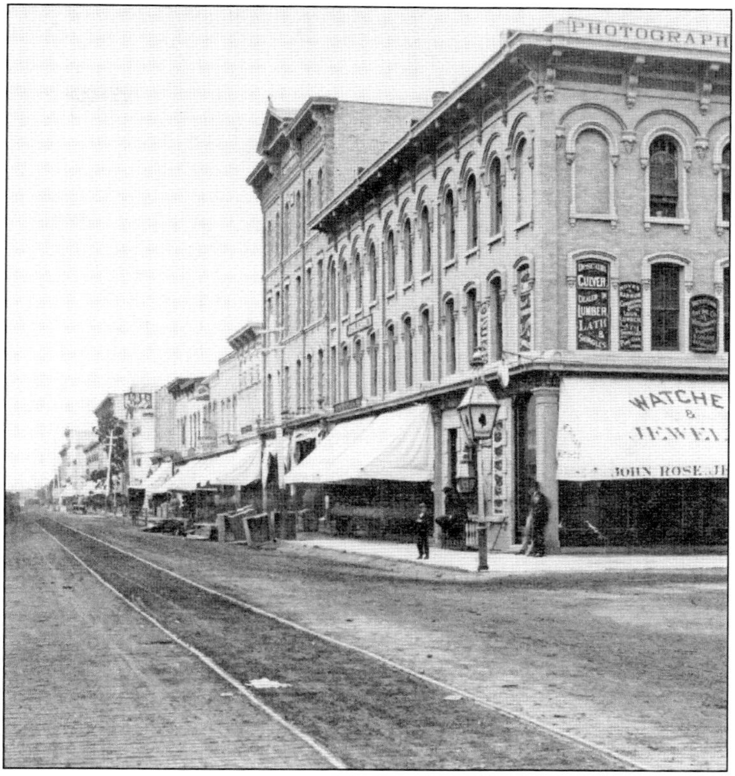

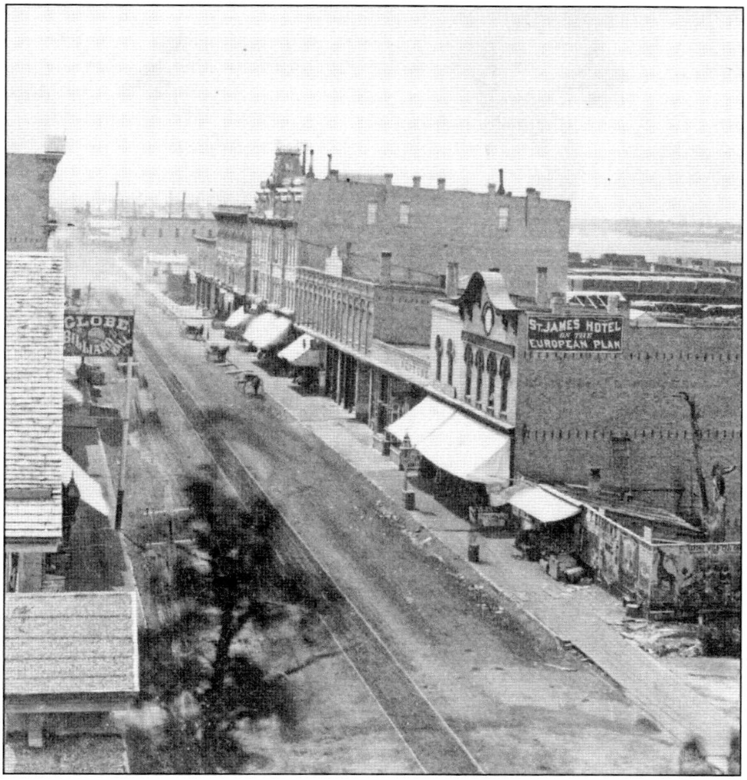

Looking south on Water Street from about Fourth Street, Bay City of the early 1880s looks like a thriving lumber town of the era. The fence surrounding the small shack to the north of the St. James Hotel is being used as a billboard for one of P.T. Barnum's shows. Sides of buildings, fences, and windows were popular places for advertisements of all shapes, sizes, and colors.

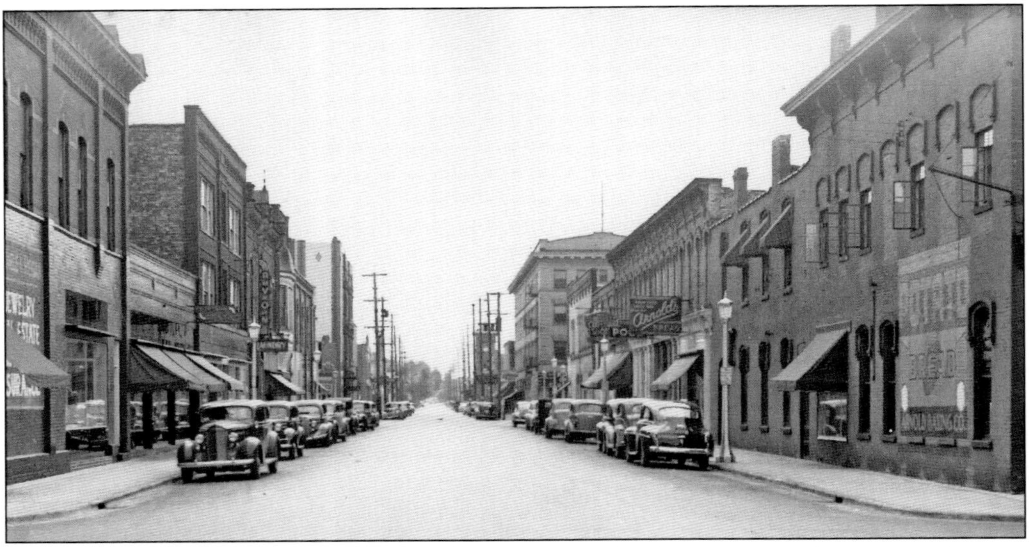

Looking south down Saginaw Street from Fifth Street in the 1940s, one would see many familiar landmarks. Arnold's Bakery with its instantly recognizable neon sign is at right. A corner of the Wenonah Hotel is visible, as is the Art Deco–inspired Centre Theatre façade, both at the corner of Center Avenue. The sign for Caris' Red Lion is barely visible on the corner across Center Avenue from the theatre.

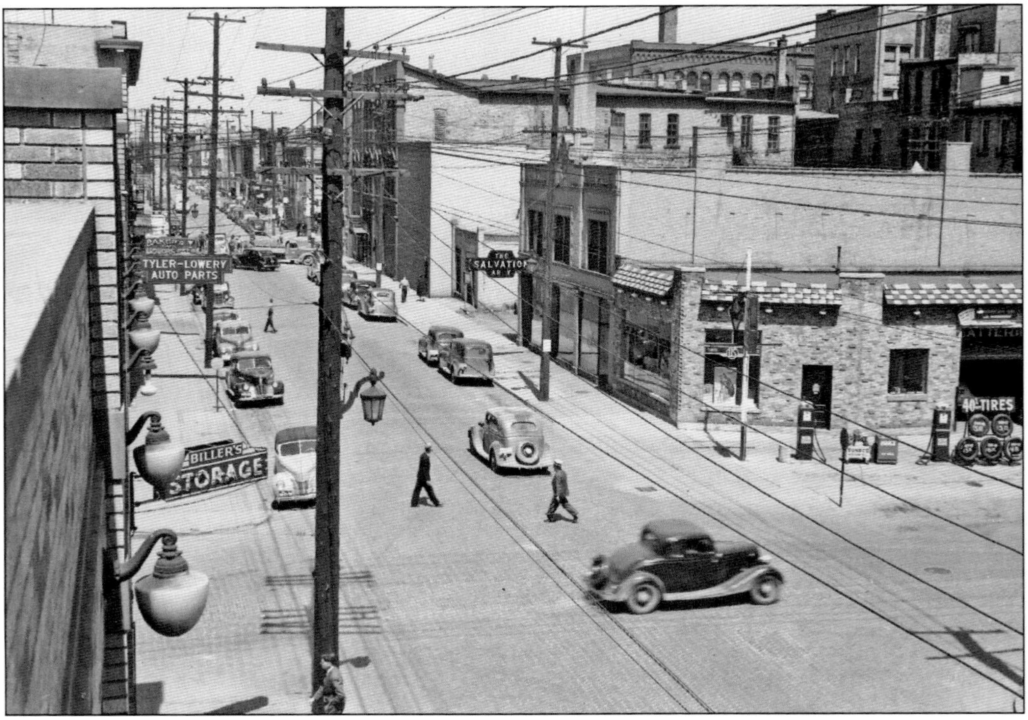

Reverse the angle from the previous photograph, and one sees Saginaw Street looking north from south of Sixth Street. This section of Saginaw Street has seen more radical changes in the decades since the 1940s, when this photograph was taken. The area today is much more open, especially on the west (left), where the planetarium now stands. The former Salvation Army building is about all in this one-block section that still stands.

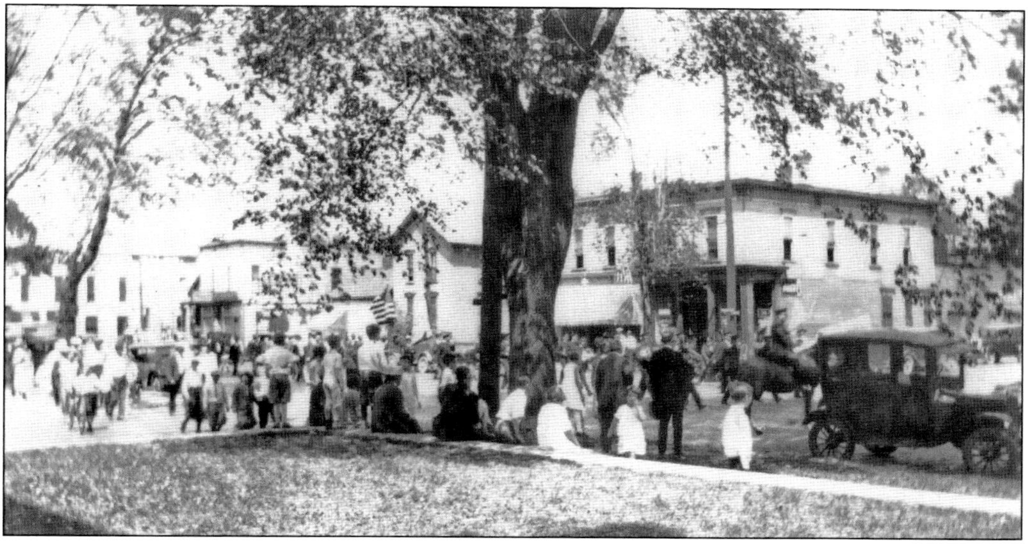

This photograph of the Memorial Day parade in 1926 was taken from the front lawn of the armory (now the museum), looking northeast along Washington at Ninth Street. Much of the older building stock along this section of Washington was replaced in the 1960s in favor of less ornate structures of cinderblock. The building to the right of the tree was replaced by a single-story structure that has been a nightclub for many years.

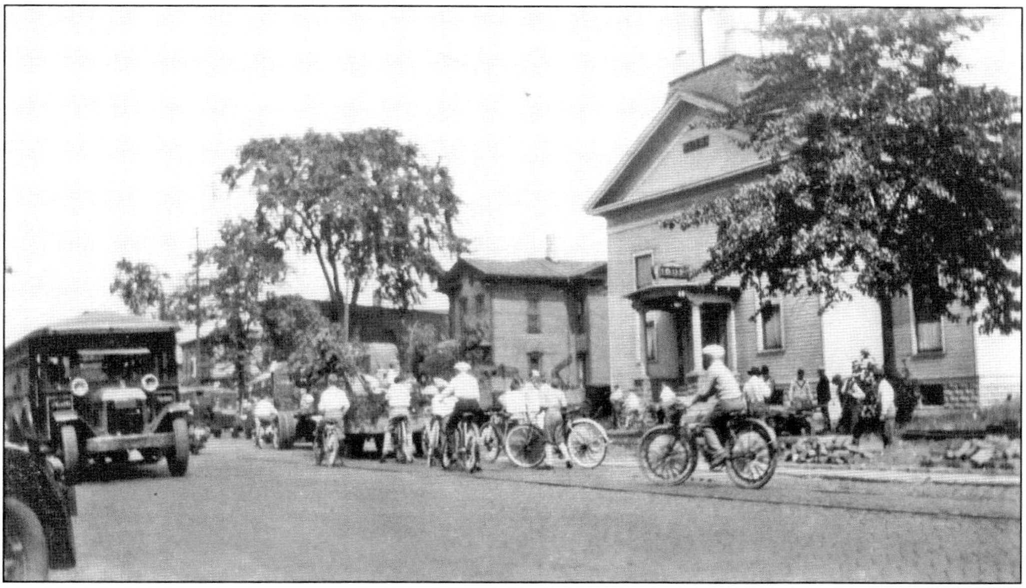

This view of Washington Avenue looking northeast from the front of the armory was taken in 1939 and shows the Independent Order of Odd Fellows (IOOF) hall at 314 Washington Avenue, between Ninth and Tenth Streets. Originally a Presbyterian church built in 1861, the building served the IOOF for many years. It was razed in the early 1990s, and a McDonald's restaurant now occupies the site.

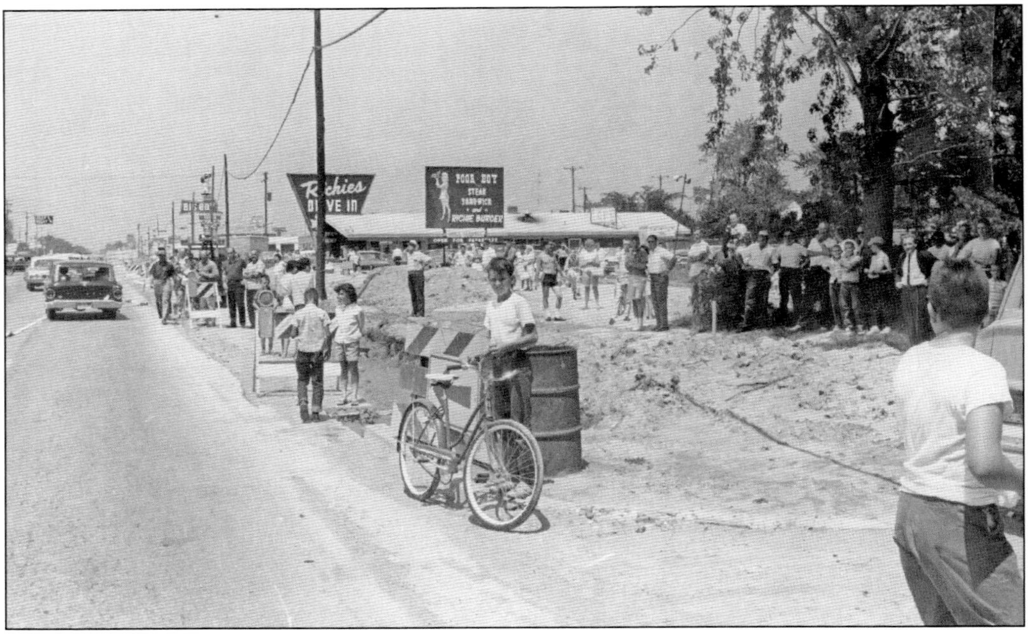

Euclid Avenue, the four-lane that defines Bay City's western boundary, has certainly seen many changes. The Texan Restaurant (with its distinctive sign) stood watch for decades at the corner of Midland Avenue until late 2014, when it was razed for new development. Likewise, Richie's Drive In, pictured here in the 1960s, was a mainstay of the drive-in crowd and a landmark north of where Discount Tire now stands.

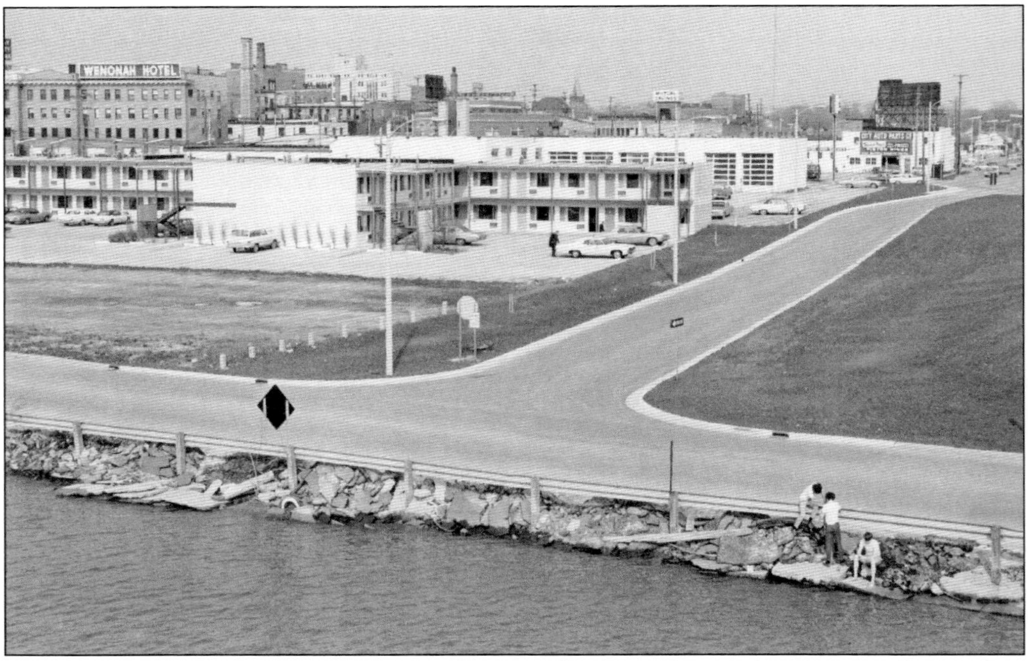

This view of downtown from the west has dramatically changed since this photograph was taken in the mid-1960s. The Imperial 400 Motel (later the Gateway Regency Motel) was removed in the 1990s to make way for the current Doubletree Hotel. An automobile dealership was due east of the motel. The Wenonah Hotel eventually disappeared, and public space now abounds.

Two

Edifices of Government

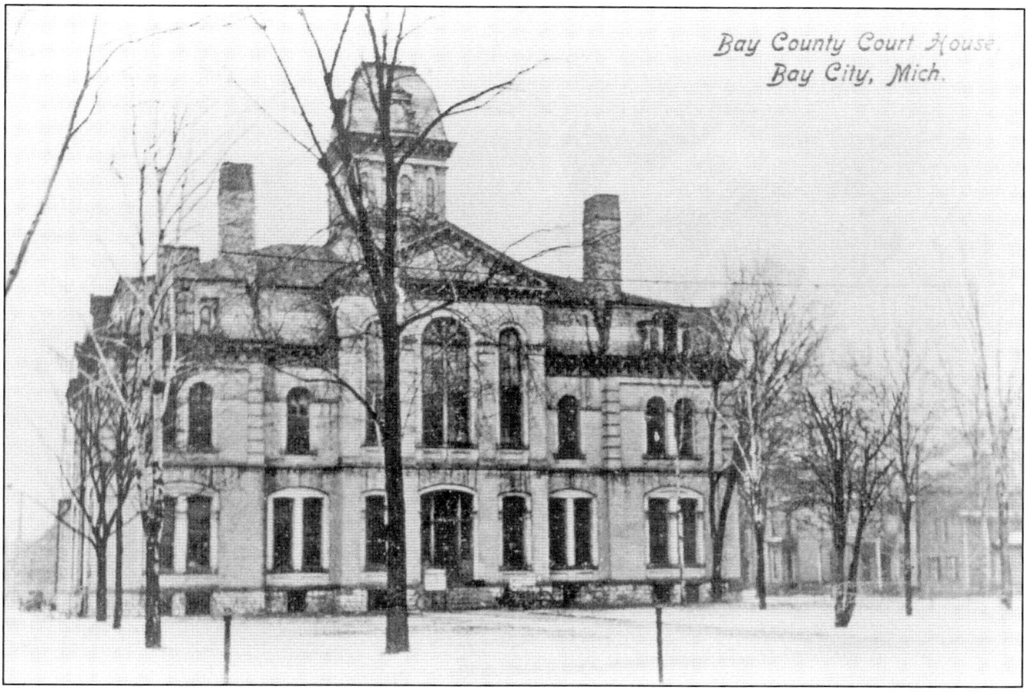

As the settlements that eventually became Bay City grew in size, the need for offices to house officials and city business became apparent. As the county seat of Bay County, offices were also required for county business, including courts and jail facilities (the 1867 County Building is pictured here). In addition, a federal presence has long existed in Bay City, not only through the post office, but also with a substantial federal court seat.

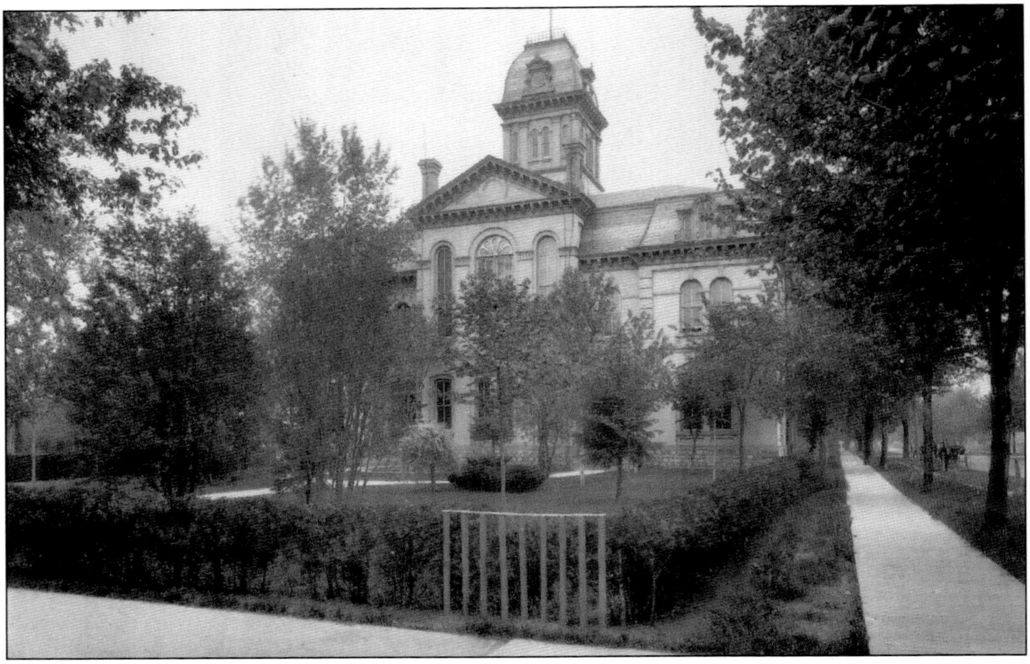

County offices were originally housed in a small wooden building at the corner of Fourth and Water Streets. In 1867, a Second Empire–style building, designed by Cyrus Watkins, was built on the north side of Center Avenue between Jefferson Street and Madison Avenue. The mansard roof featured a cupola, which while designed as a practical solution for ventilation, became one of the distinct features of the building.

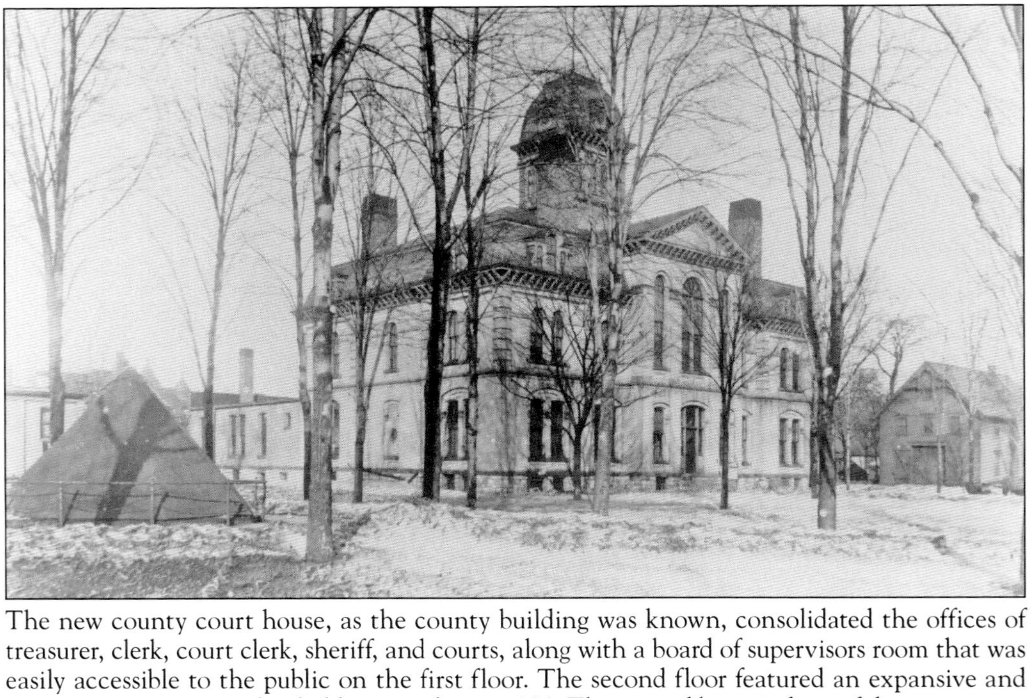

The new county court house, as the county building was known, consolidated the offices of treasurer, clerk, court clerk, sheriff, and courts, along with a board of supervisors room that was easily accessible to the public on the first floor. The second floor featured an expansive and impressive court room that held seating for over 100. The central bay windows of the court room looked south over Battery Park.

By the late 1920s, it was apparent that the 50-plus-year-old court house was significantly outdated and too small. Local architect Joseph Goddeyne was commissioned in 1931 to design a new building. In 1932, despite being in the midst of the Great Depression, the county offices and courts moved to temporary housing across the street at the Ridotto, and the aged building was torn down. A new Art Deco skyscraper of nine stories was erected on the site and still serves today. At right is the steel skeleton of the new building. This new, modern county building opened in 1934 and included a suite of museum rooms on the second floor occupied by the Bay County Historical Society (below). In the 1960s, more space was needed for the courts, and the society moved to renovated space at 1700 Center Avenue.

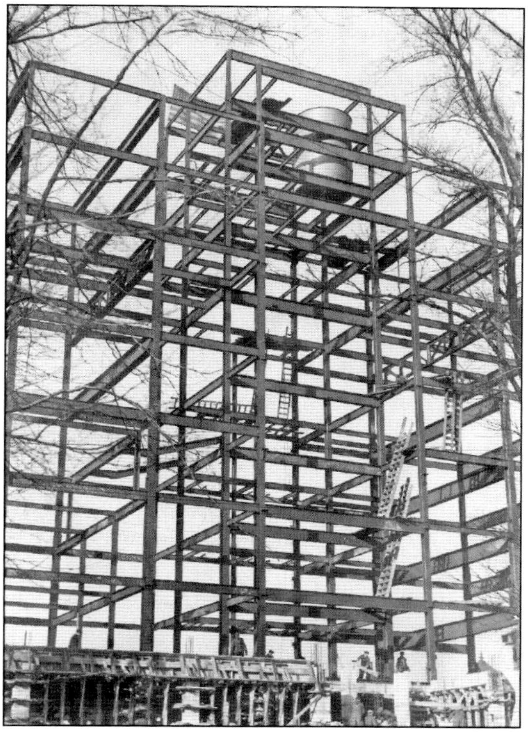

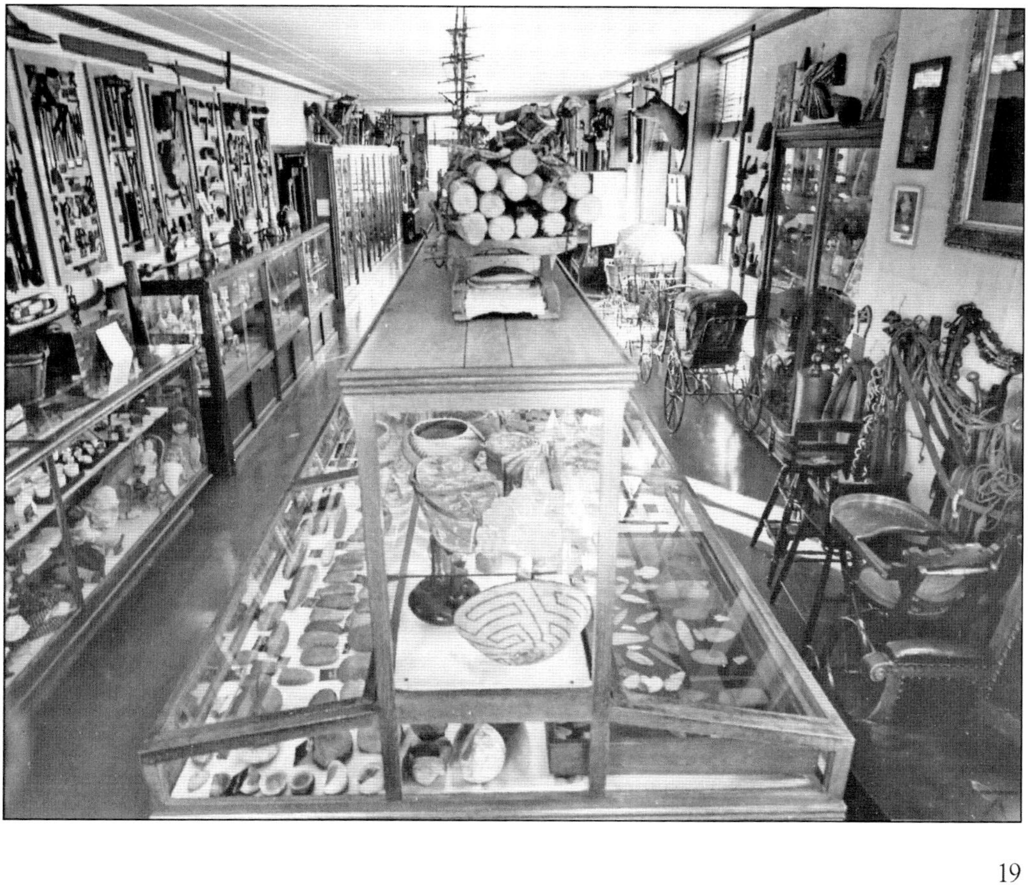

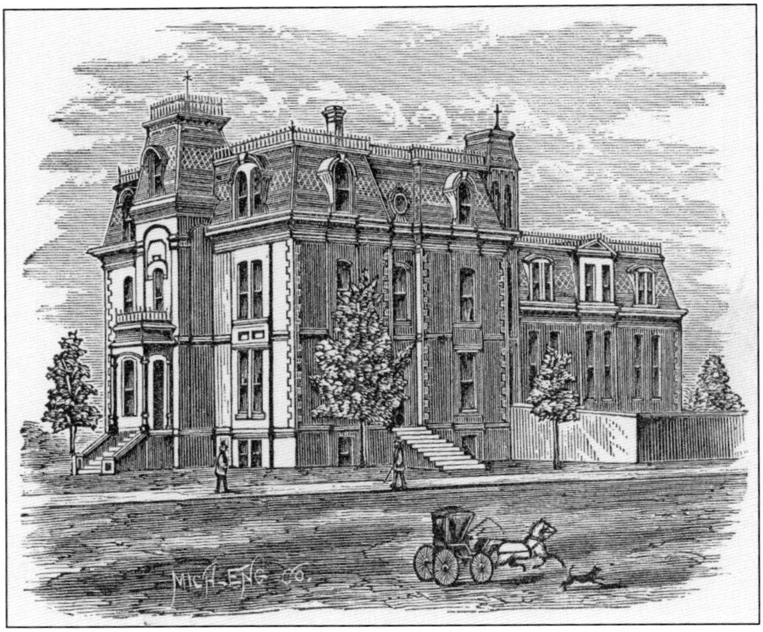

The Bay County Jail, often referred to as the "County Hotel," was built in 1872 to handle the various horse and cattle thieves, drunks, prostitutes, murderers, arsonists, and gamblers from the lumber era. This Second Empire–inspired building was located across Center Avenue from the county courthouse and was designed by the same architect, Porter and Watkins. It was the first proper jail, as the county had previously used temporary housing for inmates.

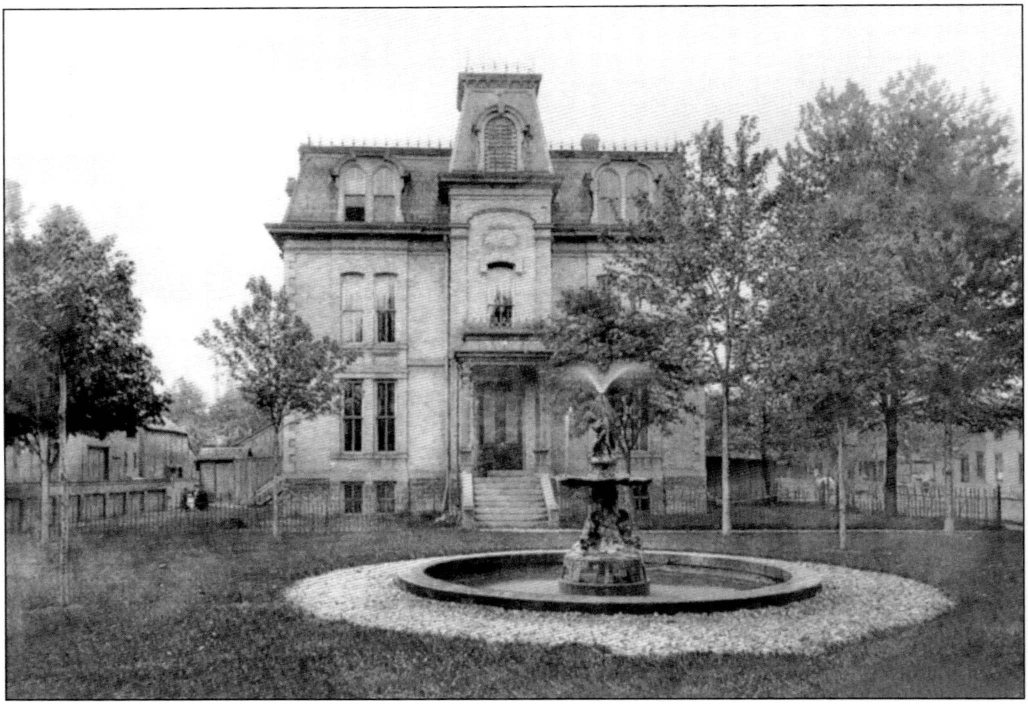

The county jail looked north over Battery Park and included the sheriff's residence, with a parlor, dining room, pantry, and upstairs bedrooms. The actual jail was located in a two-story wing at the back, with a separate entry on Jefferson Avenue. It featured 16 five-by-seven-foot cells with iron bars and floors and ceilings of boiler plate. Female inmates had separate accommodations on the third floor above the sheriff's quarters.

In 1883, the county purchased leg irons with balls and chains so jail inmates could work off the cost of their incarceration. At the time, splitting wood was the only task available; however, harder work was found in tasks like excavating sewers. The chain gang also offered a form of public disgrace that helped deter some would-be petty criminals looking for free room and board at the County Hotel.

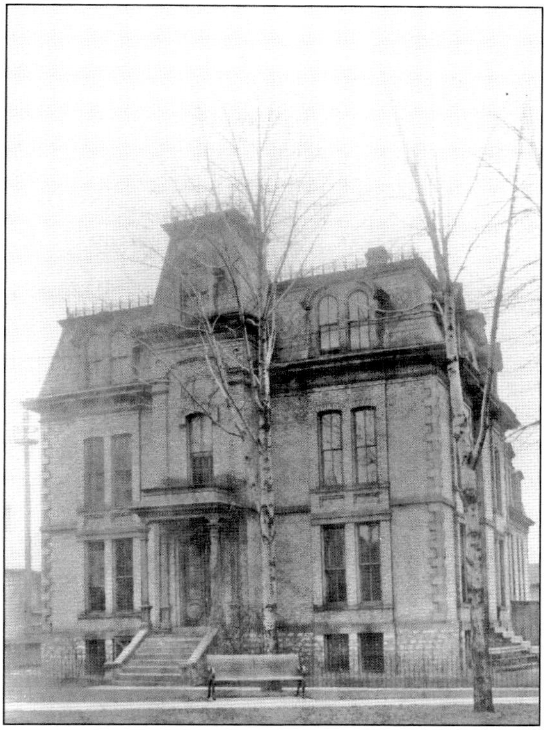

The jail stood for almost 70 years before it was torn down in the mid-1930s. The new jail, a Public Works Administration project, was built on the same site. This utilitarian building became a county storage facility when the current law-enforcement facility was built a couple blocks north in 1978. It was eventually razed in 2003 to make way for the new Alice and Jack Wirt Public Library.

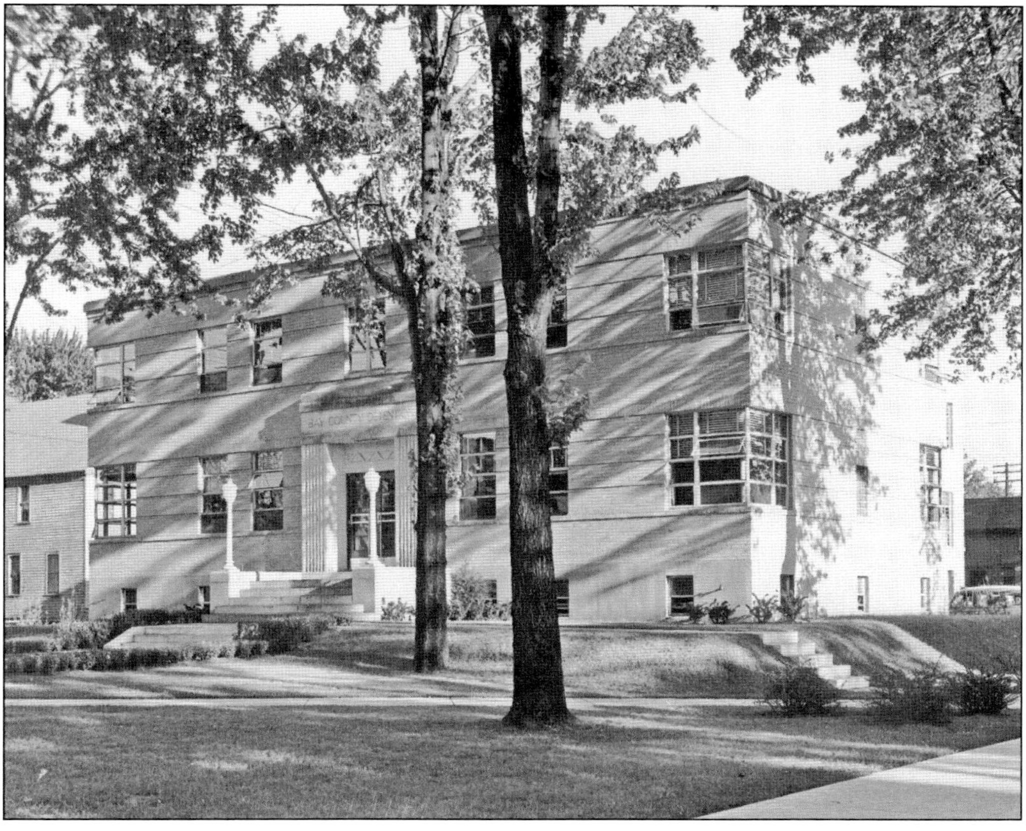

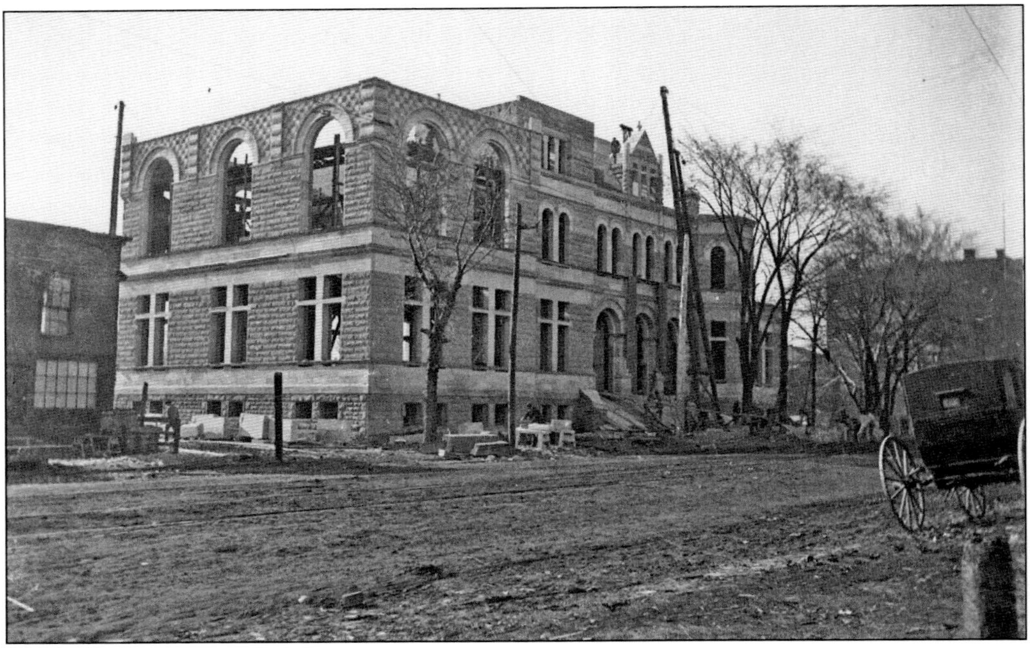

The first major federal building was built in 1893 at the north end of Washington Avenue, between Third and Second Streets. Amateur photographer Thomas Webster took this photograph in 1893 of the Romanesque structure under construction. It has generally been referred to as the post office due to its most visible function, but federal offices and courts have also occupied the building.

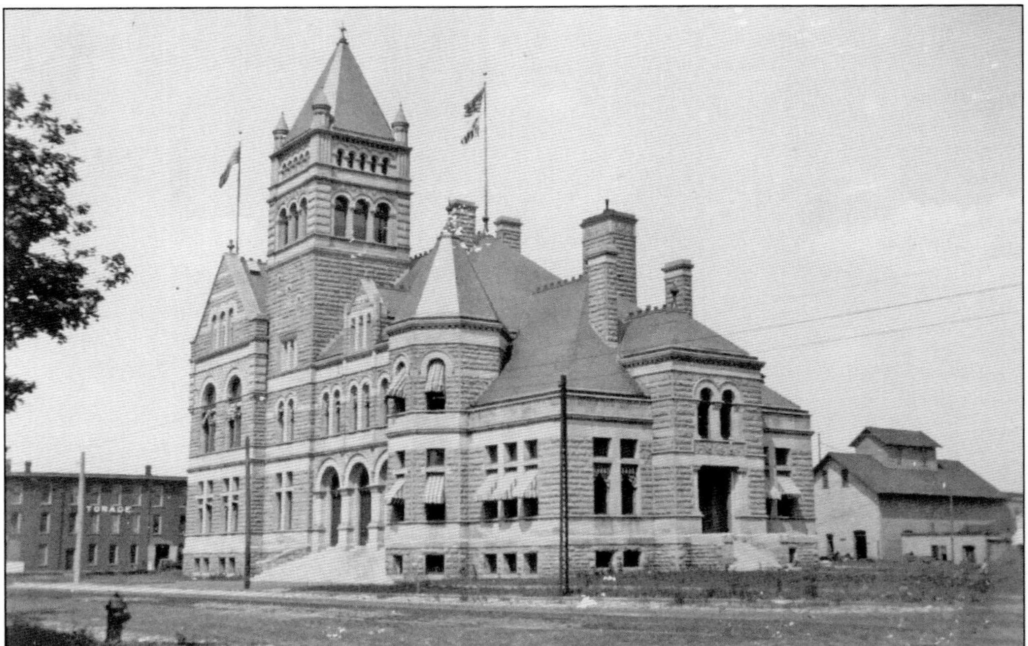

Capt. Benjamin Boutell or one of his associates took this photograph after the federal building opened to the public in December 1893. The first floor featured the post office, while the second floor held the federal court room, judge's office, jurors' room, and offices for customs and revenue agencies. Additional offices were housed on the third floor.

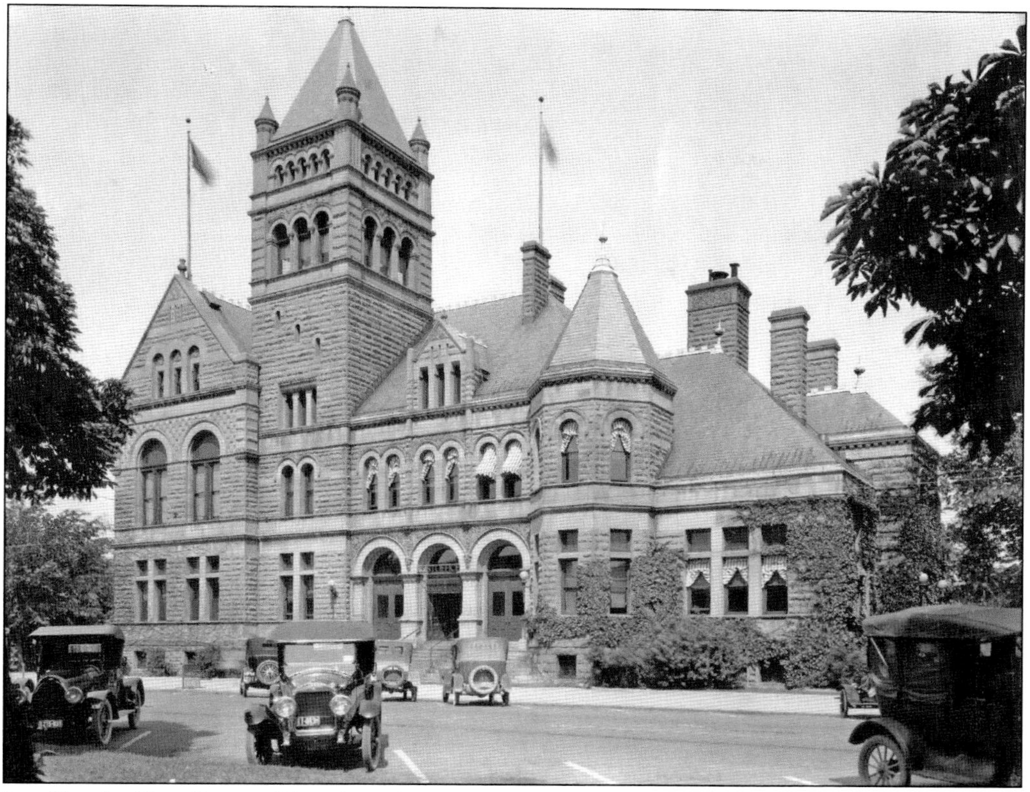

Just like the First Baptist Church and city hall, the federal building's distinctive features made it an easily identifiable structure in any view looking north on Washington Avenue. In fact, the design of the prominent five-story tower has been commonly mistaken for city hall in some photographs due to their similarities, though city hall's tower is much taller.

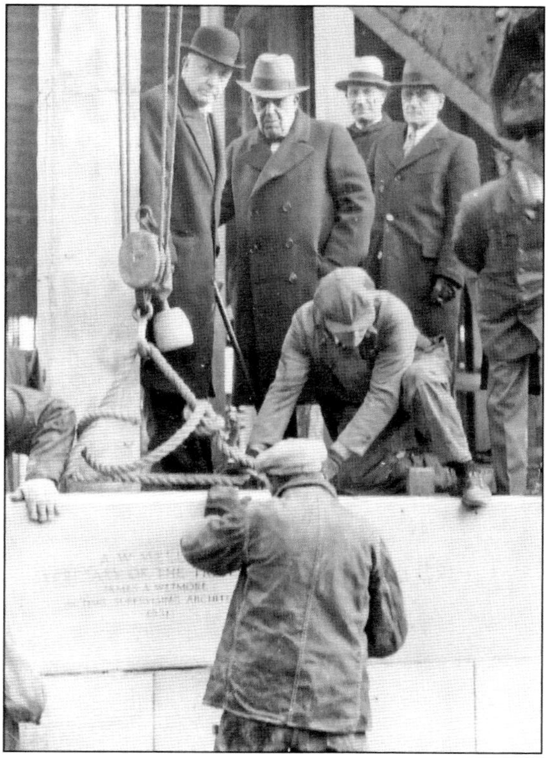

The original federal building received criticism for having a number of faults that were not properly addressed and rectified in the years after it was built. Federal appropriations were made in 1930 for a new building, and the old one was razed later that year. Much of the stone was reused in a residence near the corner of Lincoln and Sixth Streets. The cornerstone of the present federal building was laid on December 9, 1931.

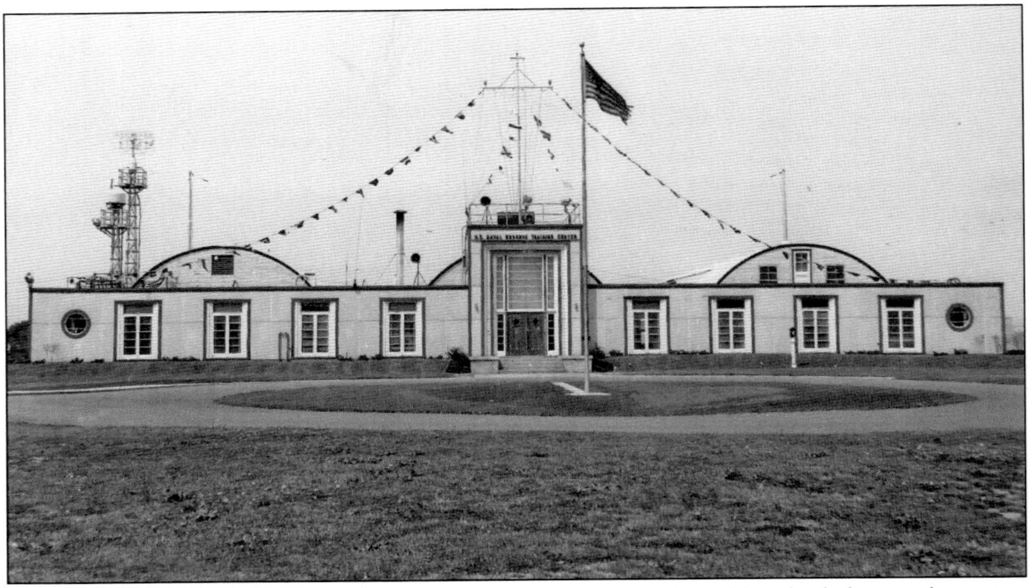

The US Naval Reserve Training Center was a Quonset hut–style building built for naval training in 1949. According to a 1961 Change of Command brochure, the Bay City Naval Reserve Training Center was "one of a chain of similar centers stretching across the length and breadth of America. The purpose of these centers, as is that of the entire Naval Reserve, is to provide a pool of trained manpower upon which the Navy can call in time of emergency." Surface Division 9-74 was organized in September 1946. The Navy approached Bay City about erecting a training center on a suitable site, and the Middle Grounds were chosen.

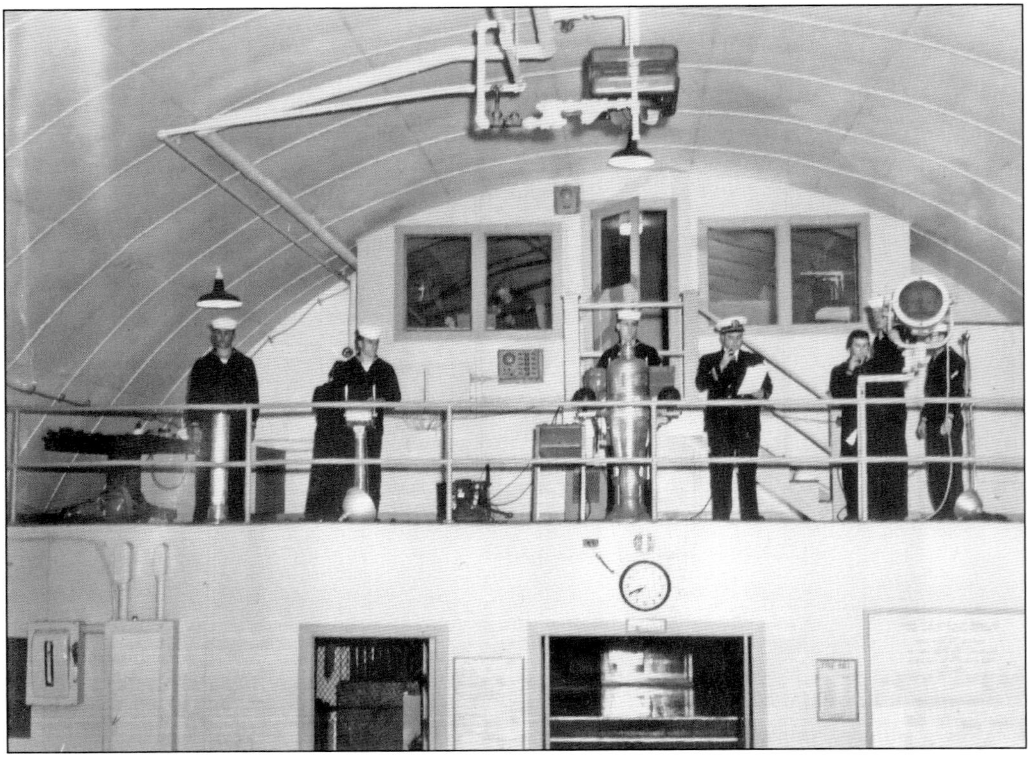

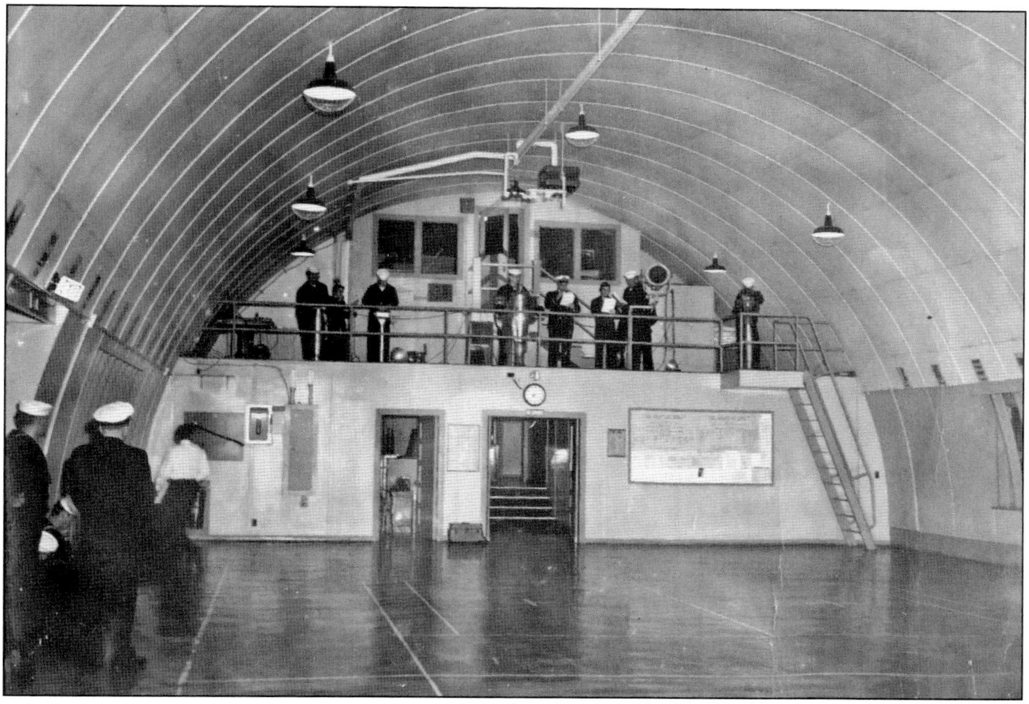

Above, recruits practice on the simulated bridge inside the center, while below, recruits are assembled to help welcome the 1962 Armed Forces Day queen. As of 1961, Naval Reserve Surface Division 9-74 had a complement of 200 enlisted men and 15 officers. The building served until the mid-1960s and around 1967 become the home of the Boys' Club, which eventually razed it in favor of a new building on the Middle Grounds location in 1975.

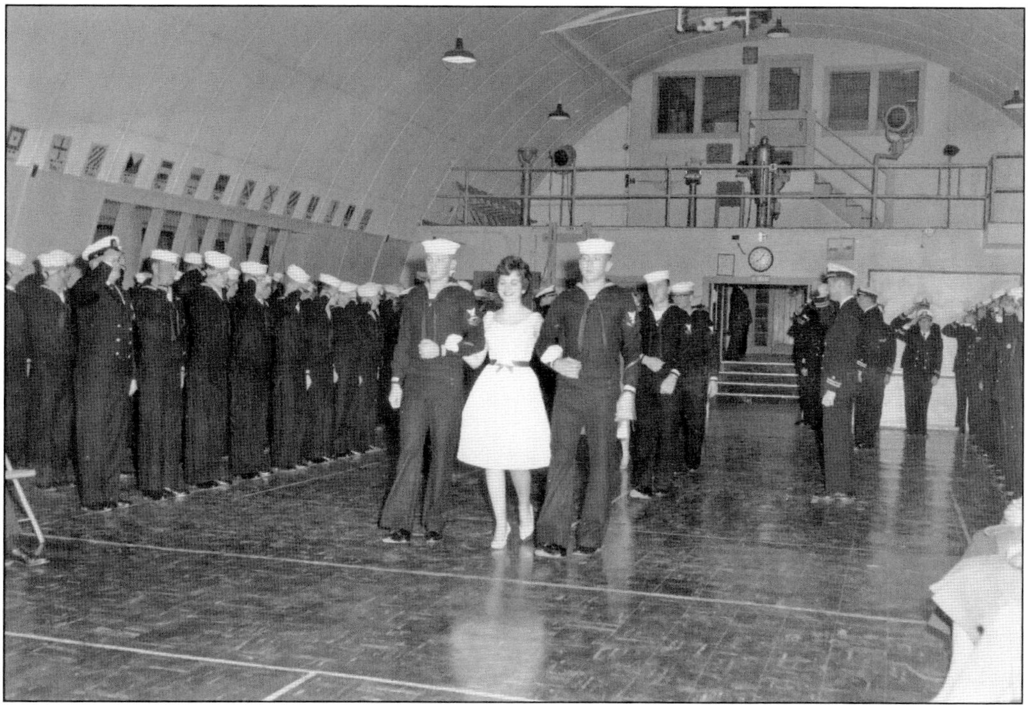

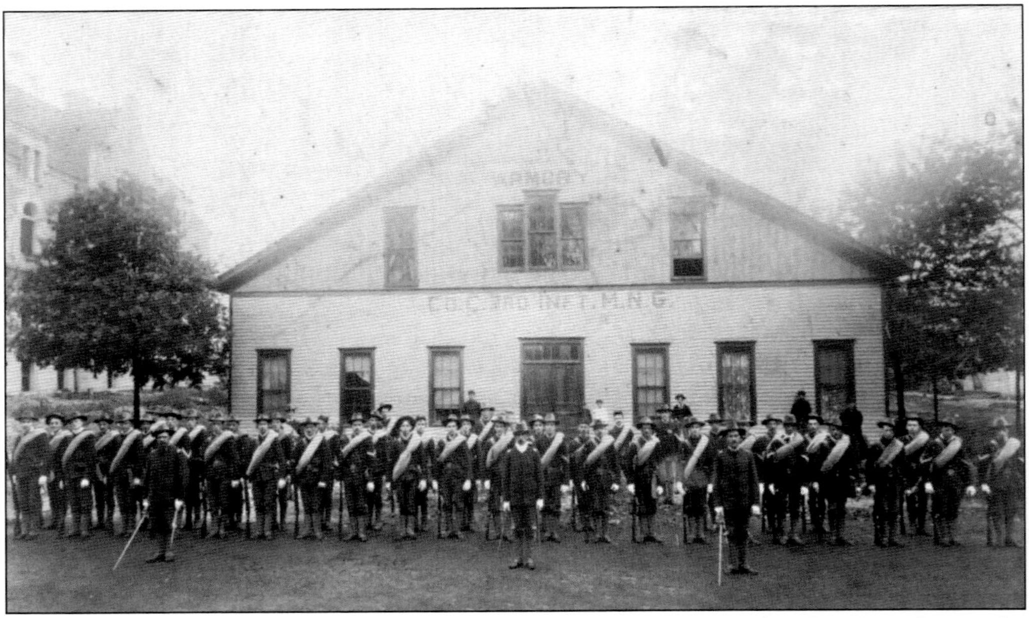

The Michigan National Guard was organized out of local militia units such as Bay City's Peninsular Guard. These units regularly met at local halls for organizational practice and drilling. Bay City's first National Guard armory was located next to city hall at Washington Avenue and Ninth Street. It was a wooden-framed multipurpose building that also housed a bowling alley. Here, the men of Company C, 3rd Infantry, are gathered for a photograph around 1898.

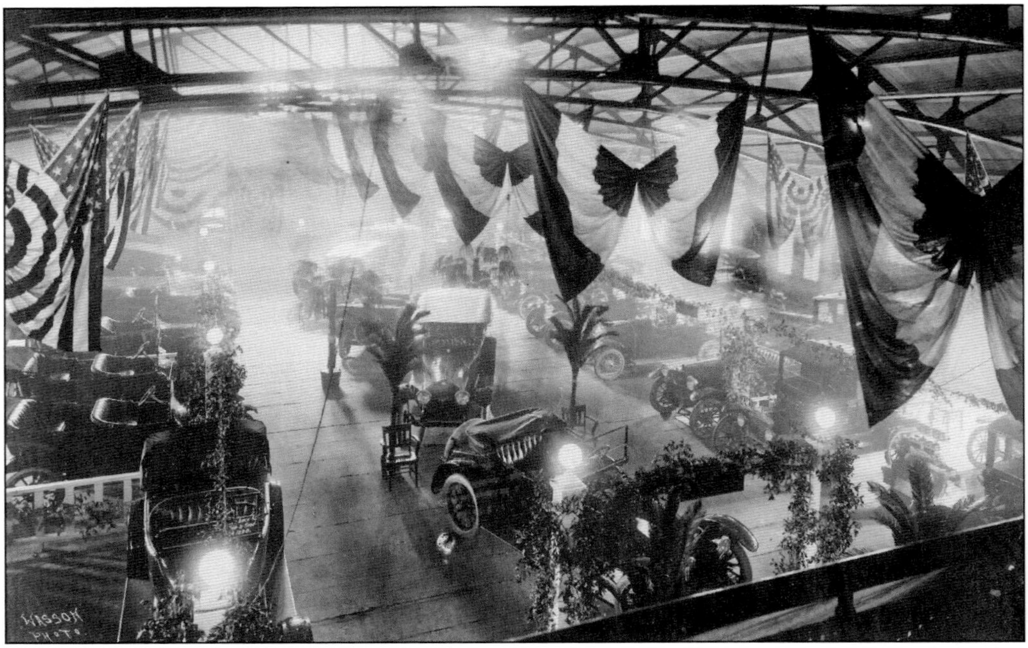

The original armory was razed, and a new Pratt and Koeppe armory went up in 1910. Pres. William Howard Taft dedicated the building during a ceremony in September 1911. The new building served until the 1980s as both armory and event space, featuring Golden Gloves boxing, automobile shows (like this one in 1916), and dances. The Bay County Historical Society later acquired the building for a museum, which opened in 1988.

Three

Monuments and Murals

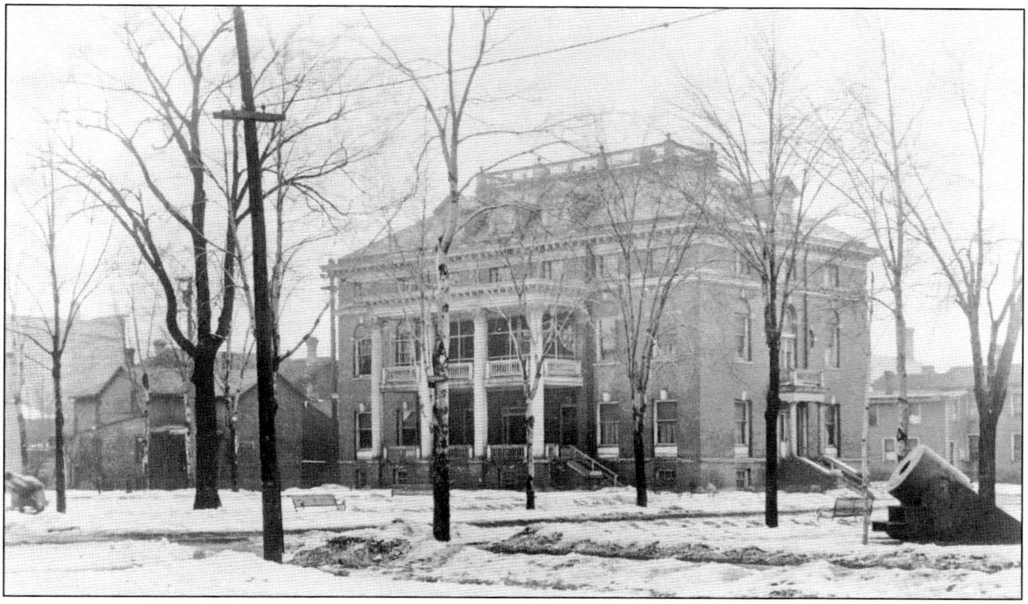

Monuments are a visibly public way to remind citizens of certain occasions like triumphs, tragedies, sacrifice, and war. Many of Bay County's monuments are still here to this day, such as the monument to Chief Ogemawkegato in Roosevelt Park, the doughboy statue in Pershing Park commemorating the sacrifices of World War I soldiers, and the veterans' memorial outside of the Bay County Building. One of the ordinance monuments is pictured in Battery Park around 1906.

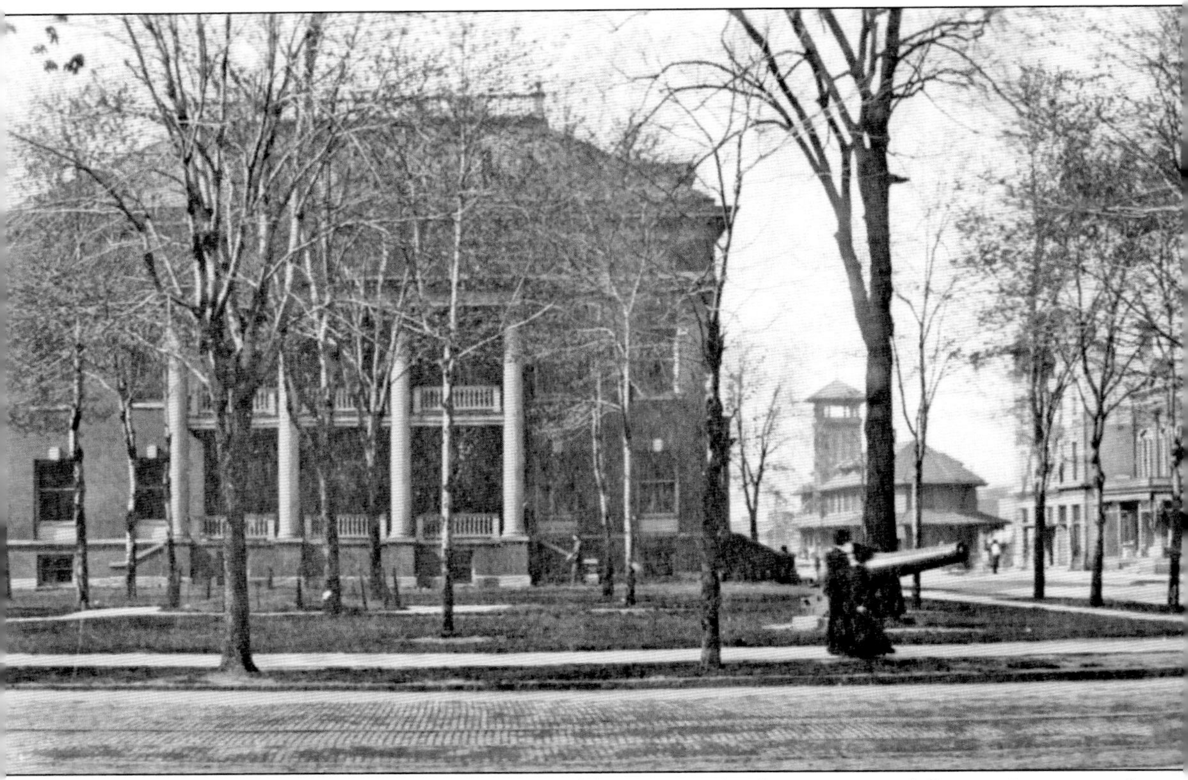

Battery Park was the name given to the public area on the four corners of Center Avenue and Jefferson Street. This photograph, taken around 1906, shows the north side of Center Avenue at Jefferson with the Bay City Club at left, the Pere Marquette Depot in the center background, and the Bay County Building at right. In 1904, Congressman George A. Loud of Bay City secured two artillery guns originally from the USS *Hartford*, which were placed in Battery Park. One is seen

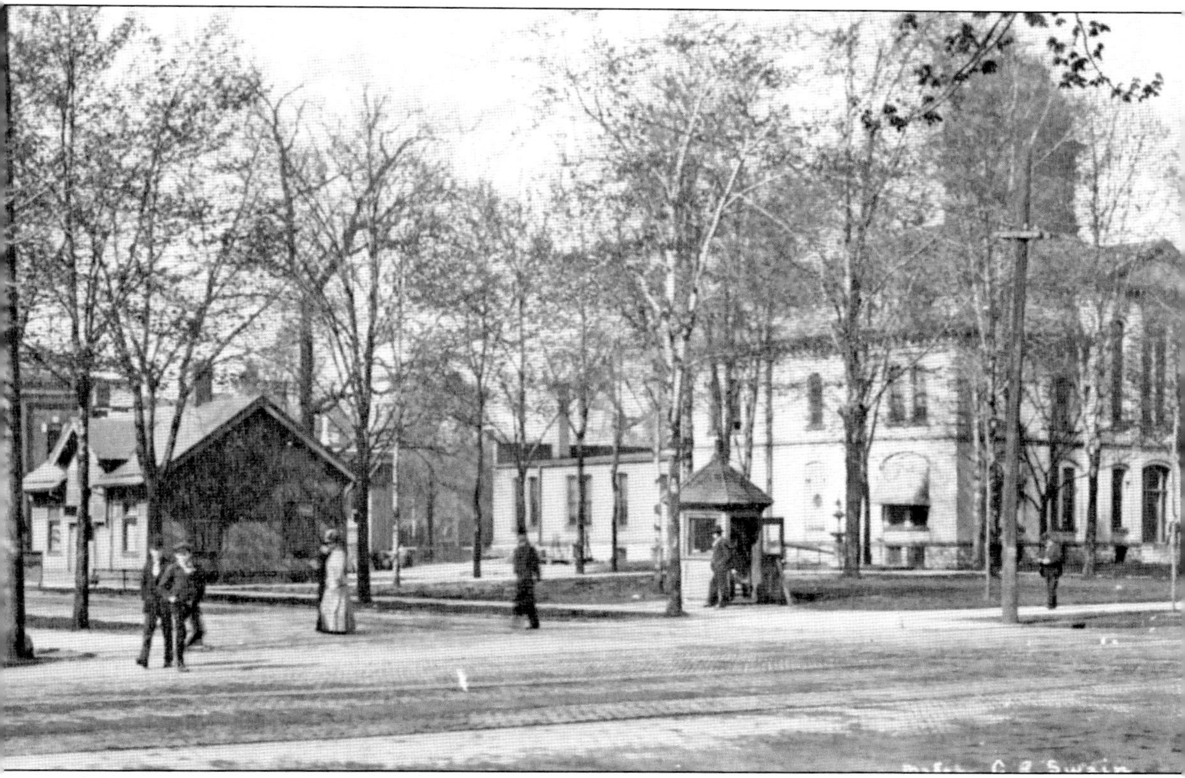

at left center while the other was placed across Center Avenue to the south. They were joined in 1907 by two large artillery mortars of Civil War vintage from Fort Sumter, also acquired by Congressman Loud. These war relics were placed on the eastern corners of Battery Park, and one can be seen in the photograph on the preceding page.

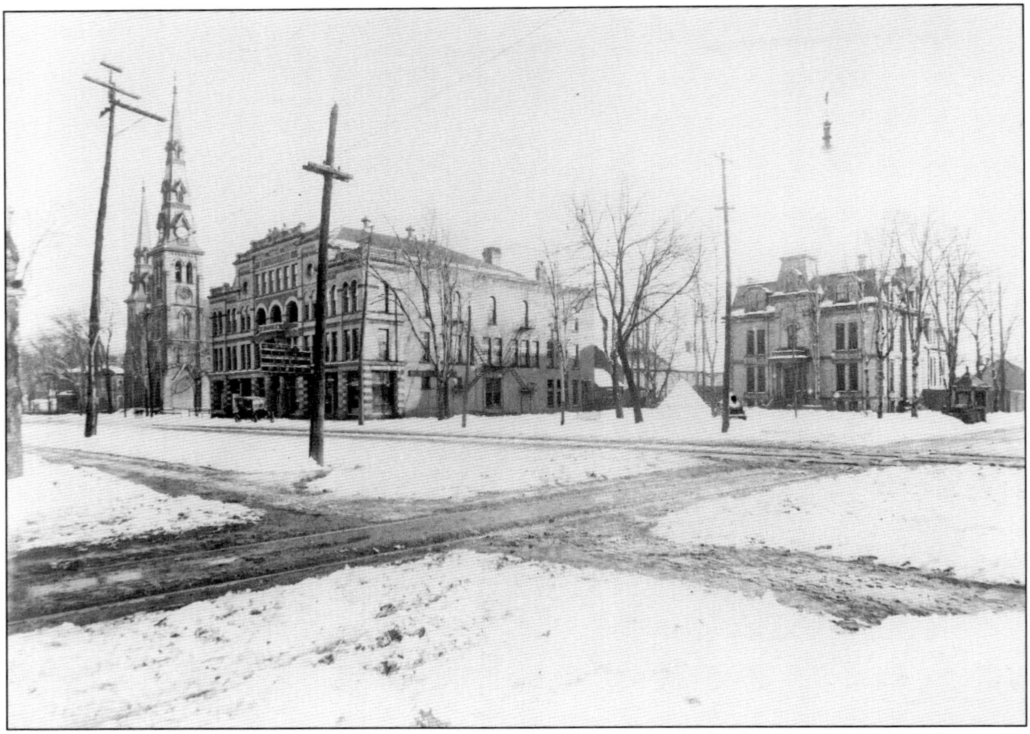

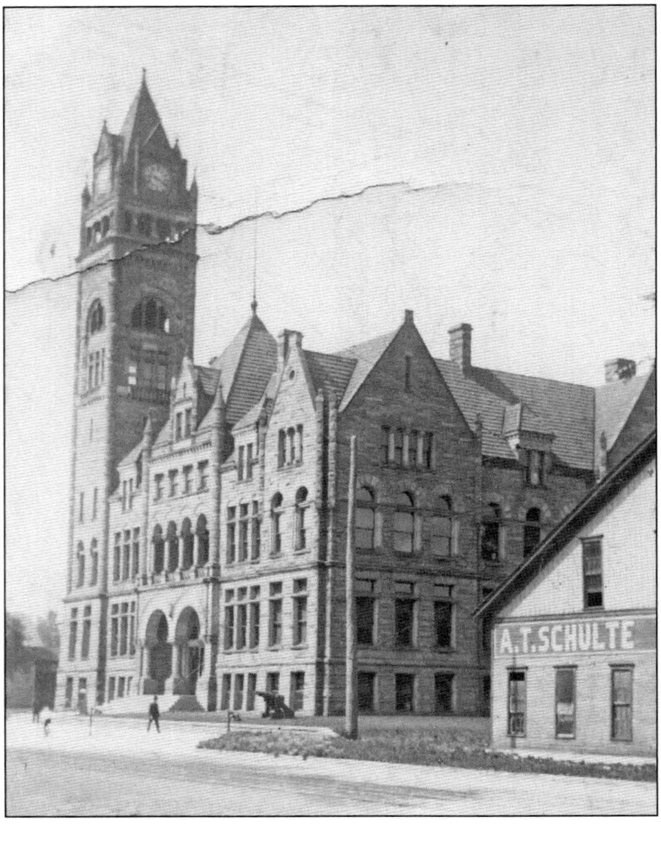

The buildings surrounding the southeastern section of Battery Park included the Ridotto at left and the Bay County Jail. In this wintry scene from around 1915, the twin towers of the First Baptist Church across Madison Avenue are also visible. One of the Fort Sumter mortars is at center right. All four of the mortars quickly became popular photograph backdrops.

In addition to Battery Park, two war relics were placed around city hall. Two guns from the USS *Portsmouth* were also placed on the grounds of Sage Library. All eight of these monuments (25 tons in total) were turned over to the Bay County Salvage Committee with ceremony in 1942 and sent off to the smelter for the World War II scrap drive.

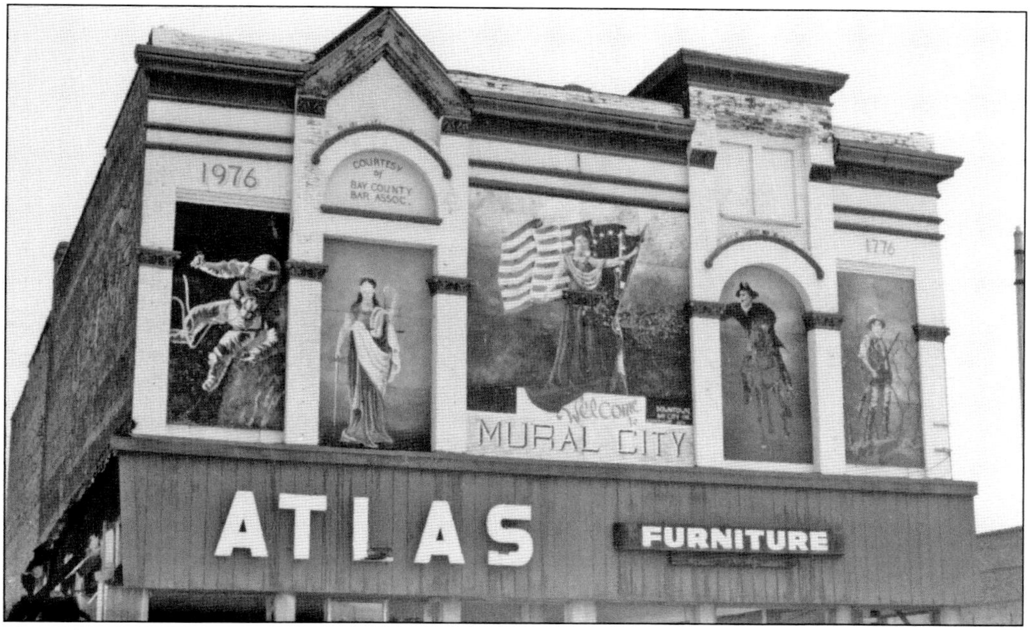

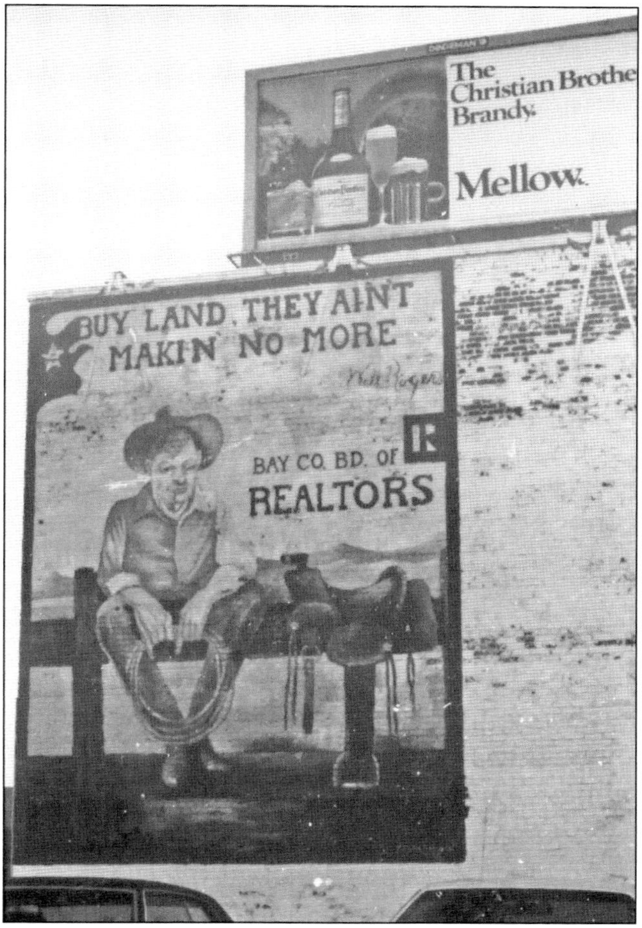

"Mural City" was a branding initiative started by Downtown Bay City Inc. in 1976. John R. Willertz, mayor of Bay City, officially proclaimed the name for the large number of bicentennial murals around the downtown area. His proclamation noted that by 1977, some 50 murals would make Bay City a major tourist destination. Costumed tours of the murals and a major marketing campaign ultimately drew nationwide attention. Above is the Atlas Furniture building at 500 Washington Avenue, which features five panels depicting space exploration, justice, a woman with a flag, Paul Revere, and a pioneer, with a sign proclaiming, "Welcome to Mural City." At right is a mural depicting Will Rogers sitting on a fence, with his saying, "Buy land, they ain't makin' no more." This mural was located on the side of the former Eagles club at 201 Washington Avenue. (Right, courtesy of Stephen Kent.)

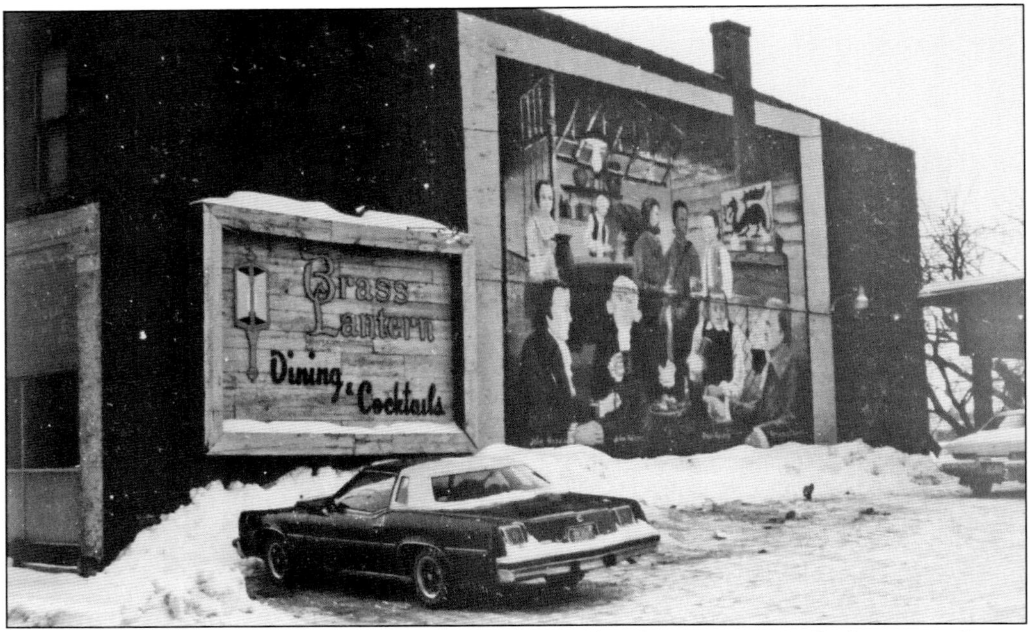

The majority of Mural City's murals were the work of local artist Terry L. Dickinson, a former math teacher at Bay City Central who quit teaching in 1974 to pursue a passion for mural painting. After Dickinson's stay in Bay City, he branched out to other communities, and his work can be seen throughout Michigan. Above is one of Dickinson's murals, identified as *Founding Fathers at Tavern*. It was located on the building directly to the south of the former Brass Lantern Restaurant, which was eventually torn down. Below is a mural on the side of the former Cum-Craft hobby shop on Adams Street (to the north of the former P.M. Depot), depicting 18th-century warships with the saying, "If we merely celebrate their war we've missed the essence of our heritage." (Both, courtesy of Stephen Kent.)

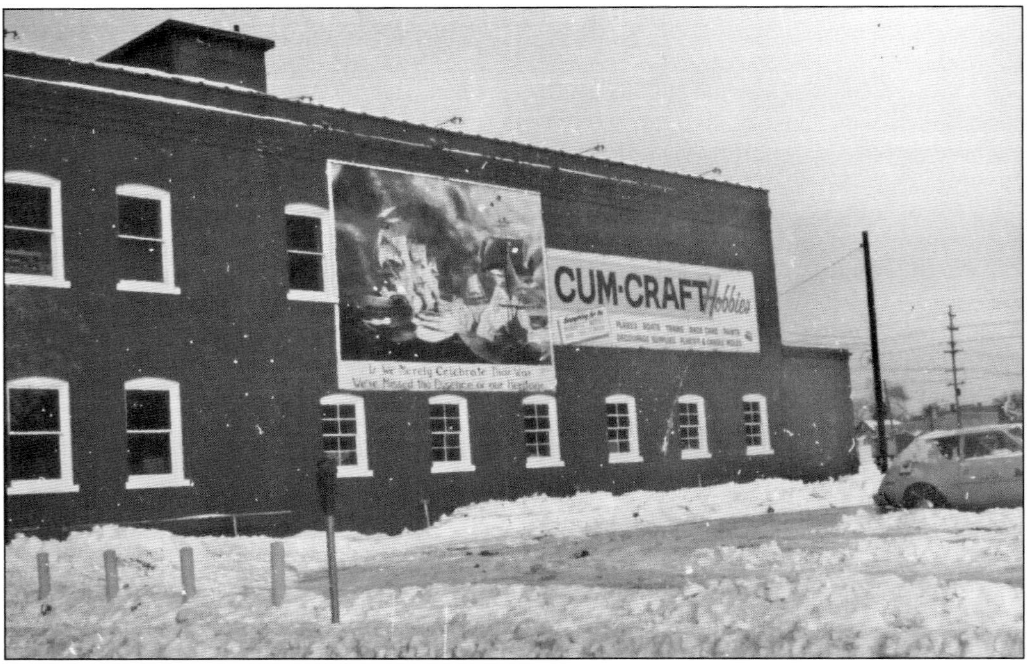

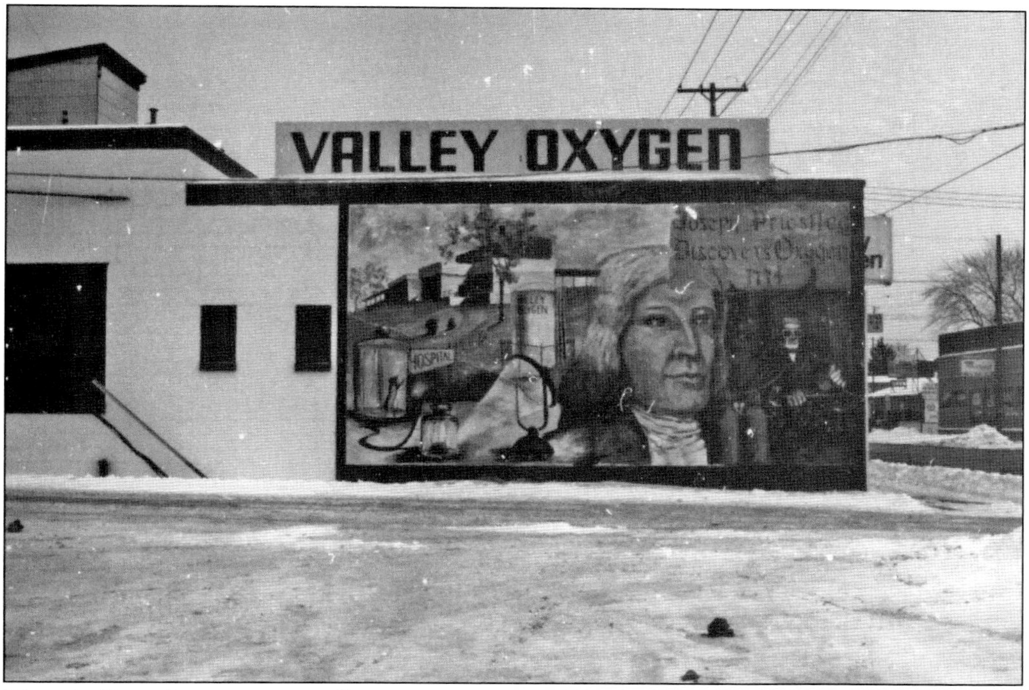

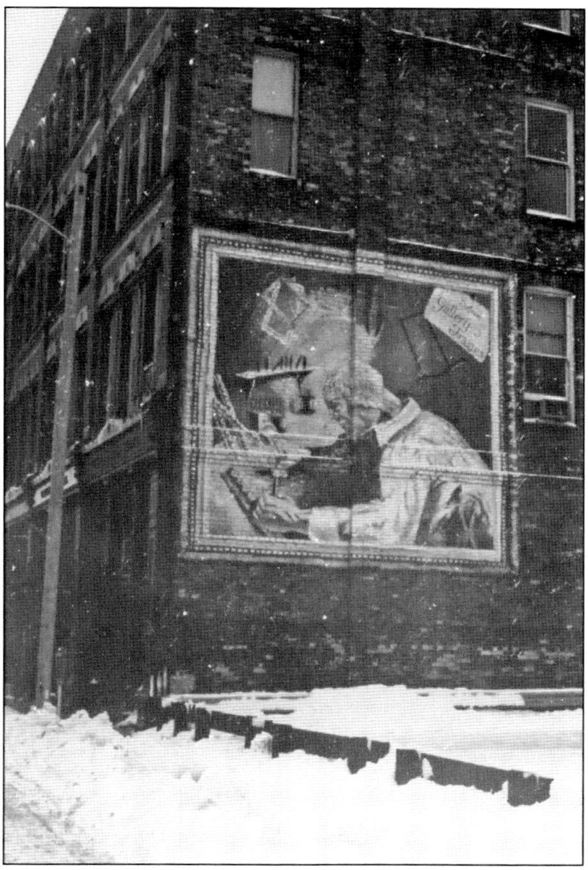

Though 50 works were reportedly completed, an inventory of murals around Bay City from the early 1980s lists 29 works of varying topics of local and national significance. Of these, two are listed as removed, while one is listed as not up yet. The condition of most is listed as good. Three artists are identified, including Scott Shaver and J. Spring in addition to Dickinson. Several are unattributed. The bulk of the murals with patriotic themes date from 1975–1976 and were painted by Terry Dickinson. The photograph above shows the Valley Oxygen building at 311 Columbus Avenue. This 1977 Dickinson mural depicts Joseph Priestly discovering oxygen in 1774. At right is another Dickinson mural, this one of a framer with "Nielsen Gallery of Frames" in the corner, which was located on the northeast side of the Shearer Building. (Both, courtesy of Stephen Kent.)

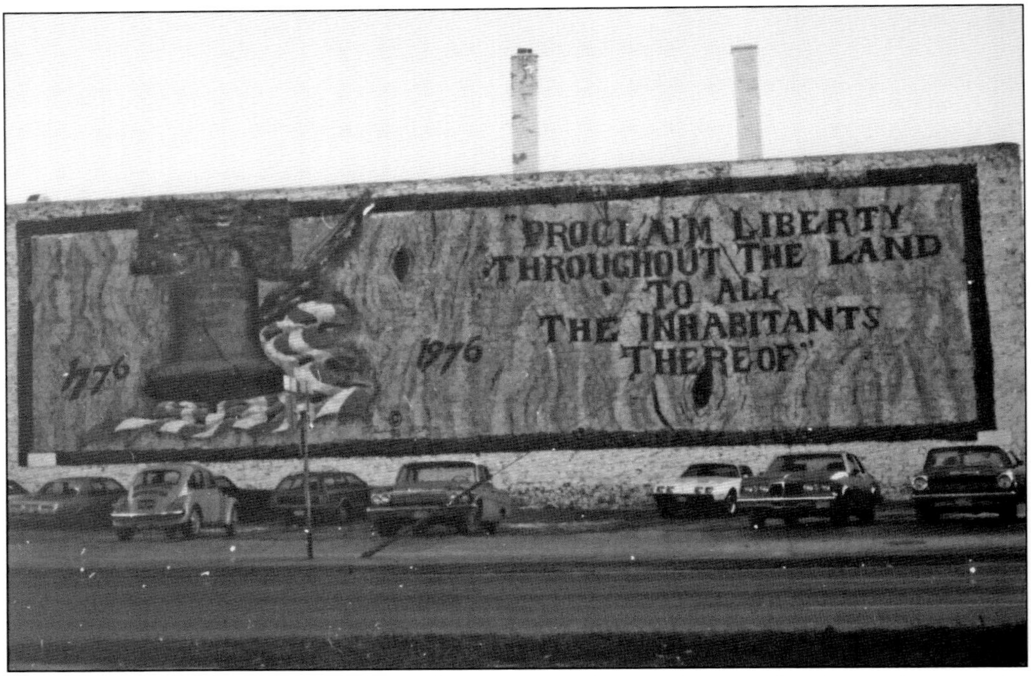

The *Liberty* mural was Terry Dickinson's first in Bay City and is one of only two that remain. Located on the north side of the Dunlop building at Seventh Street and Washington Avenue, the mural was covered by siding for many years and rediscovered in 2013 by workers making building improvements. It measures 100 feet long and 25 feet high and was completed in less than a week in September 1974. (Courtesy of Stephen Kent.)

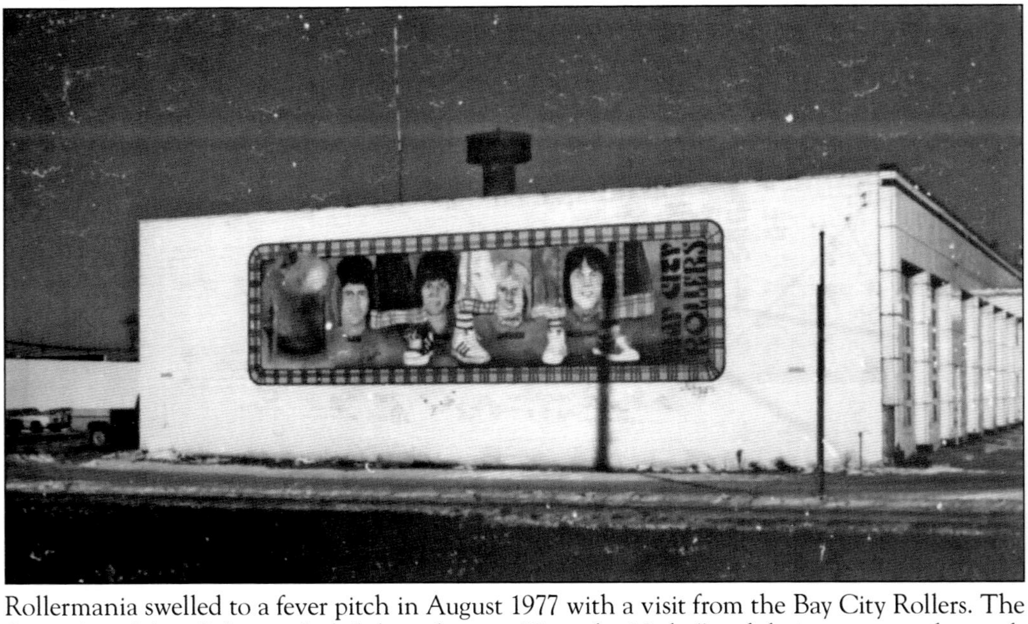

Rollermania swelled to a fever pitch in August 1977 with a visit from the Bay City Rollers. The Scottish rock band's hits included the infectious "Saturday Night," and their name was the result of a dart throw at a map. The *Bay City Times* headline branded their visit the "Biggest thing Since Bridge Fell In." This mural was painted on the back of the Metro Transit Authority building on Water Street in honor of their visit. (Courtesy of Stephen Kent.)

Four

BUSINESSES AND BLOCKS

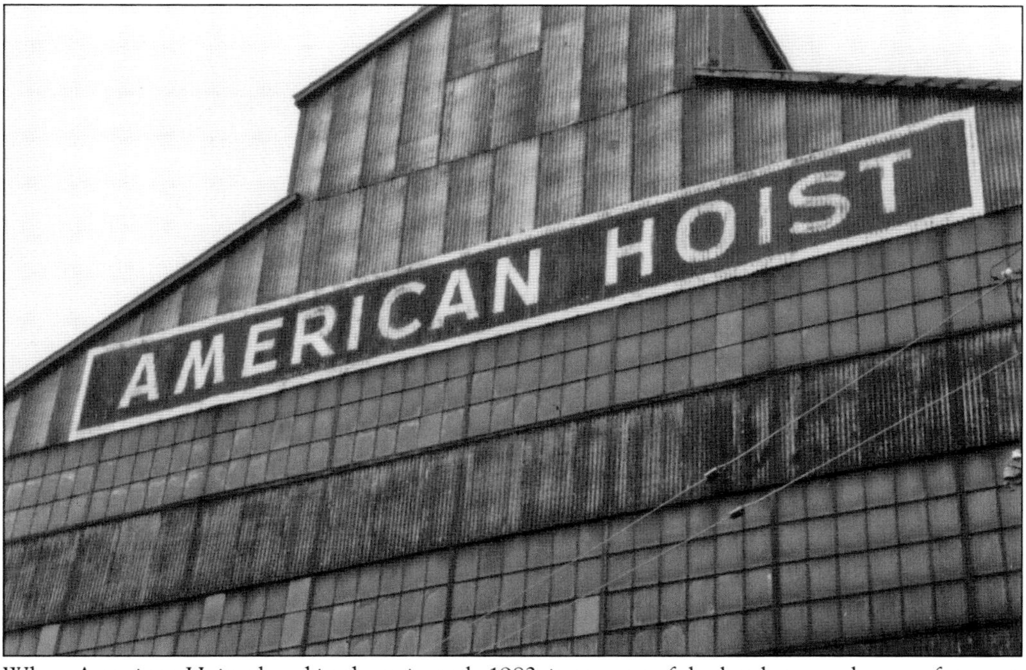

When American Hoist closed its doors in early 1983, it was one of the last large-scale manufacturers left in Bay City, and the loss was certainly felt within the community. Many businesses have come and gone throughout the years, including some that have had significant history in the community. Launched as Industrial Works in the 1870s and later Industrial Brownhoist, American Hoist had been manufacturing on the same site for over a century.

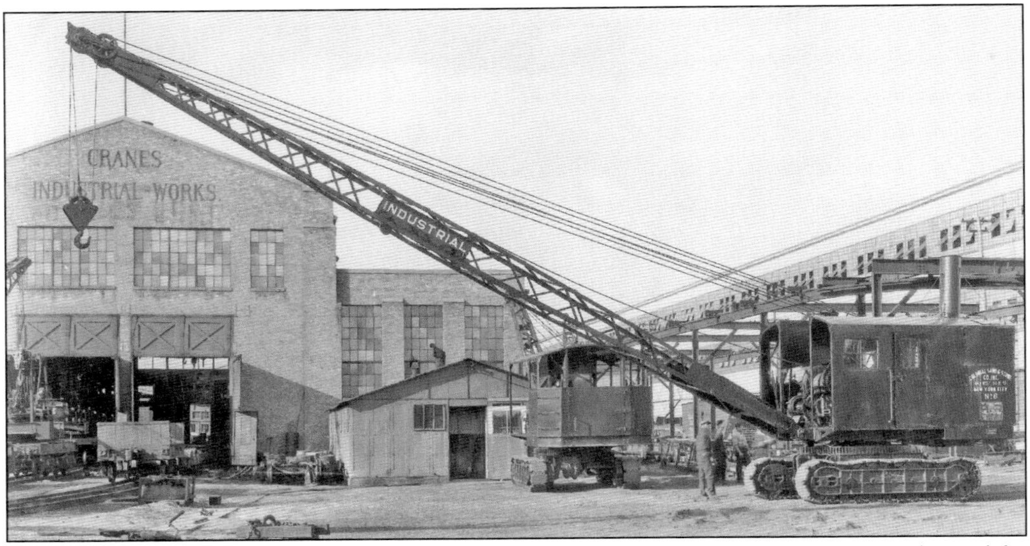

Industrial Works was known worldwide for its rail-mounted wrecking cranes, primarily used for cleaning up debris from rail accidents. Other products included rail-mounted and traction machinery such as the steam crane pictured here. Its manufacturing complex, on the riverfront, came to occupy an area roughly from Eleventh Street south to the foot of Columbus Avenue and from Saginaw Street to the Saginaw River; with 1,800 employees, 59 buildings, and 29 acres in 1920.

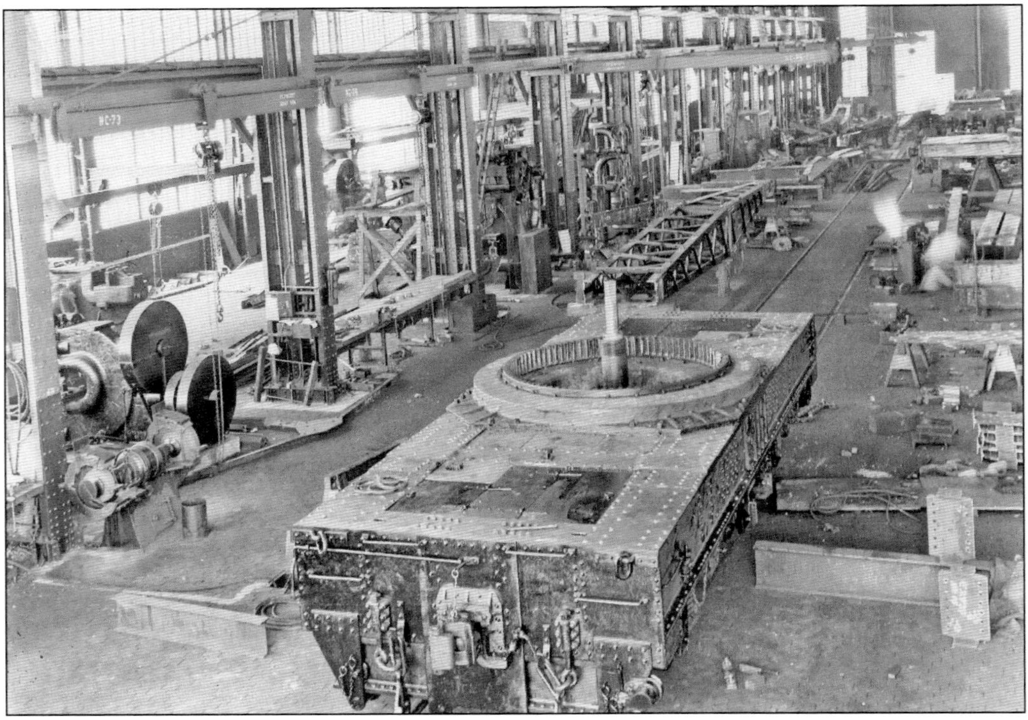

This is a rare photograph of the interior of one of the Industrial Brownhoist fabrication buildings around 1935, showing a railcar base with the main gear and shaft where the crane cab would later be placed. A section of crane boom is seen in the center background. These massive buildings were used until the company closed in the 1980s and were torn down decades later when the site was redeveloped.

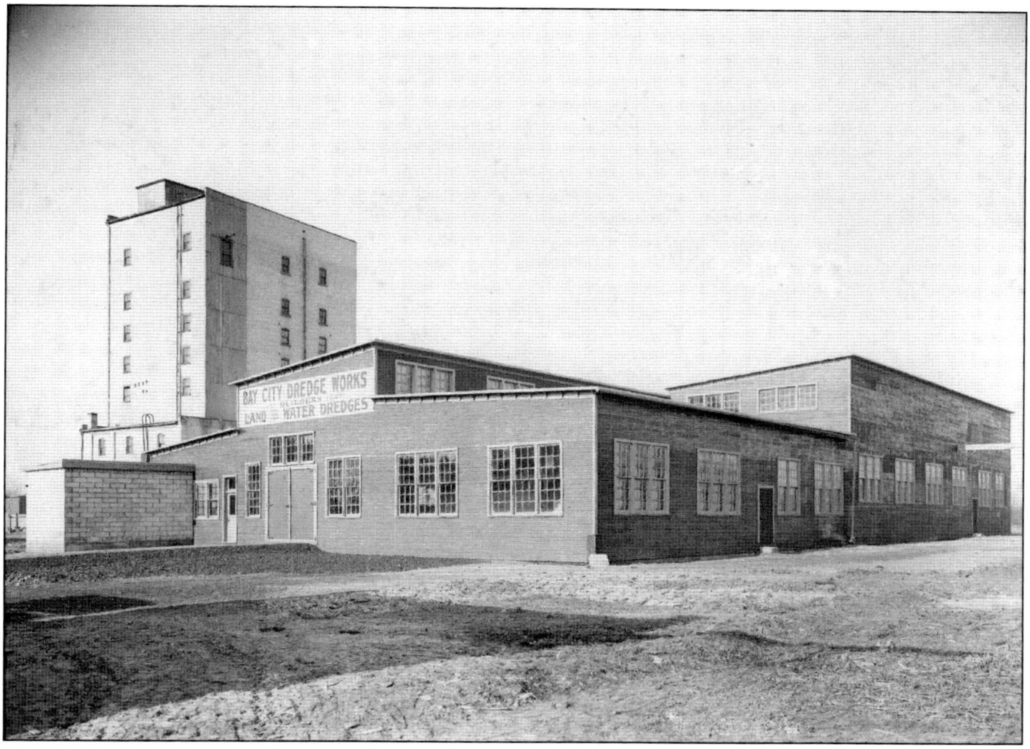

Bay City Dredge Works was started in 1913, and its initial products included dredging machines and mechanical shovels that were sent all over the world from the factory at 2611 Center Avenue. In 1931, the company was reorganized as Bay City Shovels and operated as the city's fourth-largest employer at that time. In 1960, Bay City Shovels was sold to Unit Crane and Shovel of Milwaukee, Wisconsin. Currently, Bay Cast Corporation operates on the site. One of the first land dredges built by Bay City Dredge Works in 1914 had a .75-yard capacity dipper and a 38-foot-long boom (below). One of its walking dredges is preserved as a National Engineering Landmark in Florida for its outstanding contribution during the 1920s to help create the Tamiami Trail, a major highway from Tampa to Miami across the Everglades.

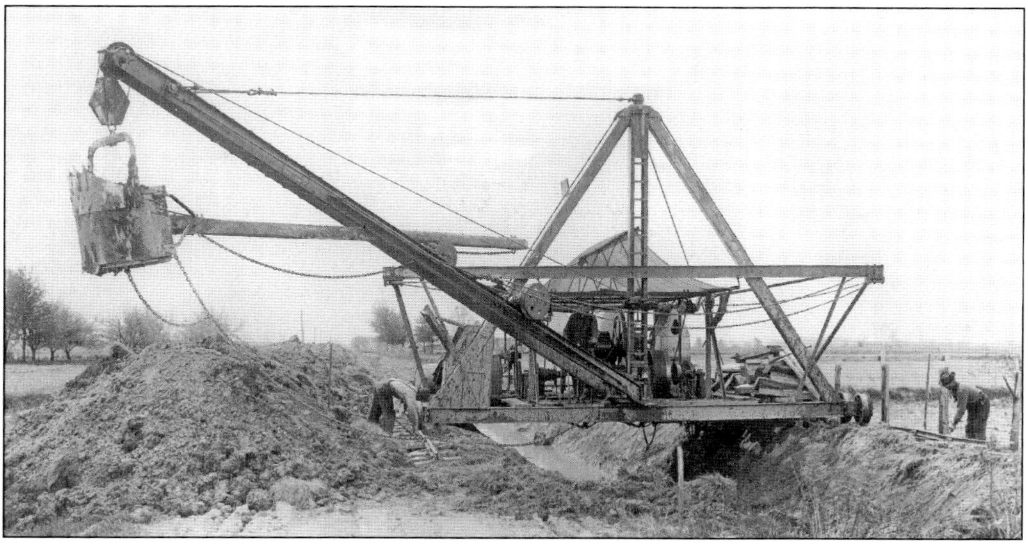

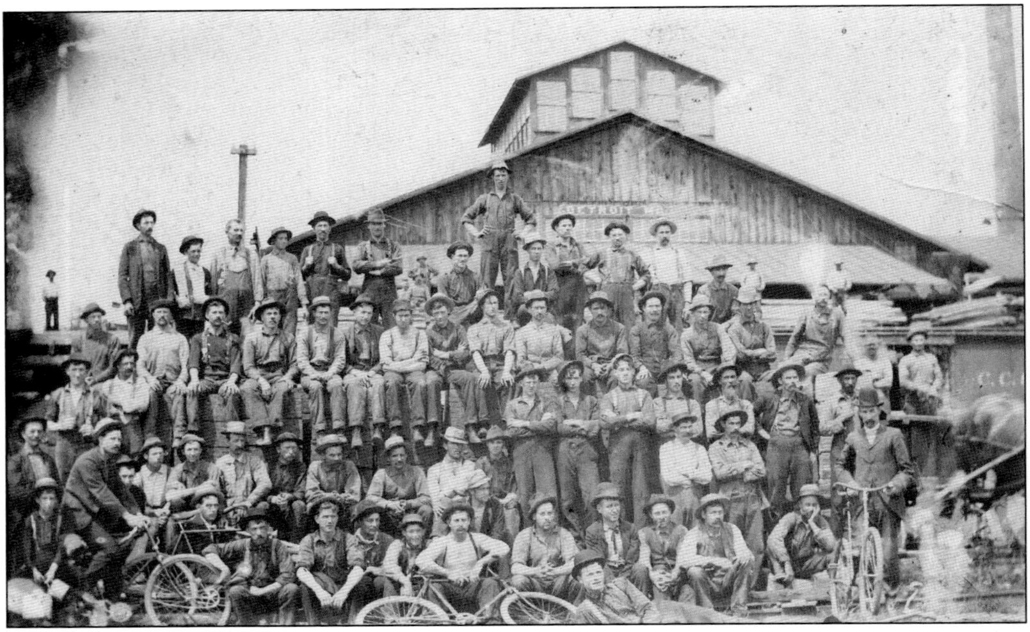

Bay City's largest industry to date revolved around the cutting, processing, and shipping of lumber for the world market. During the heyday of the lumbering industry (1860–1890), over 100 mills operated along the banks of the Saginaw River. The Detroit Mill was located at the foot of North Sherman (where Powertrain currently stands). In 1882, the peak year, a total of 858,344,000 board feet of lumber was shipped from the Saginaw River.

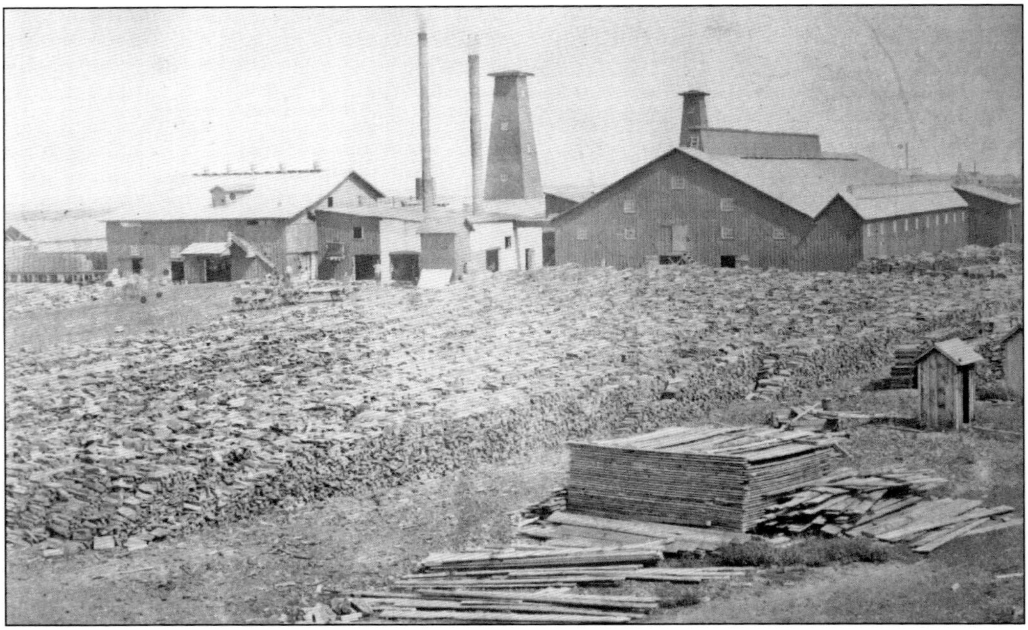

J.R. Hall owned what was once the largest shingle mill in the Saginaw Valley. The production from that mill alone accounted for half of all shingles produced in Bay County. Located in Essexville, along the river at the foot of Scheurmann Road, the mill could cut 6,000 shingles per hour. This photograph of the mill dates from 1874. In 1882, a total of 176,376,500 wooden shingles were shipped from the Saginaw River.

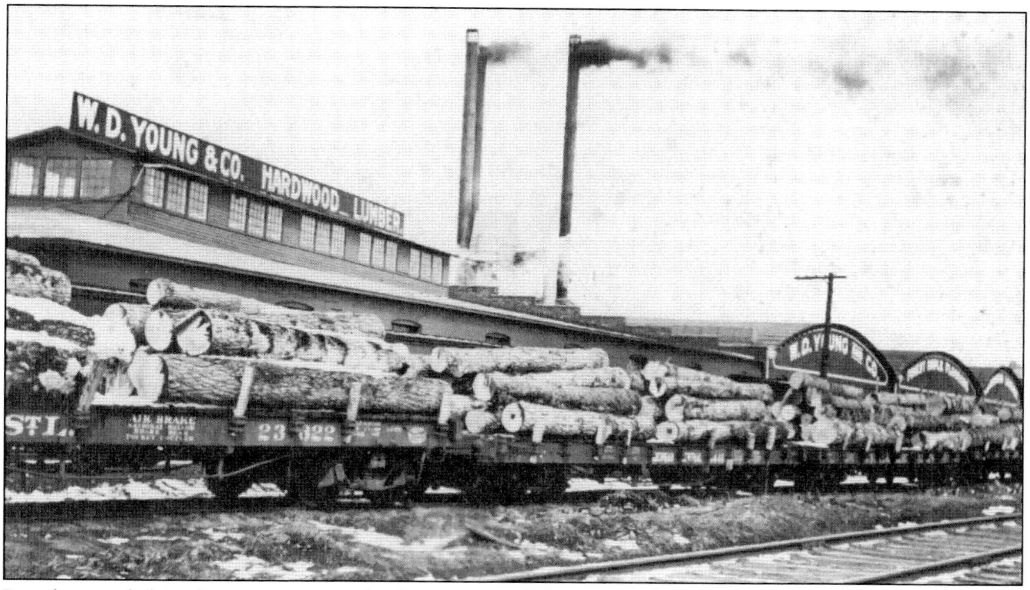

Lumber and shingles were certainly the most proliferate products shipped; however, there was a thriving market for other items made of wood. W.D. Young and Company manufactured hardwood flooring at its plant, which was located in the Salzburg area of the west side, on the south side of Salzburg Road near the train tracks east toward the river. It was once known as the world's largest manufacturer of hardwood flooring.

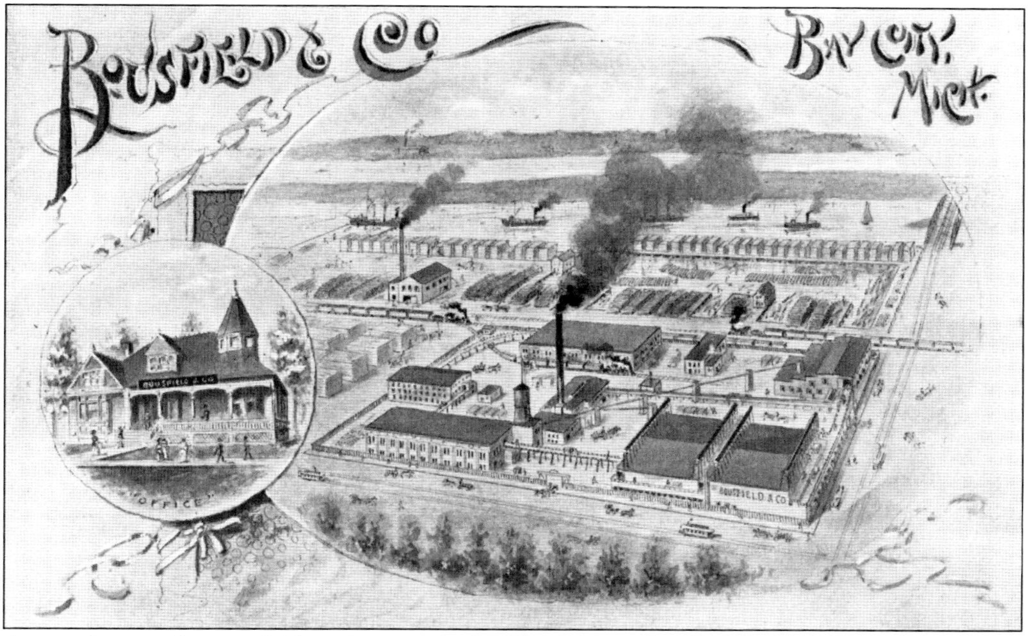

As pine became less available, other wood-related industries developed that relied on the sturdier products that could be developed from the previously untapped hardwoods. Items such as wooden pails, tubs, broom handles, and curtain rods became important commodities. In the 1880s, Bousfield and Company, located at the foot of Thirty-Fourth Street in Portsmouth, became the world's largest factory to produce woodenware items such as washtubs, churns, pails, wooden bowls, and utensils.

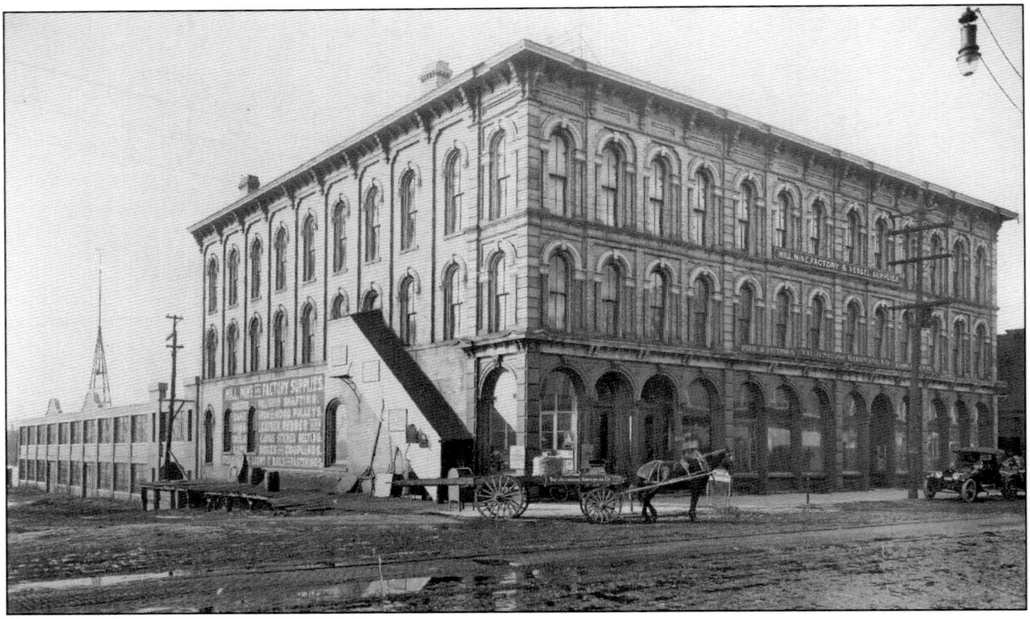

The Jennison Hardware Company had the distinction of once being the largest and oldest wholesale and retail hardware firm in the state of Michigan. Started by Charles E. Jennison in 1850, its second building (above) was built in 1870 at Fifth and Water Streets. Destroyed by a fire in March 1924, a larger building was rebuilt on the site. That new building along with an addition along Fifth Street toward the river and a steel warehouse on Water Street between Second and Third Streets were the hub of Jennison's business until it closed. The post-1924 hardware building and the steel warehouse have been renovated into condominiums. Below is Jennison's lock department, displaying many shapes, sizes, and styles of padlocks alongside hasps, door knockers, and brass house numbers.

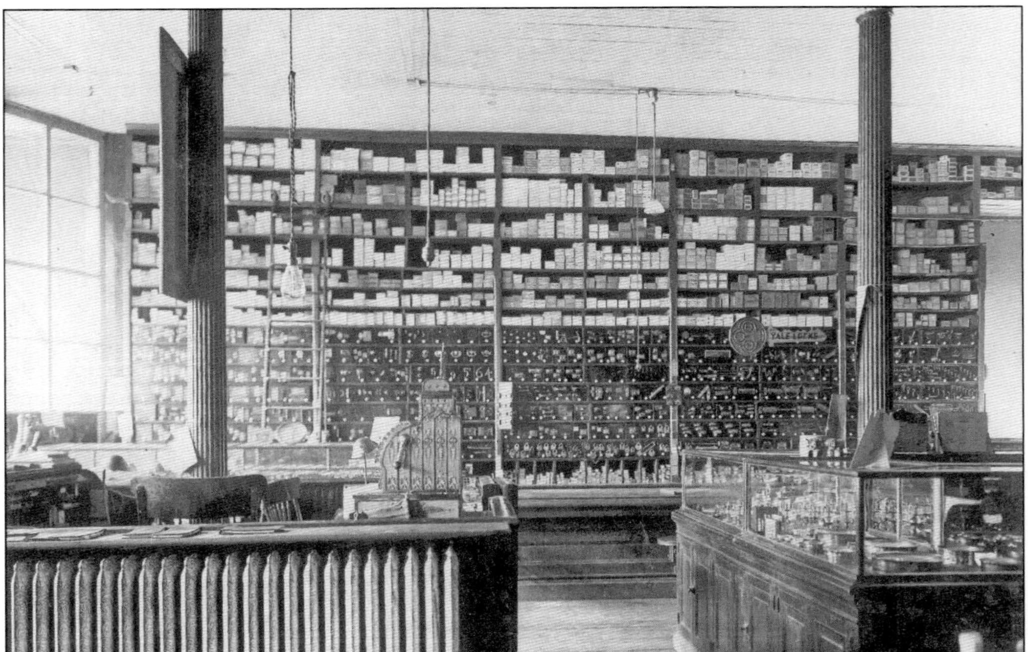

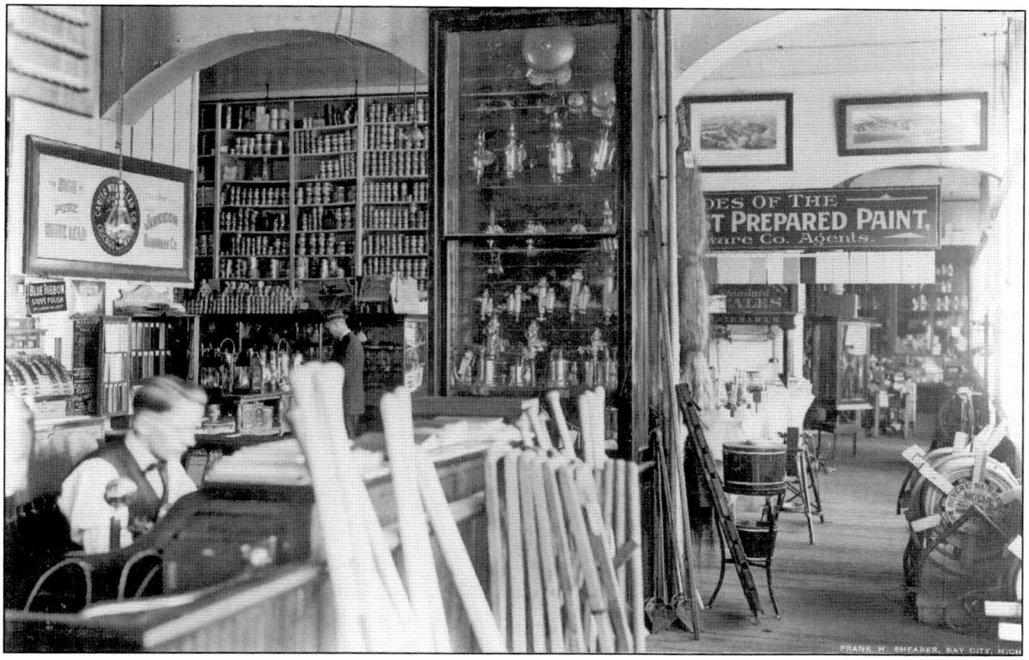

The Jennison Hardware Company advertised mill, mine, and factory supplies in the early 1900s. Above, the interior of a packed hardware store displays many more of the products sold by Jennison. Security bells, brass valves, lanterns, and rubber hose sit outside of the paint department. An early paint sample cabinet can be seen behind the head of the employee at the desk. Below is a continuation of the above image; it shows the area to the left of the seated employee, who appears in both. Visible in this photograph are many types of brass valves on shelves reaching to the ceiling and showcases holding a good selection of brass nozzles. In the background are wooden axe and shovel handles.

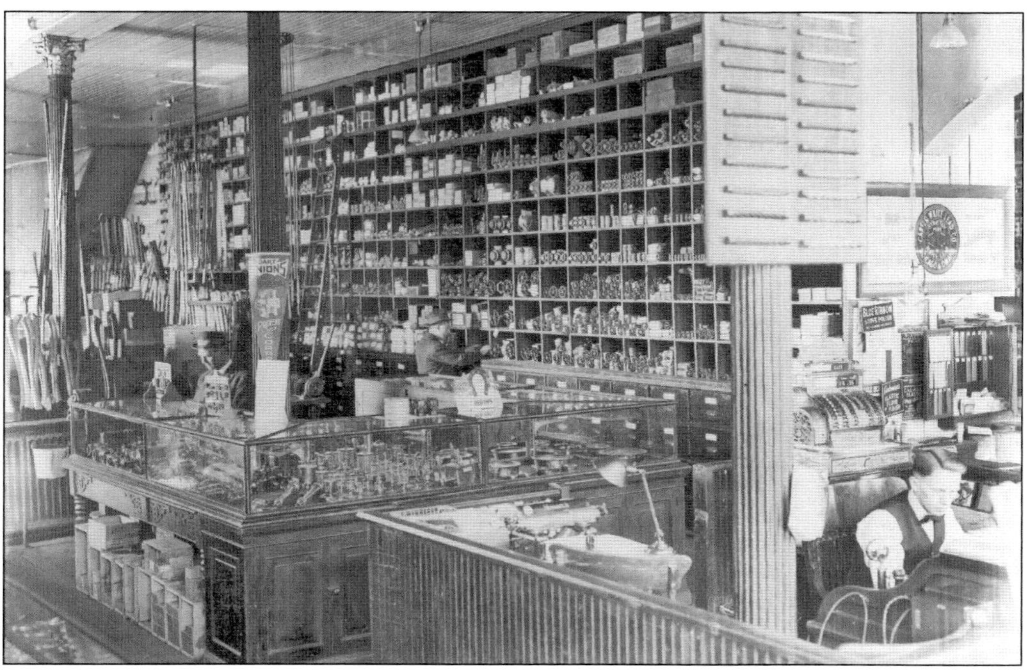

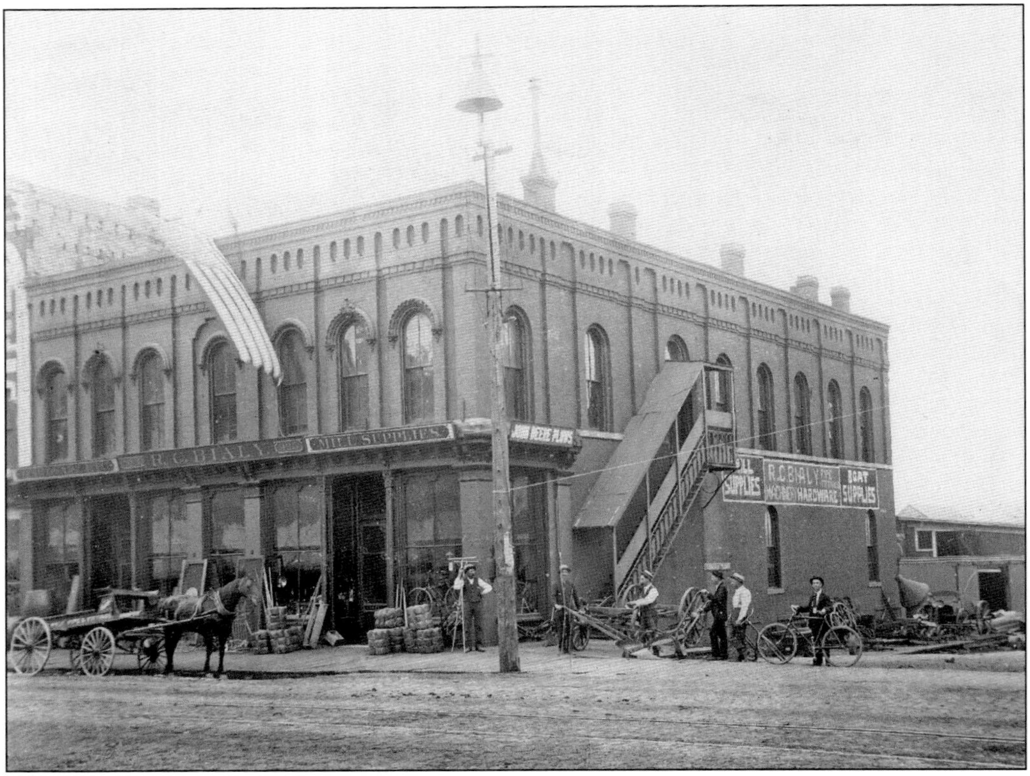

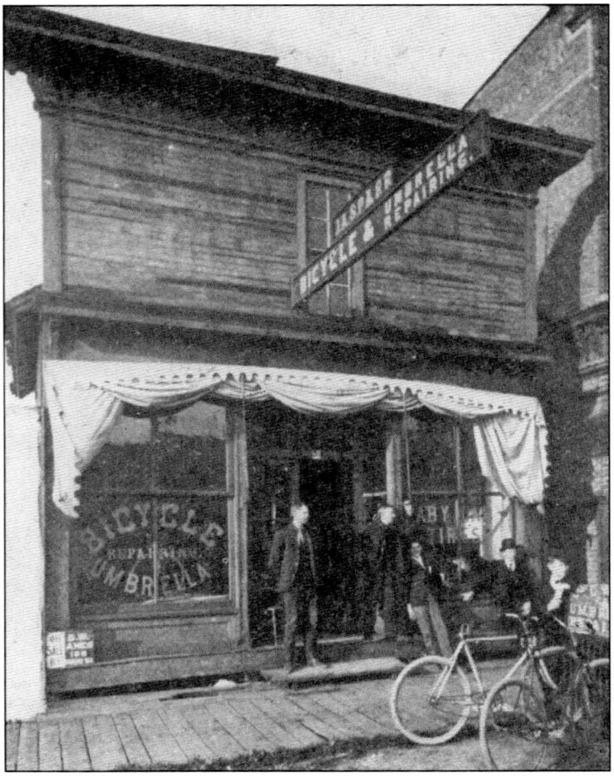

Robert C. Bialy, brother of local businessman Mendel J. Bialy, ran a hardware company located at Fourth and Water Streets (925 Water Street), pictured here around 1885. This building was destroyed by fire in February 1914. In the late 1800s, hardware stores furnished many different types of machinery products, including mill machinery and parts, farming machinery (including plows), pipes and fittings, bicycles and parts, wagon parts, and marine supplies.

J.A. Sparr ran this bicycle and umbrella repair shop at 513 Third Street around 1905. According to promotion of the time, "Mr. Sparr is a Bay City boy, and a surgeon of no common cast when bicycles and umbrellas have broken ribs. He has a complete outfit for repair work, is a mechanic of acknowledged skill, is busy every day and at his post six days of the week."

The Bay City Hardware Company started in 1902 with Robert V. Mundy as the first chairman and sold hardware and farm implements. Located at 1009–1015 Saginaw Street, the brick building was in the middle of the block between Third and Fourth Streets, on the west side of the thoroughfare. On July 12, 1952, a massive fire broke out that was considered the most costly and spectacular fire in the city up to that time. According to department sources, a total of 110 firefighters worked the scene, including Saginaw and local auxiliary. Flames shot 100 feet into the sky, and it took two and a half hours to contain with a crowd of 4,000 people watching. After the total loss, the company moved to a new location on Sherman Street and operated until 1978. The site is now a parking lot.

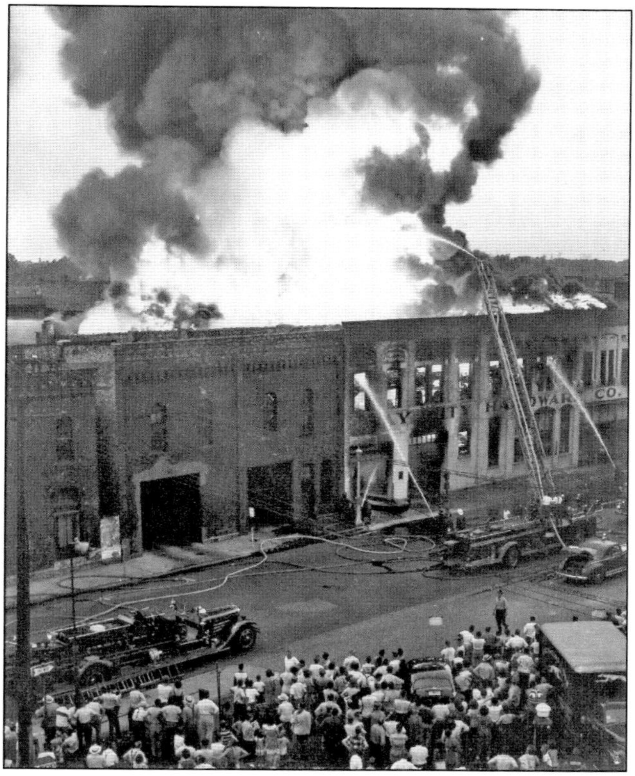

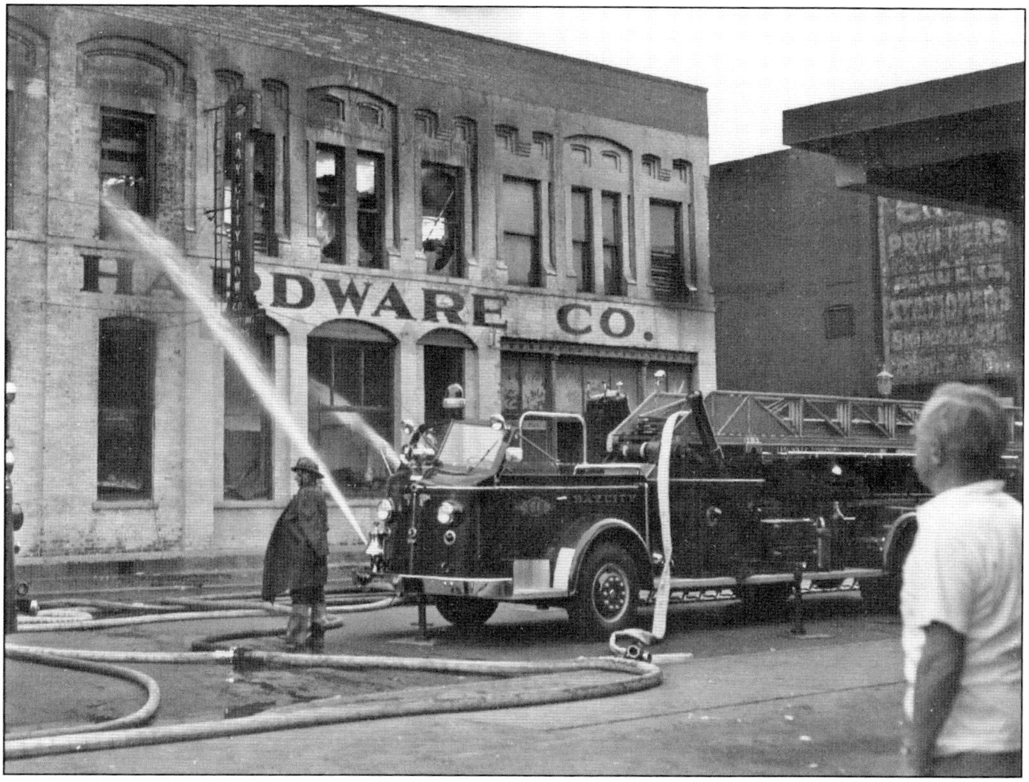

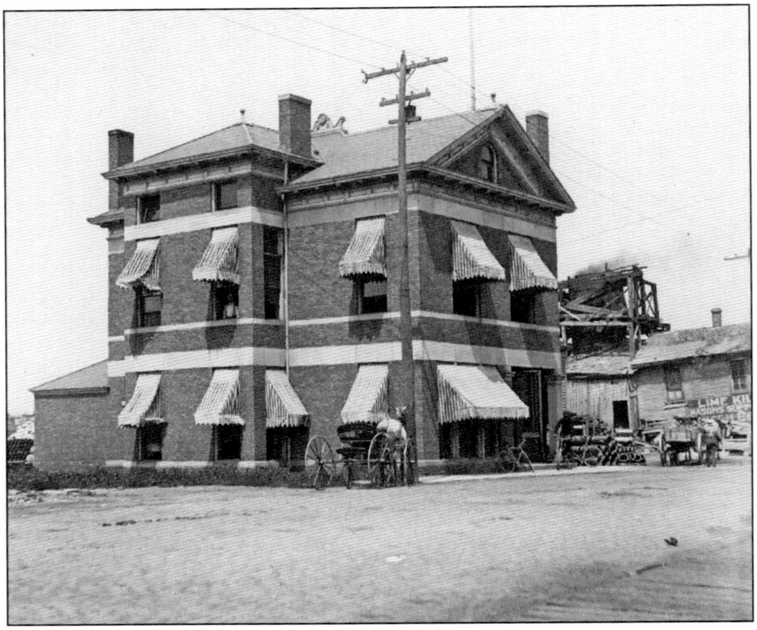

Brothers William H. and Fred E. Boutell (sons of Capt. Ben Boutell) and cousin Lorenzo Boutell ran Boutell Bros. and Company at Second and Water Streets. Dealers in coal and mason's supplies, they became one of the leading fuel companies in the city. They manufactured Kelley Island White Lime, handled the highest grades of Lehigh Valley coal (more heat, less clinkers), and carried a complete line of high-grade masonry supplies.

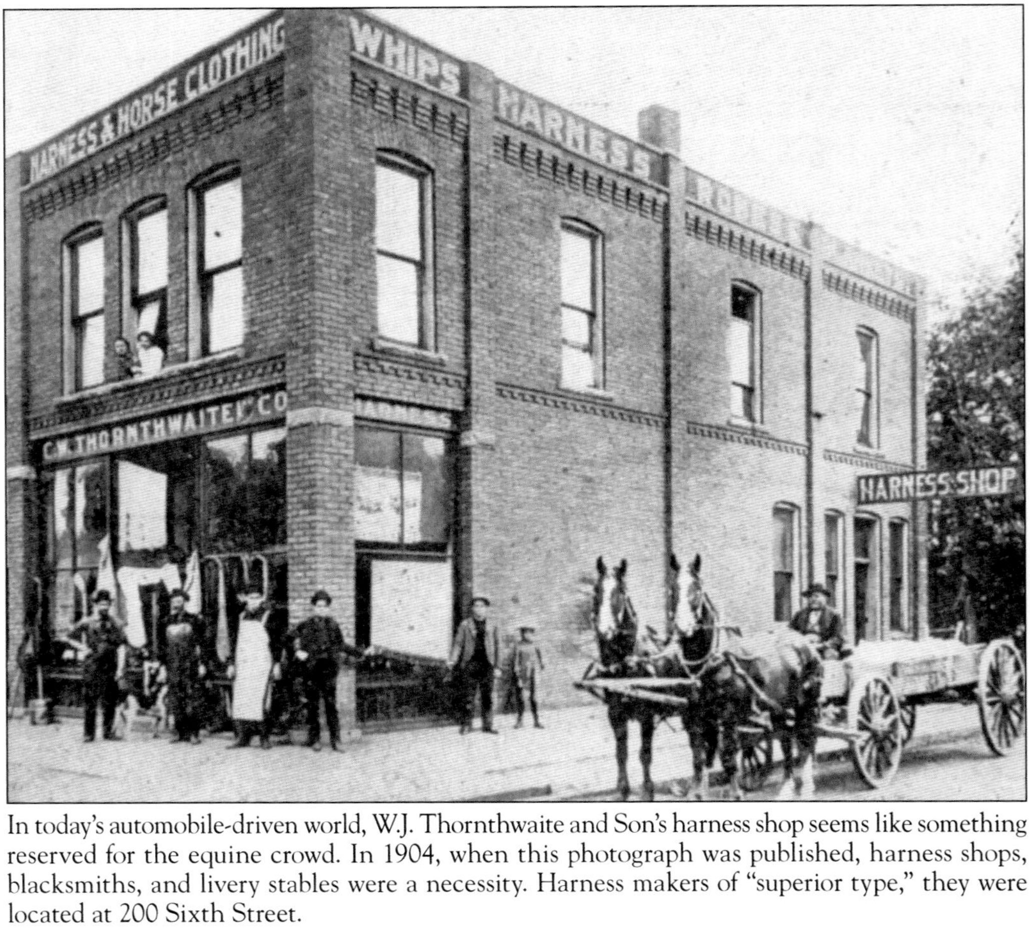

In today's automobile-driven world, W.J. Thornthwaite and Son's harness shop seems like something reserved for the equine crowd. In 1904, when this photograph was published, harness shops, blacksmiths, and livery stables were a necessity. Harness makers of "superior type," they were located at 200 Sixth Street.

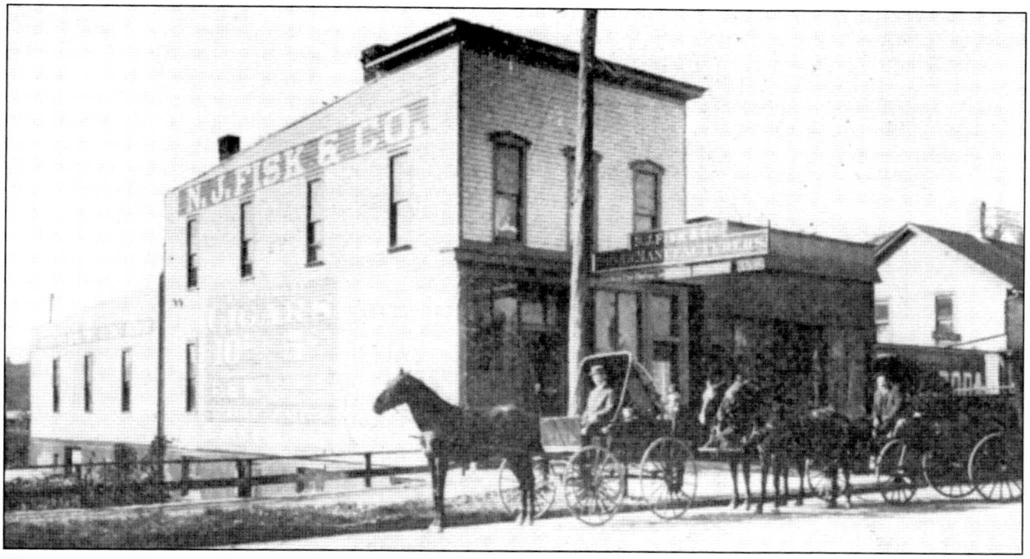

Cigar manufacturers N.J. Fisk and Company organized in 1896 at 208 East Midland Street in West Bay City. By 1906, they were manufacturing 75,000 cigars a month, including the F.&W., Socrates, F.&W. Jr., Michigan Central, and King Buck brands. Adda Fisk, who worked for the family business, was listed as a "stripper" in the 1902–1903 city directory. Like many professions, cigar manufacturing had its own terminology to describe the various tasks. A stripper stripped the tobacco leaves during the preparation process. Below is the interior of the packing room of the B.R. Hahn Cigar Factory, located at 206–208 Fifth Street, pictured around 1924. Notice the finished cigars on the counter ready for packing in the boxes stacked on the right. The company was one of only two active cigar manufacturers left in Bay City when it closed in 1948.

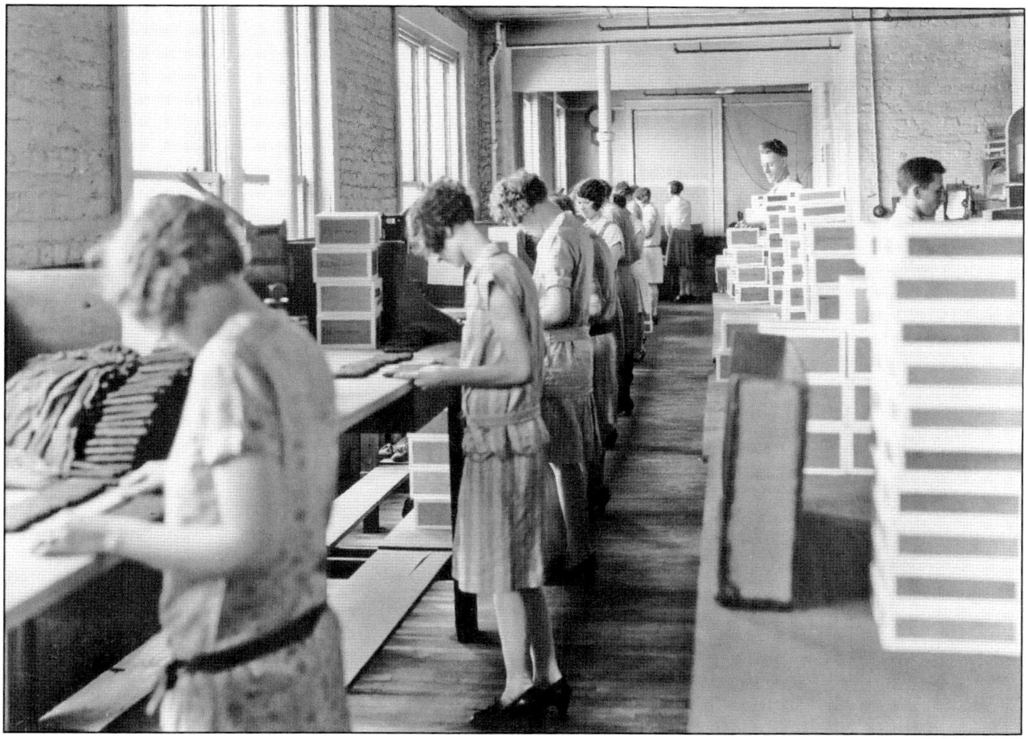

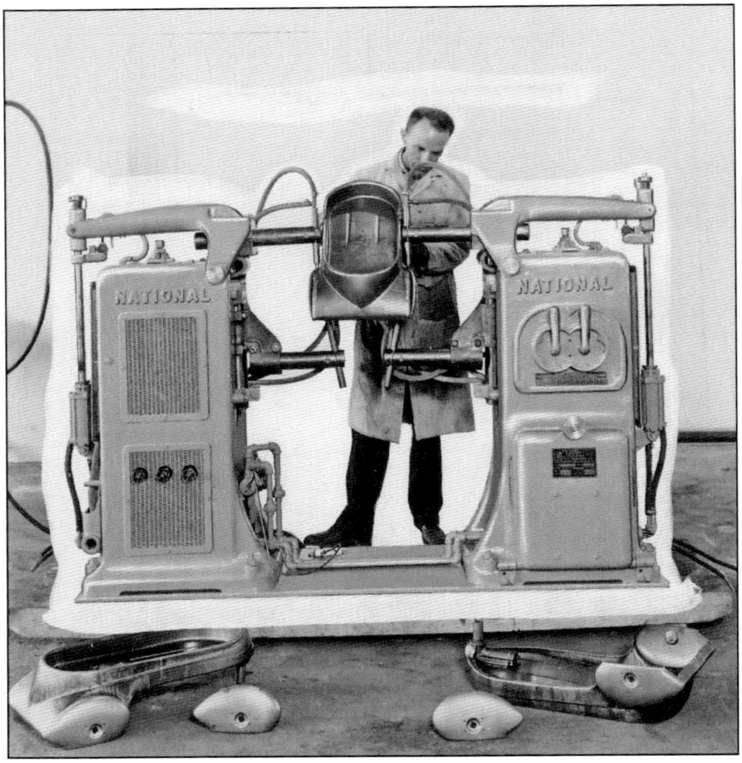

National Electric Welding Machines Co. was located at 1916 North Trumbull Street in 1960, and was one of several Bay City manufacturers of welding machines, including the Resistance Welding Corporation (RWC) and United Welders. These welding machines were made to assist manufacturers of appliances, auto parts, and many other products where welding needed to be consistent, precise, and complicated. This promotional photograph shows a National welding machine and operator.

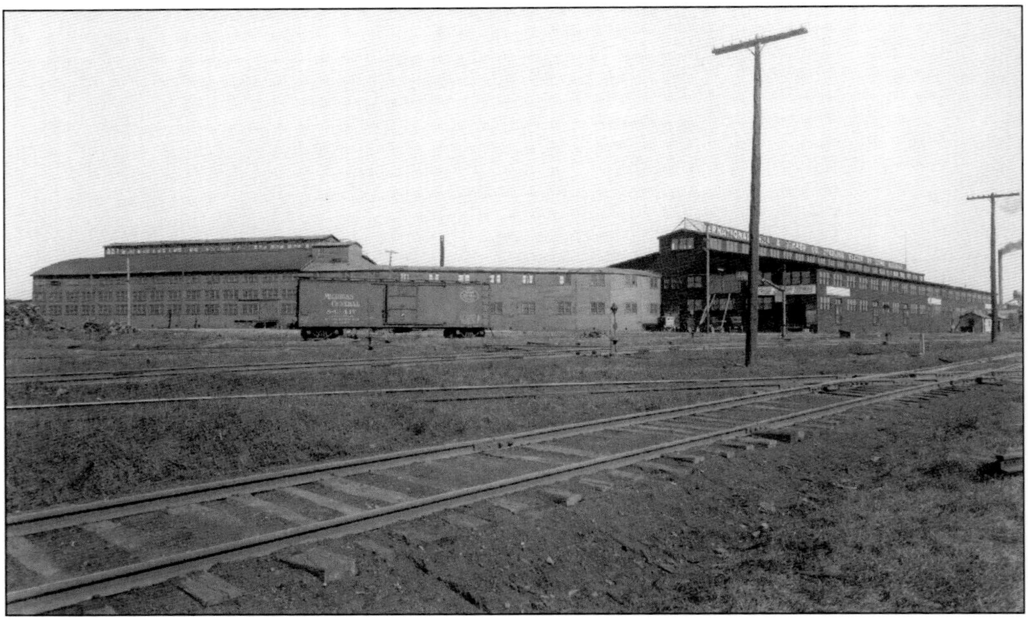

For almost 70 years, Bay City boasted three of the world's largest pre-cut housing companies. Aladdin Homes, Lewis/Liberty Homes, and Sterling Homes sold over 200,000 homes ranging from bungalows to luxury-style mansions. Illustrated catalogs helped sales well into the 1960s. Market shifts in the early 1970s caused Sterling and Liberty to close, followed by Aladdin in 1983. Shown is the mill of International Mill and Timber (Sterling Homes) on the west side, south of Salzburg Avenue, around 1920.

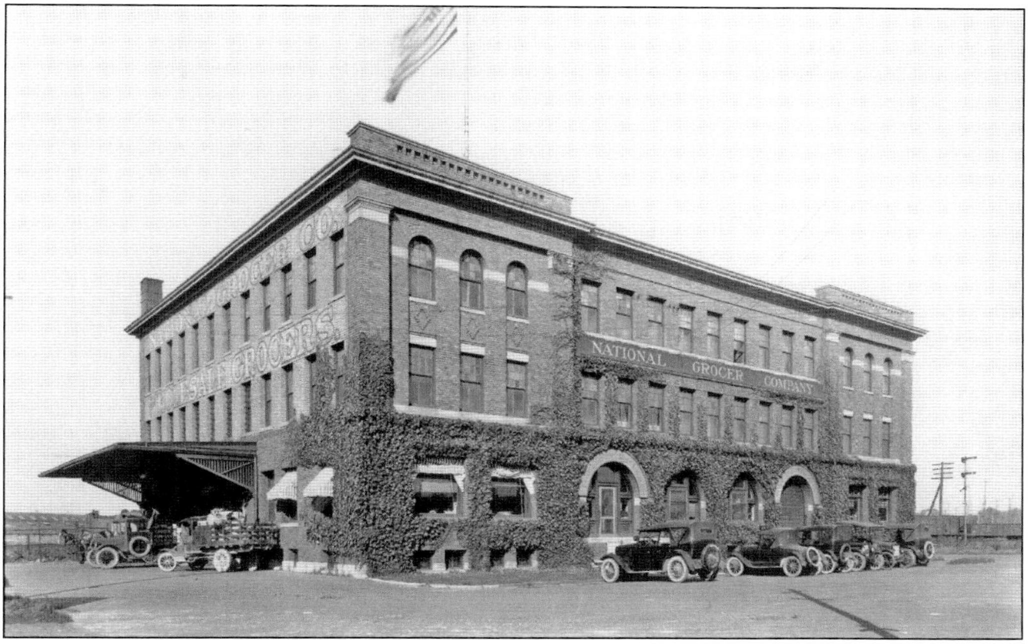

Herbert Gustin, Charles E. Cook, and Frank J. Buckley started wholesale grocery company Gustin, Cook, and Buckley in the latter part of the 19th century as a distribution center to supply local grocers. Originally located at 1001 North Water Street, the company moved to a large brick warehouse at the foot of Washington Avenue near Woodside Lane by 1910 (above, about 1915). At that time, it was a branch of the National Grocer Company. By the 1940s, the building was occupied by Bay City Milling and Grocer Company, wholesale grocers (below, about 1940). By 1959, the company moved to 715 McGraw Avenue and was servicing nearly 100 grocers within a 200-mile radius of Bay City. The firm closed in 1993. The former Washington Avenue building was torn down in 1983 for the Liberty Bridge project.

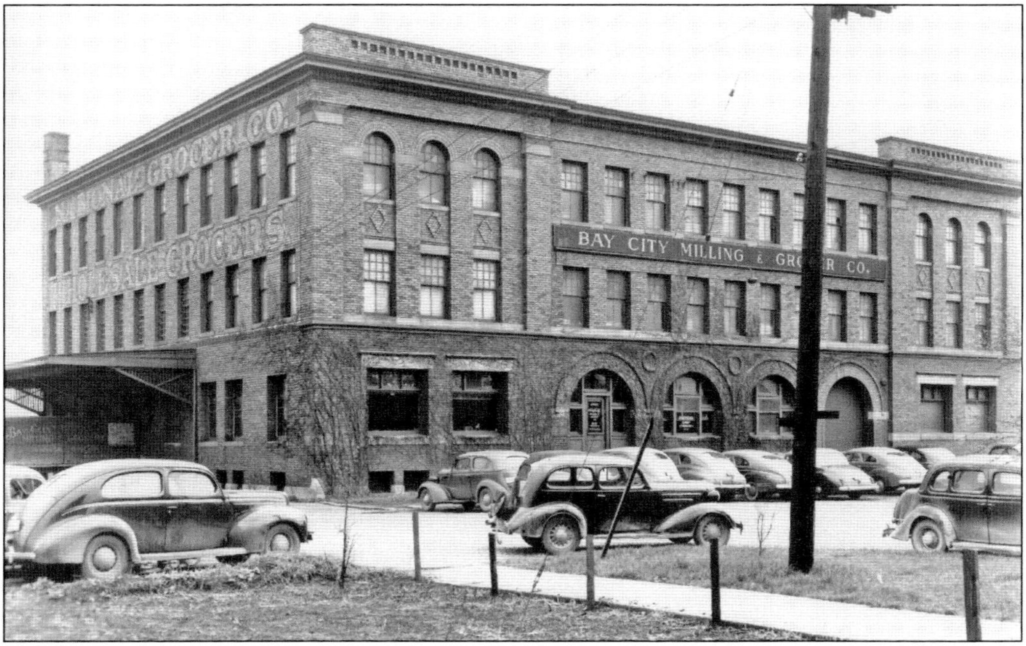

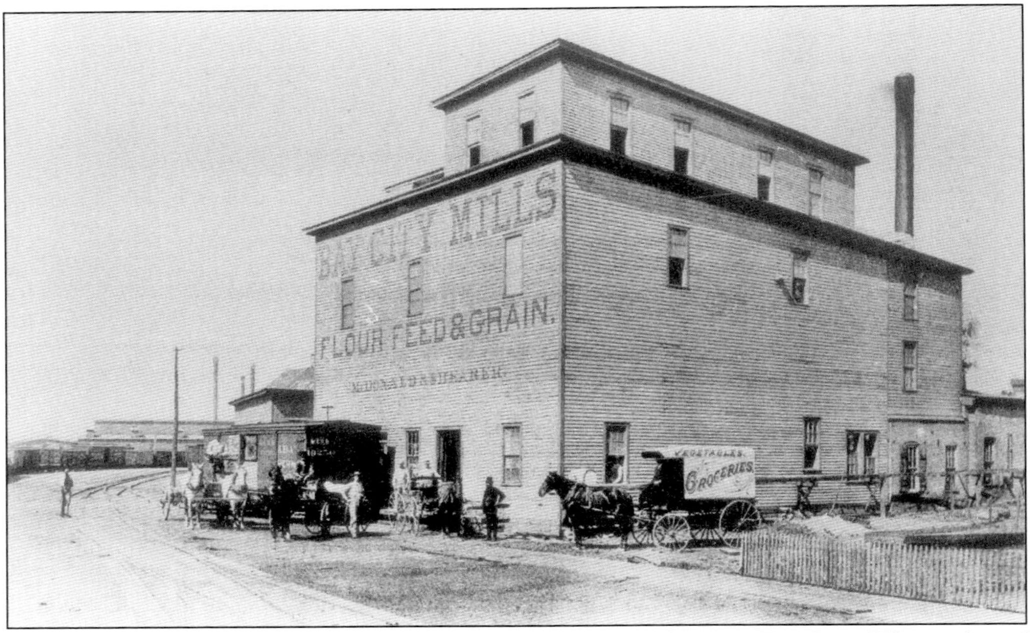

An 1898 business guide discussed the virtues of the milling industry in Bay City: "The quality of output is excelled by no other mills in Michigan grinding the same grade of wheat. Three mills pay out annually to the farmers of Bay County for grain, including wheat, corn, oats, rye, and barley." Bay City Mills was located at 1222 North Water Street at First Street.

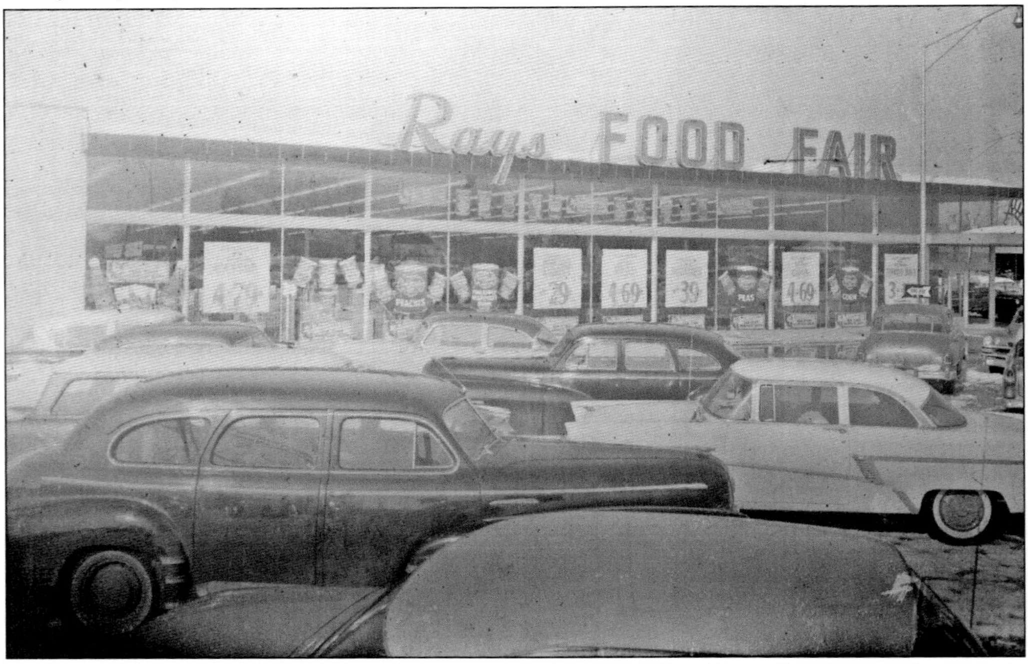

In the middle of the 20th century, grocery stores such as Ray's Food Fair offered more than simply groceries. Ray's first Bay City store opened on Washington Avenue in 1949, followed by stores on West Midland (1956), 2616 Center Avenue (1957, pictured here), Salzburg Avenue (1977) and Euclid Avenue (1978). The Center Avenue store was the last to close, in 1988. A Family Dollar store is now located on the site.

Kroger Company Grocers, known simply as Kroger, has roots in the community that go back to the late 1920s. The store pictured here around 1955 was located at 520 Center Avenue. Kroger also operated stores at 1606 Broadway Street, 109 North Henry Street, 1018 North Johnson Street, and 1029 South Madison Avenue. These smaller stores were consolidated into two large superstores by 1980, one on Euclid Avenue and the other on Center Avenue in Essexville.

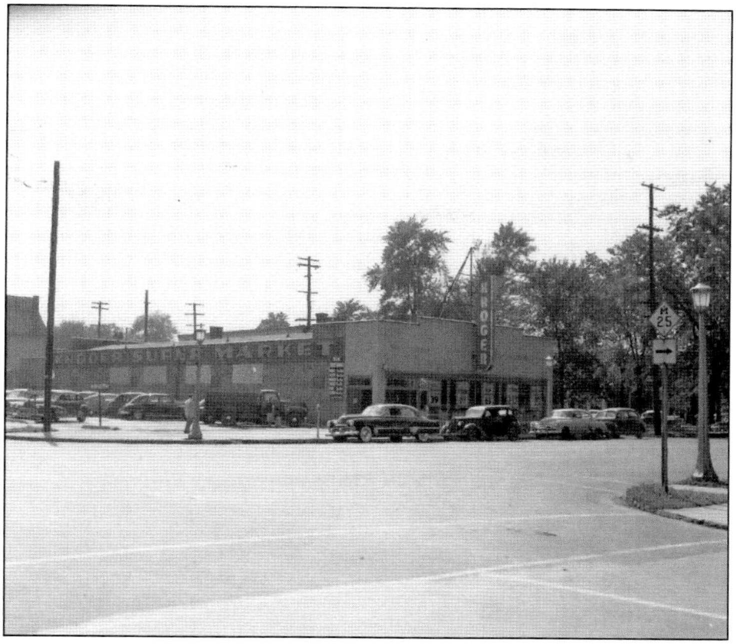

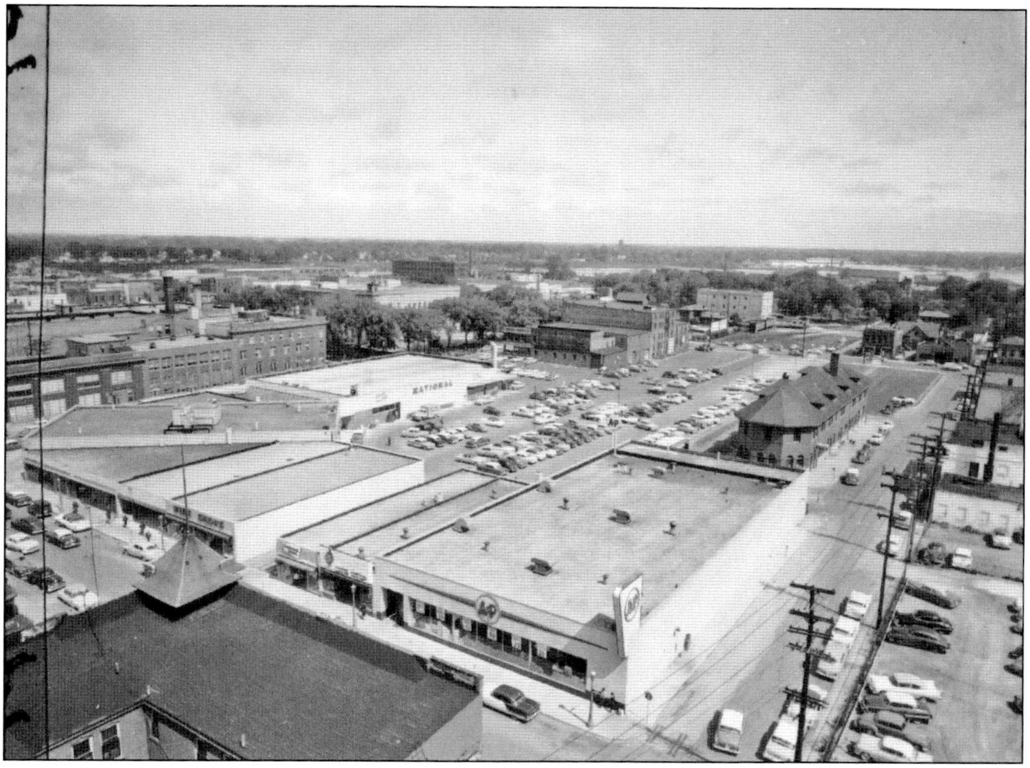

In 1936, the Great Atlantic and Pacific Tea Company (A&P) was started in Pennsylvania. Eight stores were opened in Bay City by 1938, at locations on Center Avenue and Johnson, Columbus, Midland and State Streets. By 1955, the company consolidated to one supermarket location at 501 Fifth Street (pictured here around 1957). In 1971, it opened a store at 2750 Center Avenue in Essexville, which became its sole location two years later and closed around 1979.

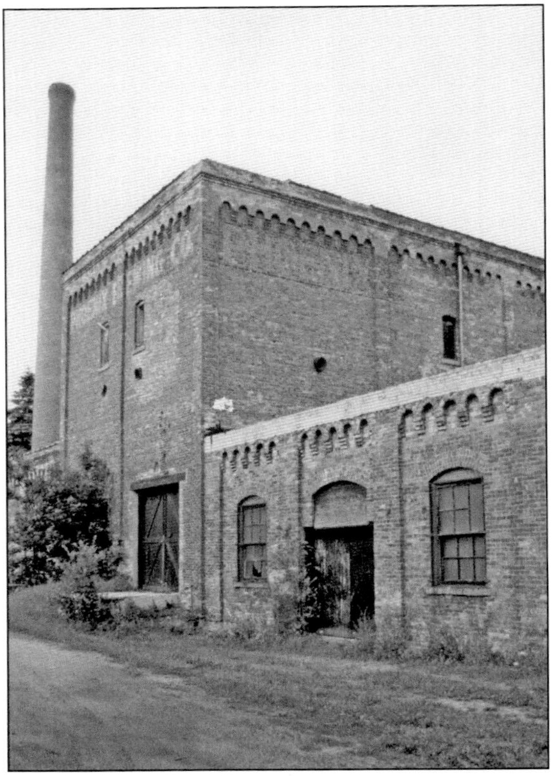

John Ross founded the West Bay City Brewing Company in 1865, with an annual production of around 5,000 barrels. Gutted by fire in 1896, it was rebuilt to an annual production capacity of 20,000 barrels, and the name changed to Phoenix, symbolizing rebirth. By 1952, the company was out of business. The building, located at 408 Arbor Street, adjacent to Vet's Park, was repurposed and demolished in 2004 after falling into disrepair.

Thomas Maguire's Sample Room was located at 112–114 Center Avenue. A 1906 business directory stated: "Since 1872 Mr. Maguire has been distributing good things to drink to the people of Bay City and has distinguished himself as a man of superior judgment in the selection of the best and in the management of sample room affairs . . . Mr. Maguire is known as the dispenser of Edgwood Whiskey, the famous 'Old Kentucky' whose superior merit has reached the borders of the earth."

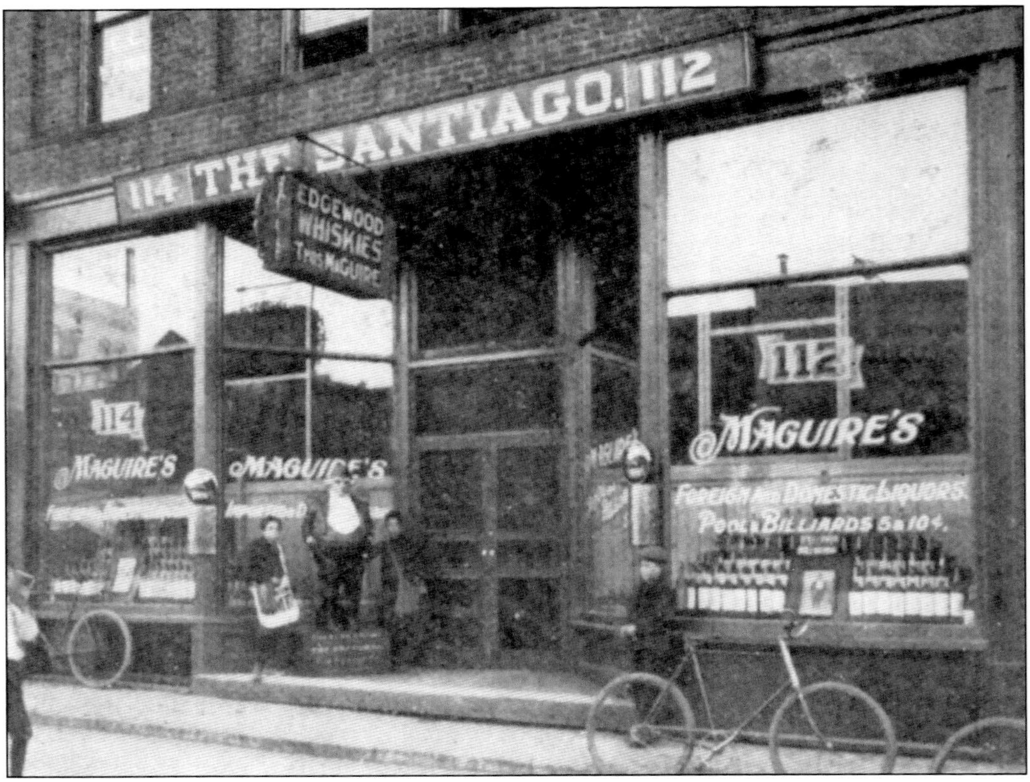

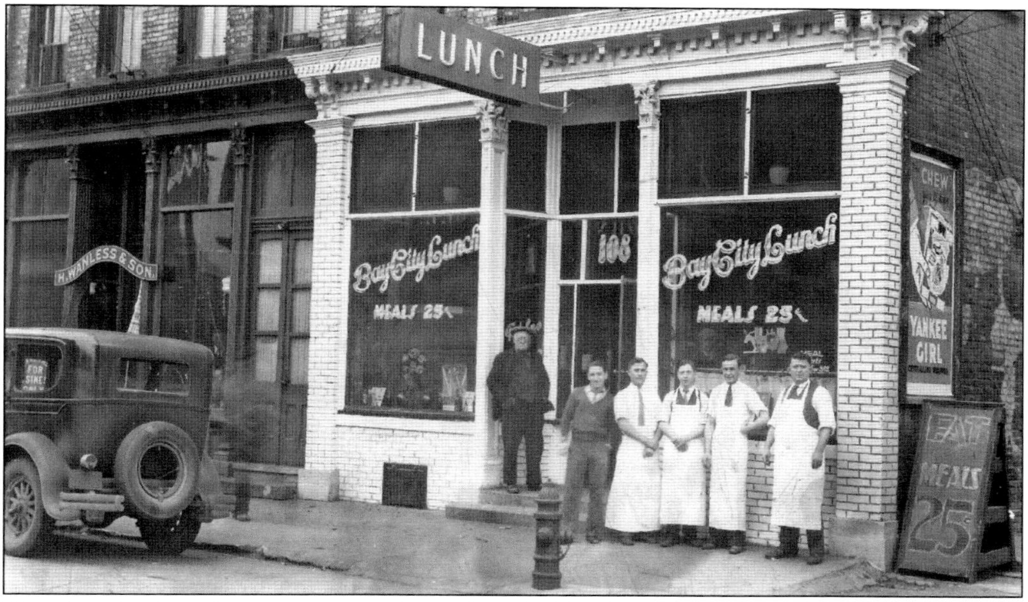

The Bay City Lunch restaurant was located at 108 Third Street in the mid-1930s, and by 1937, Nicholas Priggooris was the proprietor. He also ran Bay City Lunch Garden at 110 Third Street. The well-known restaurant was in operation until 1971. Other legendary Bay City restaurants include Caris' Red Lion, Neal's Pullman Diner, Kresge's lunch counter, and the Blackhawk Lounge and Supper Club (better known as the Brass Lantern).

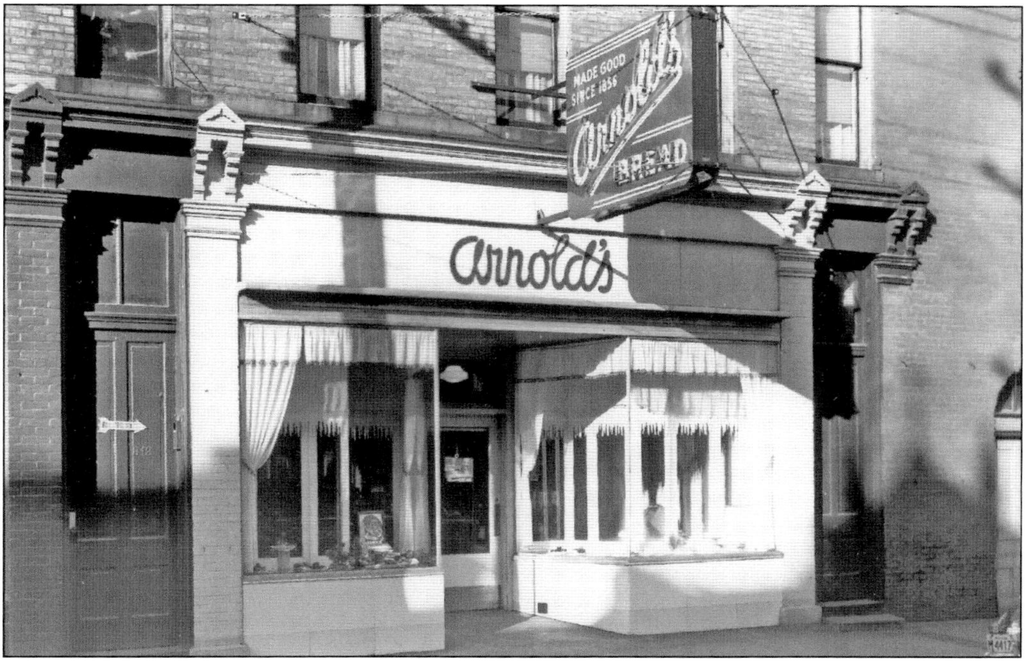

In 1856, 22-year-old German immigrant Frederick G. Arnold started Arnold's Bakery. By its centennial, it was producing a full line of breads, rolls, buns, pies, cakes, and other pastries for the retail and restaurant markets. In 1981, it was honored by the Historical Society of Michigan as Michigan's oldest active bakery. A few years later, the company ceased operations, though the Arnold's Bakery sign still adorned the Saginaw Street building for another 10 years.

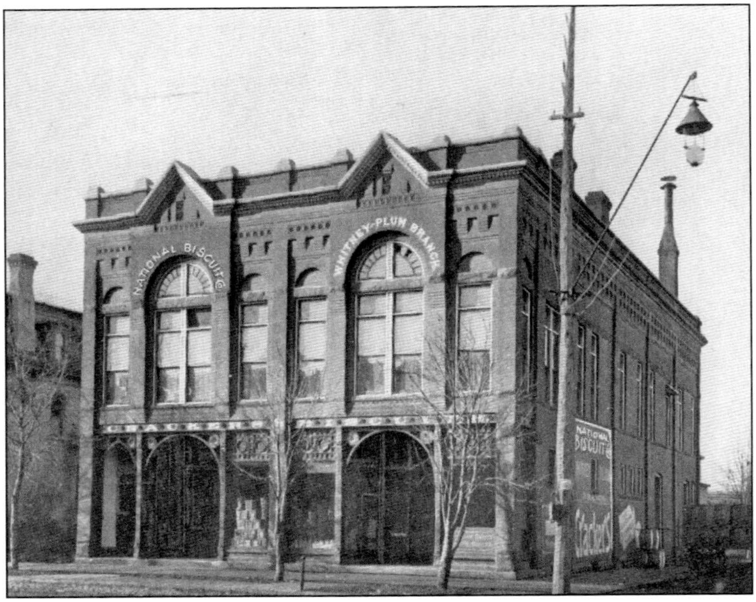

The Whitney-Plum Bakery branch of the National Biscuit Company (Nabisco) was located at 521–523 Washington Avenue in 1898. The building was later renovated and operated as the Alvarado Theater, which later became the Roxy Theater. In 1874, druggist Charles C. Whitney moved to Bay City from Alpena, Michigan. He later went into the confectionery business and ultimately started a Nabisco franchise.

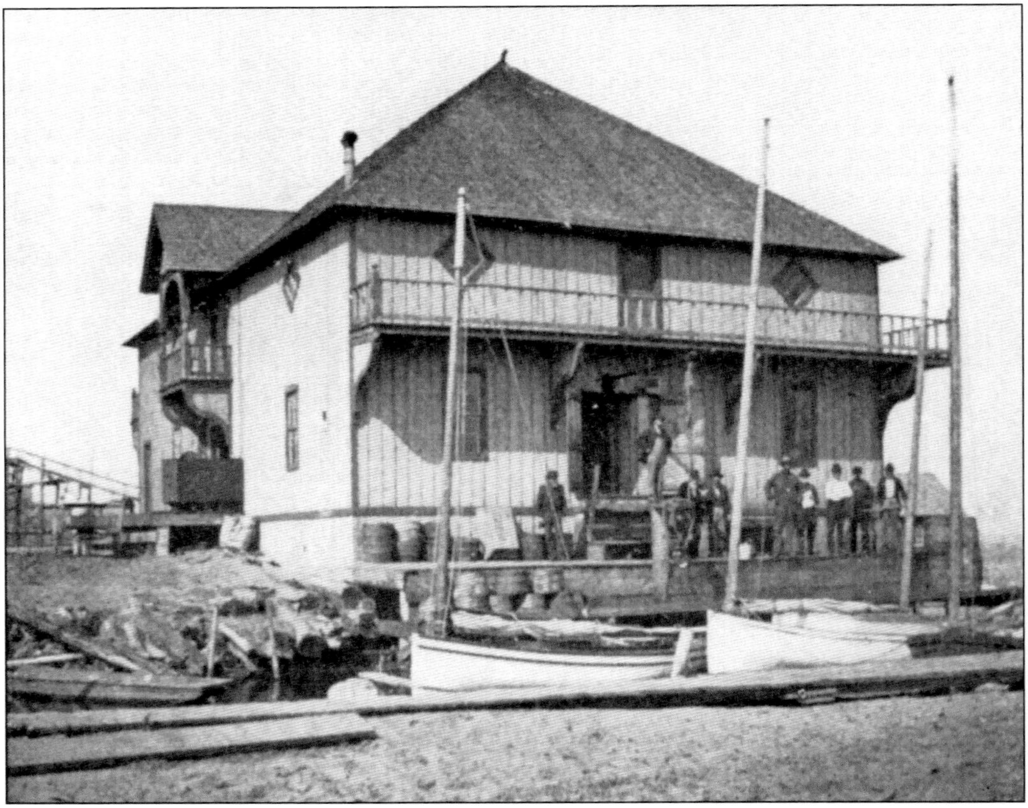

In 1905, historian Augustus Gansser wrote, "As early as 1860, the export of fish from Bay City was valued at over $50,000 annually." There were two types of commercial fishermen: those who fished the river and those who fished the bay. Fish were packed in locally built barrels with ice and shipped as far east as New York City. W.P. Kavanaugh, pictured here around 1900, was a wholesaler at the foot of Scheurmann Street in Essexville.

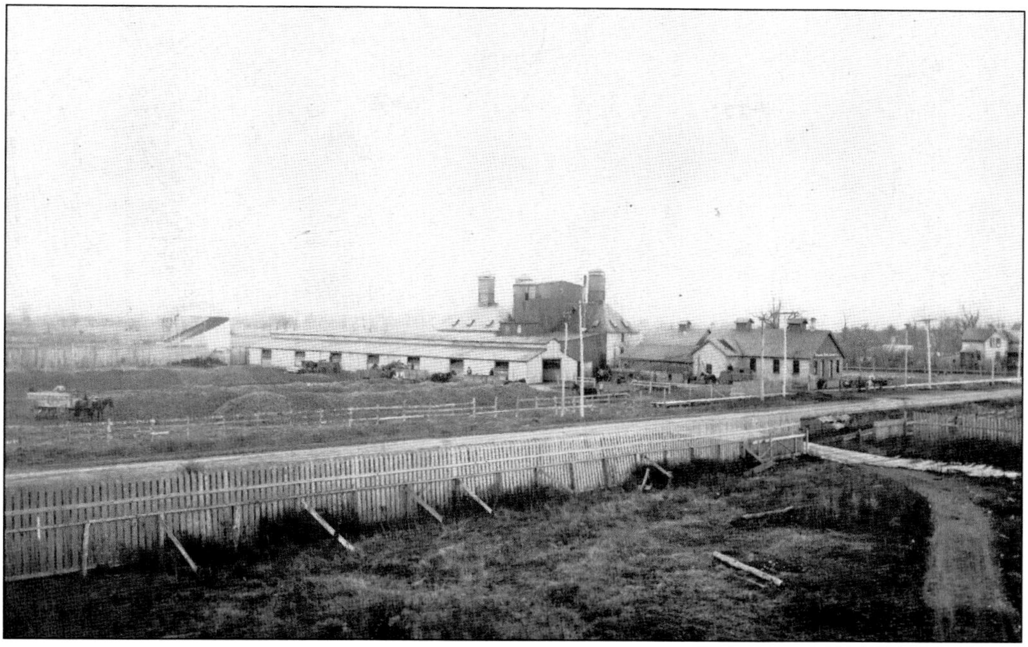

Chicory is a root-crop vegetable that looks like a parsnip and grows like a carrot. When harvested, it is sliced, dried, roasted, and ground into a product that is generally used as a coffee additive or substitute. Bay City was home to major chicory-producing factories from around 1900 to the 1930s, including the Michigan State Chicory Company, which was located on the south side of Center Avenue near Livingston Street.

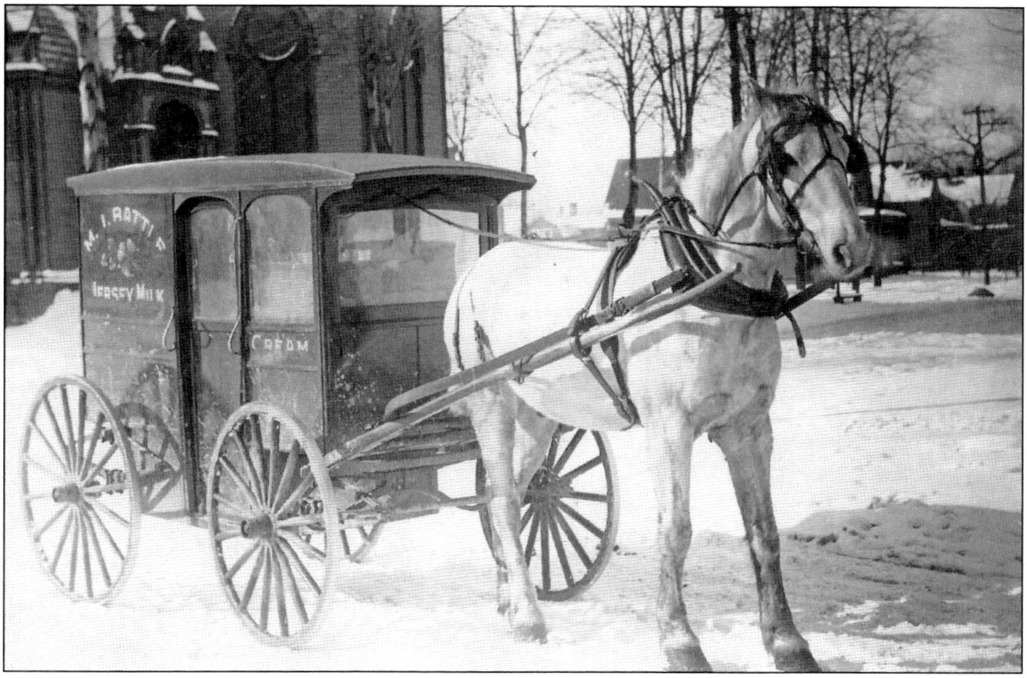

In 1929, there were 18 dairies operating in Bay City, and many had their own routes for home service delivering fresh milk. Michael J. Battle's M.J. Battle Dairy was one of those dairies; its plant was located on the north side of Center Avenue, east of Powell.

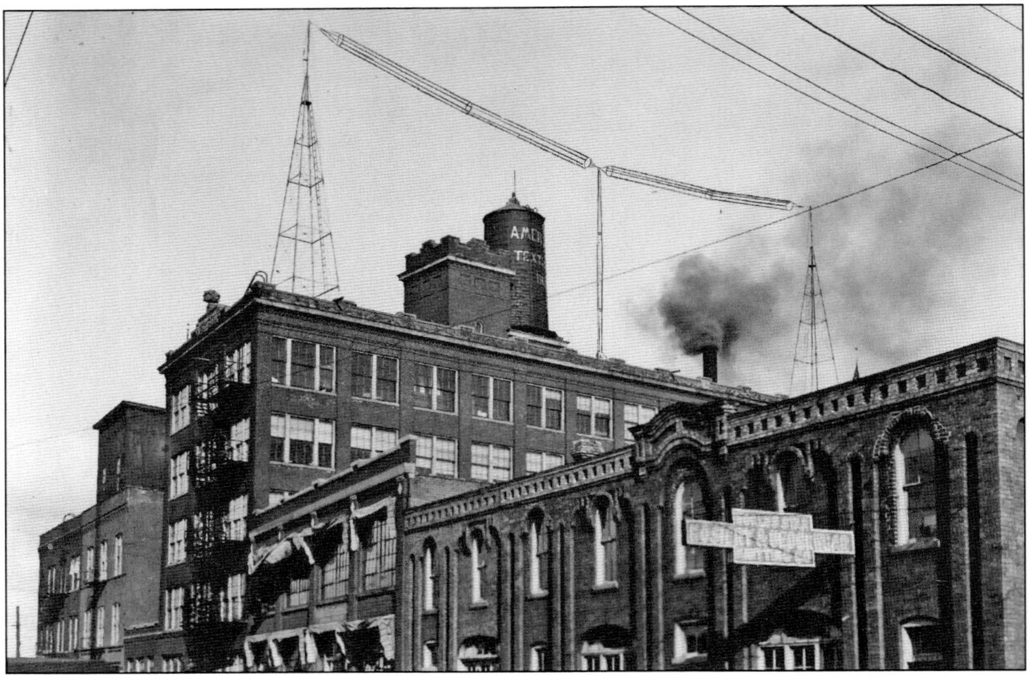

Stanley J. Northcott established the first radio station in Bay City at the World Star Knitting Company, located at First and Water Streets. WSKC operated from the mill building with two 70-foot-tall transmission towers broadcasting the signal throughout the area. The station was one of only about 750 radio stations in the entire country, and in the pre-FCC days it broadcast from coast to coast and from Central America to northern Canada.

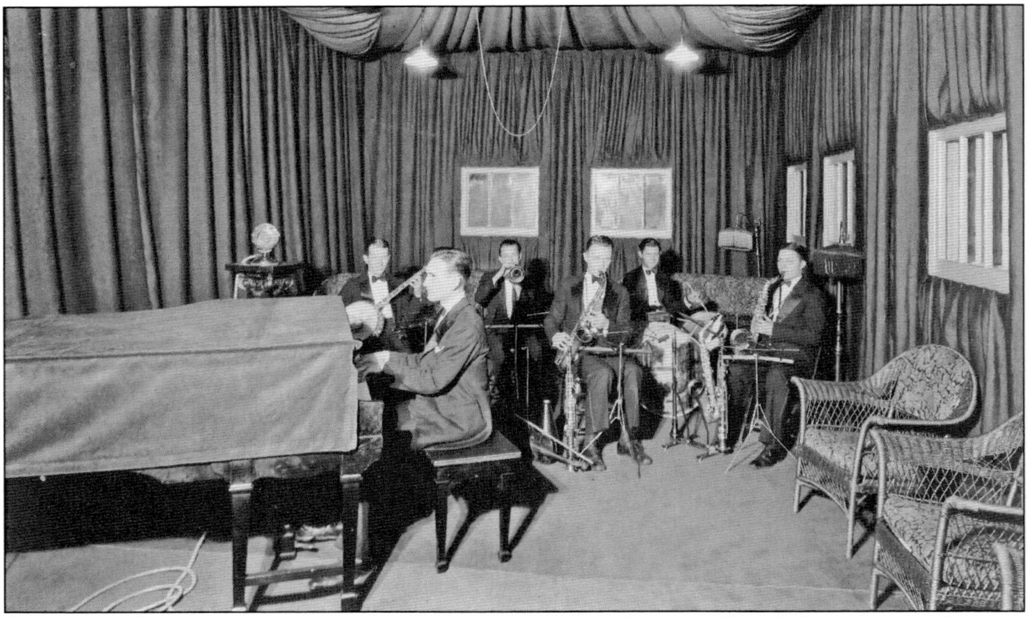

The station remained WSKC until 1928, when James Davidson purchased the station and moved it to the Wenonah Hotel, where it operated until 1960. The call letters were changed to WBCM. In the early years, the studio featured a soundproofed room, which was necessary because its broadcasts typically featured live orchestras like the one pictured here in the WBCM studio.

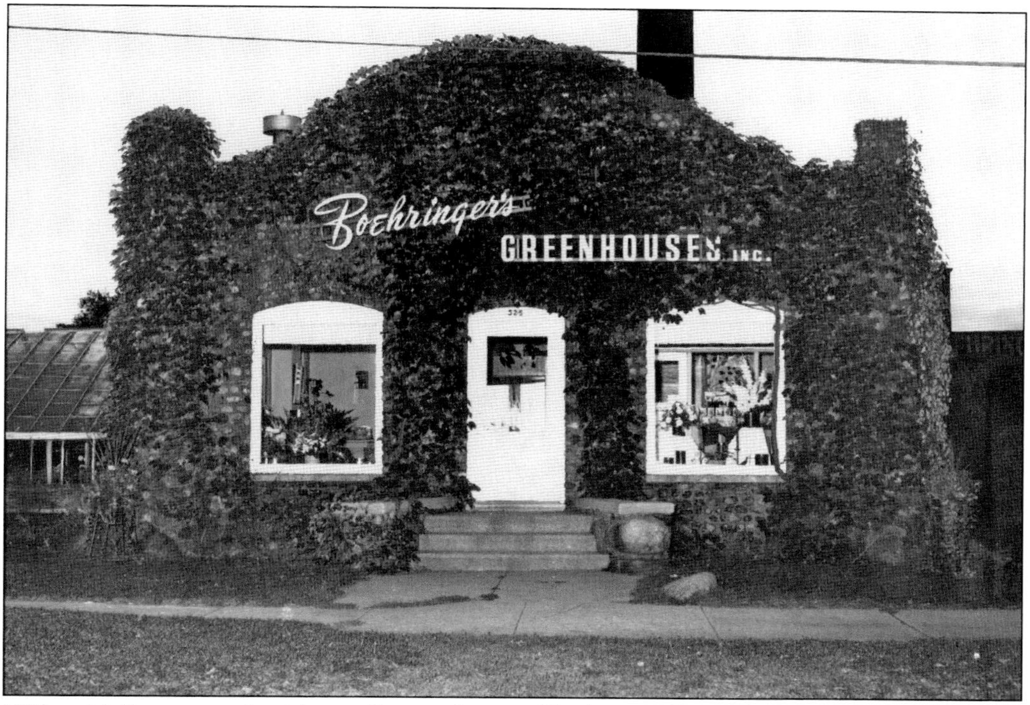

"When it's flowers, say it with ours," was a slogan of Boehringer Bros. Florists. Started by brothers Albert and Rudolf in 1893, the original one acre at 325 Park Avenue near Ridge Road (above) grew to over 20 acres with 13 greenhouses, 50,000 square feet "under glass" and 2 miles of steam pipes by 1914. In a 1915 *History of Michigan*, author Charles Moore cites a "Splendid establishment . . . from their hothouses they supply more flowers than any other single establishment in northern Michigan." Near Elm Lawn Cemetery, funeral arrangements were a staple of their business, along with choice roses, carnations, and chrysanthemums. Frederick W. Boehringer, Albert's son, started working at the greenhouse at age 12 and later inherited the business. It later moved to 114 S. Tuscola Road, shown below in 1972. Boehringer's closed after 94 years in business.

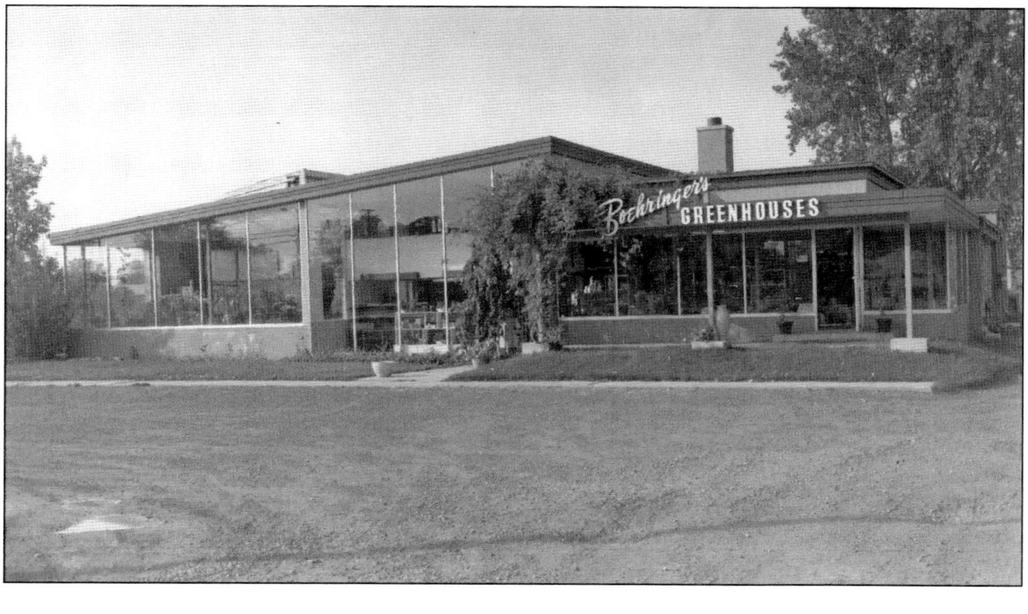

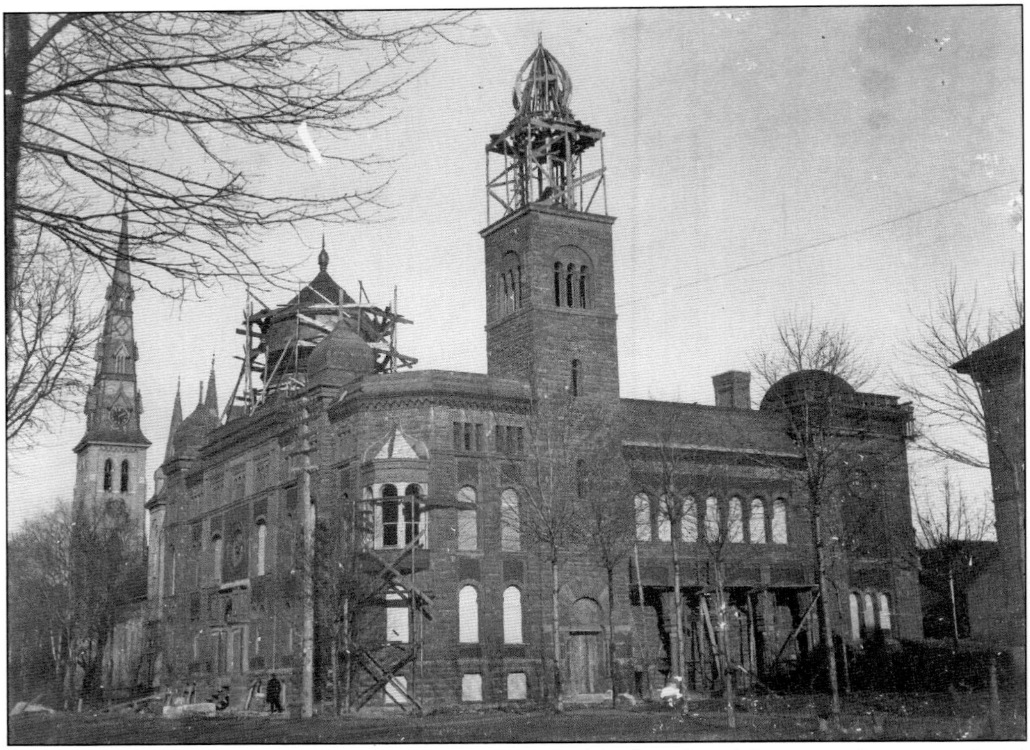

Local architects Pratt and Koeppe were commissioned by Bay City Masons to design a palatial building that could house several lodge rooms and space for Masonic ceremonies. The cornerstone of the resulting Moorish-inspired building was laid on June 24, 1891, with completion and dedication on February 27, 1893, at the corner of Sixth and Madison Streets, directly south of the First Baptist Church. It was heralded as one of the most handsome Masonic buildings in the country at that time.

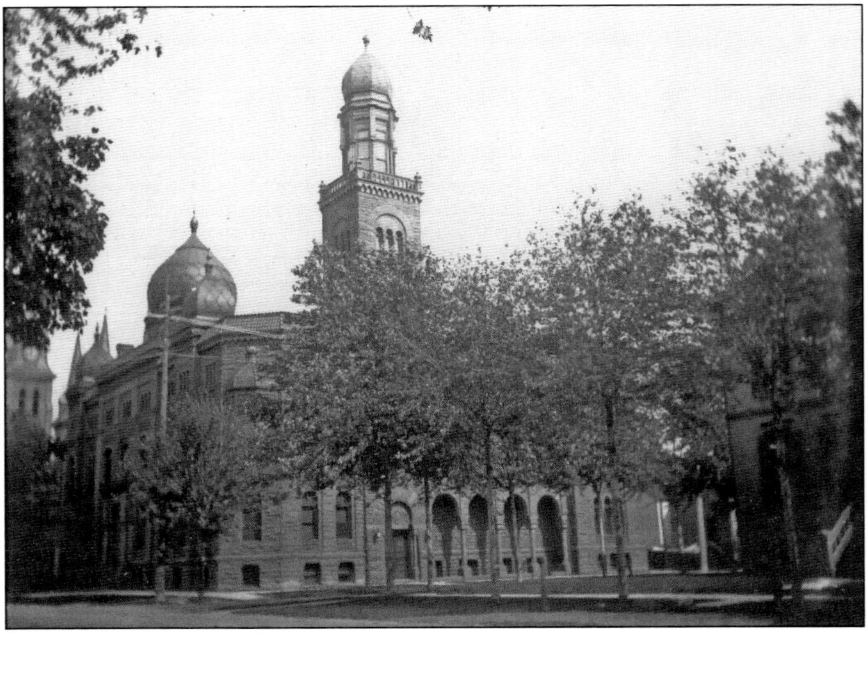

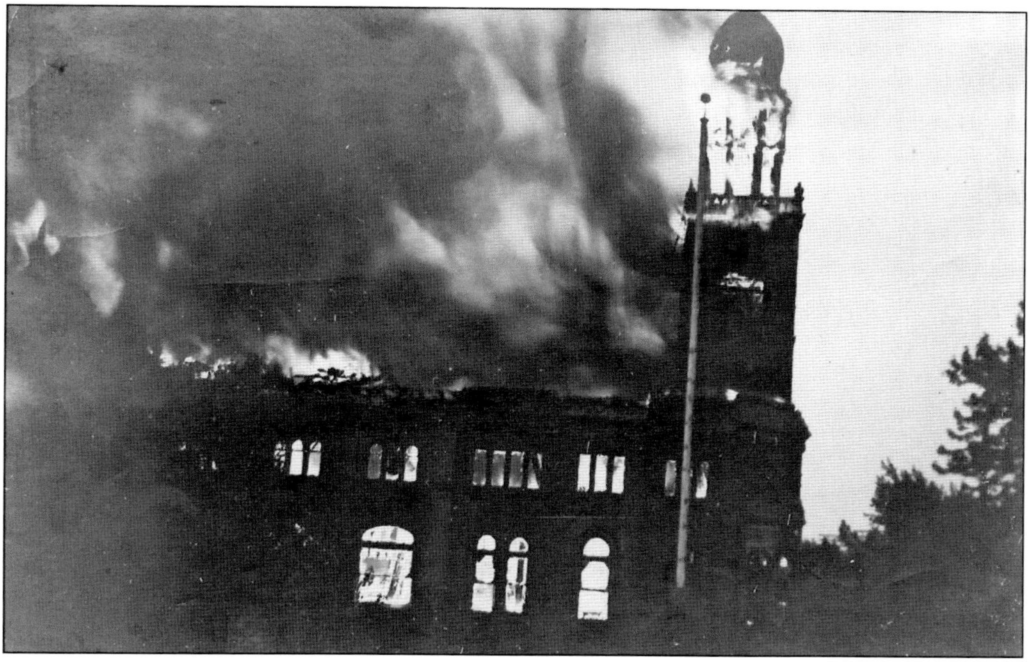

The Masons' enjoyment of their new building was unfortunately short-lived. On May 19, 1903, a major fire gutted the building and heavily damaged the roofline, including the tower. The distinctive onion domes melted under the heat of the conflagration, and copper salvaged from the domes was later made into commemorative coins for lodge members. The interior was quickly rebuilt to renewed splendor; however, the roofline and exterior were rebuilt with a bit less grandeur, as only two of the smaller domes were replaced. The building served the Masons for many years without significant updates. By the 1960s, the tower, onion domes, and all other ornamentation on the roofline had been removed.

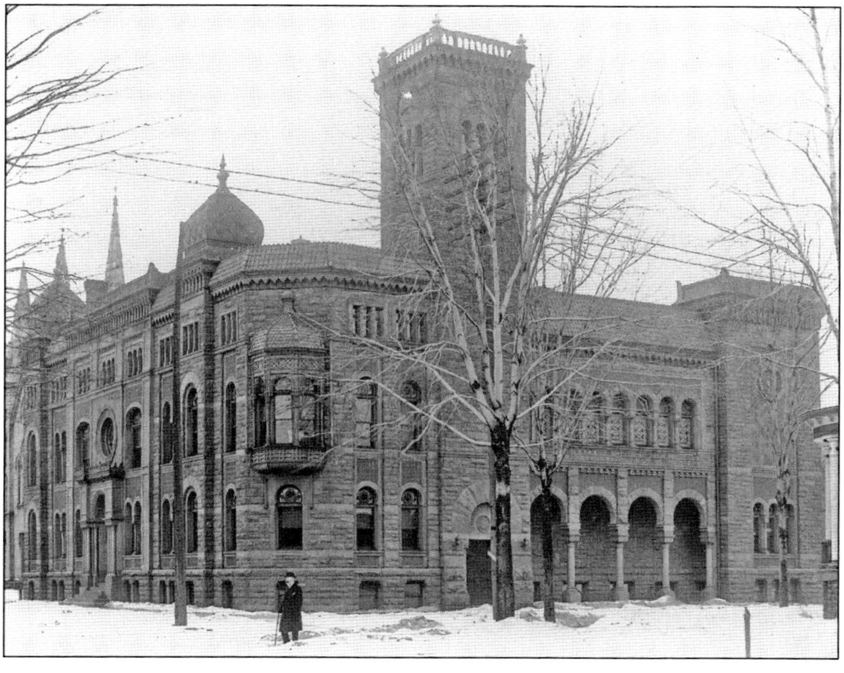

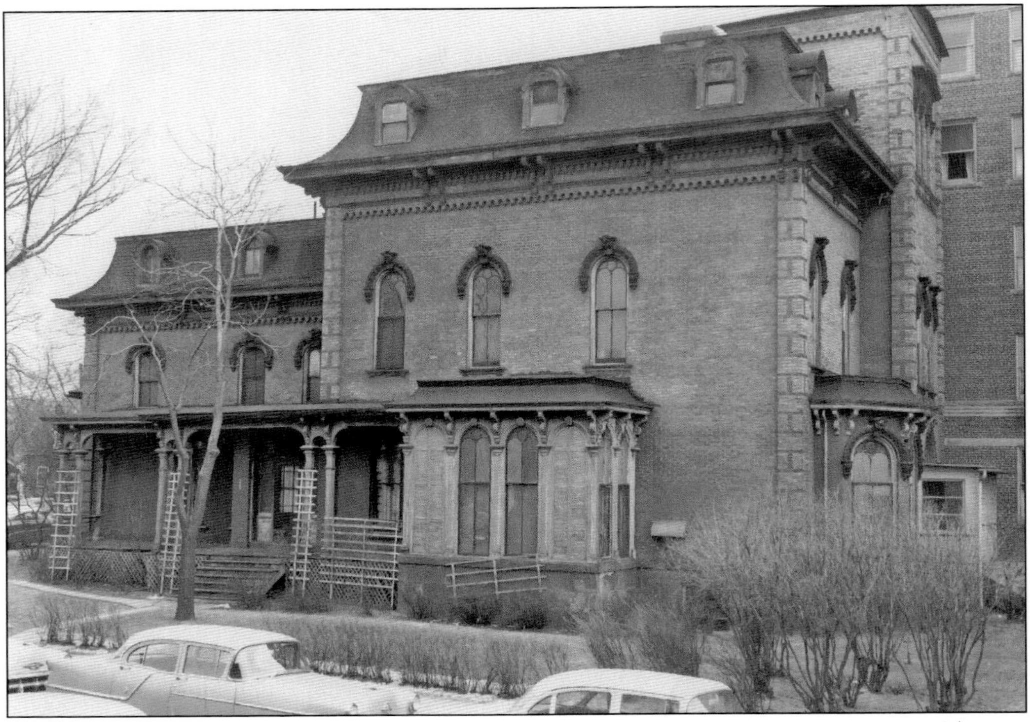

In 1899, the Sisters of Mercy were invited to found a hospital in Bay City. The sisters raised $2,500, which was matched with $5,000 from local residents to purchase the home of Hon. Nathan B. Bradley (above). On September 24, 1899, the hospital opened with a staff of six sisters, 20 beds, and a budget of $8,600. In 1917, Mercy Hospital built its most ambitious addition, a modern fireproof four-story hospital building built of brick. In 1948, Mercy Hospital dedicated a new $2.5-million five-story brick addition that increased patient accommodations from 167 to 325, making Mercy the largest hospital in the state outside of Detroit. The former Nathan Bradley home no longer housed patients and was used for storage and a chapel; in the late 1950s, it was razed for a parking lot and another addition.

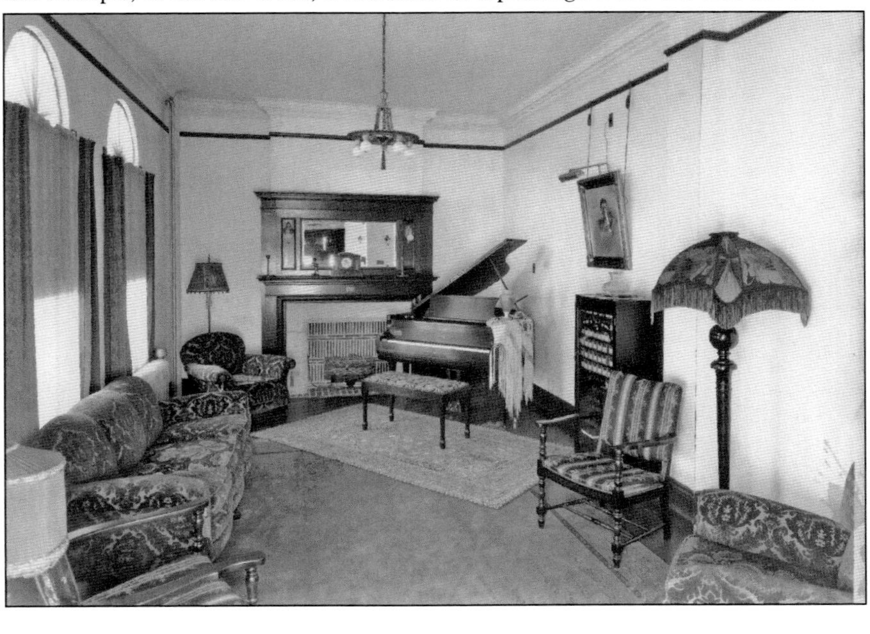

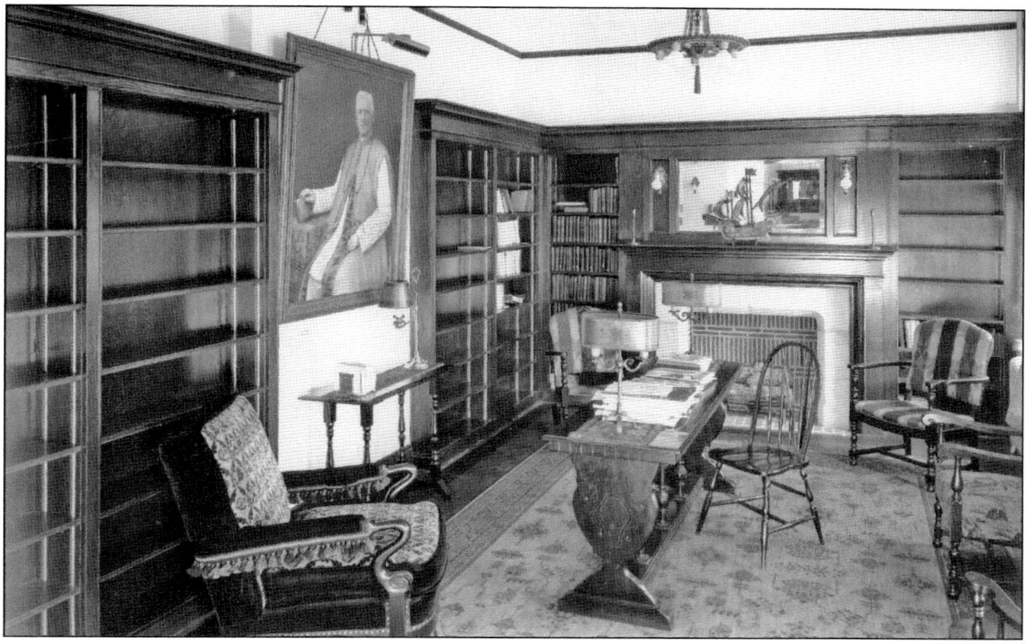

The Sisters of Mercy also started a training school for nurses at Mercy Hospital. Student nurses had eight-hour days, a half day off on Sunday, and three weeks of vacation during the year. Upon graduation, they were eligible to take the state nursing board exam; the Mercy Hospital School of Nursing program became known as one of the best in the state. In 1926, Mendel J. Bialy donated the Elizabeth McDowell Bialy Nurses Home, dedicated to the memory of his late wife. The Bialy Home at Fifteenth and Water Streets had a library (above), music room, reception room, lounge, lecture hall, demonstration room (below), chemical lab, dietetic laboratory, 66 private rooms, classrooms, two parlors (opposite, below), and a large auditorium. The school closed in 1965, and the buildings were renovated into housing now called Bradley House in 1980–1981.

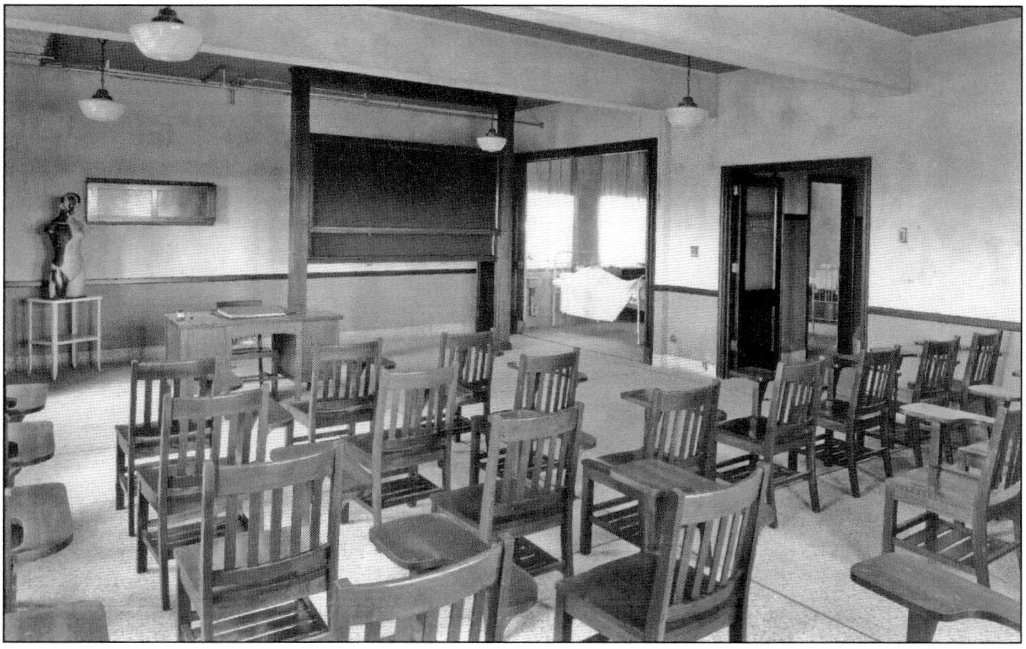

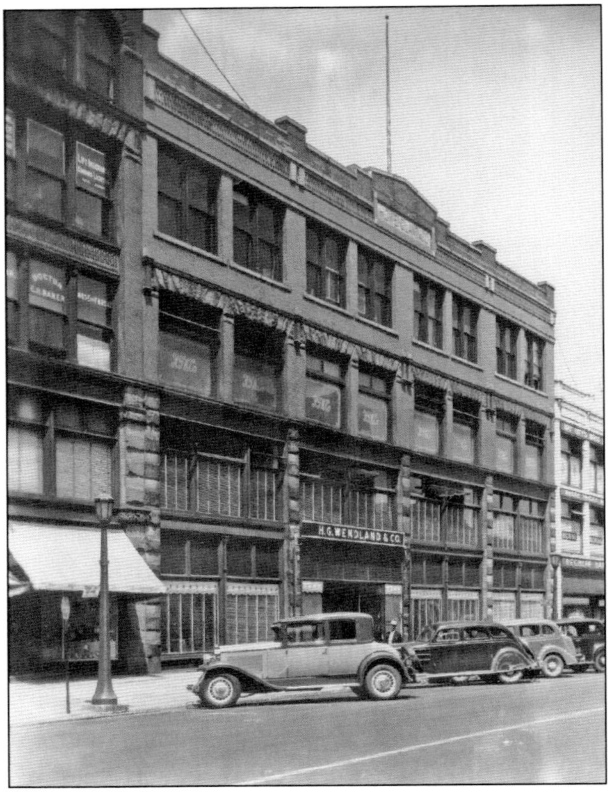

Originally a dry goods store, H.G. Wendland and Company was started in 1891 on Washington Avenue between Center Avenue and Fifth Street. In 1899, an addition was built on an adjacent lot between the building and the Crapo Block. The news of the day said this would give Bay Citians their first department store, similar to those in larger cities. "When ready for occupancy, the firm will have one of the finest dry goods stores in the state. Every present department will be enlarged and the cloak department will be placed in the present annex on the ground floor." The store would also feature a carpet department, a curtain and drapery department, three other departments to be named later, an electric elevator, and an electric cash carrier system. The two photographs show Wendland's around 1938 (left) and 1958 (below).

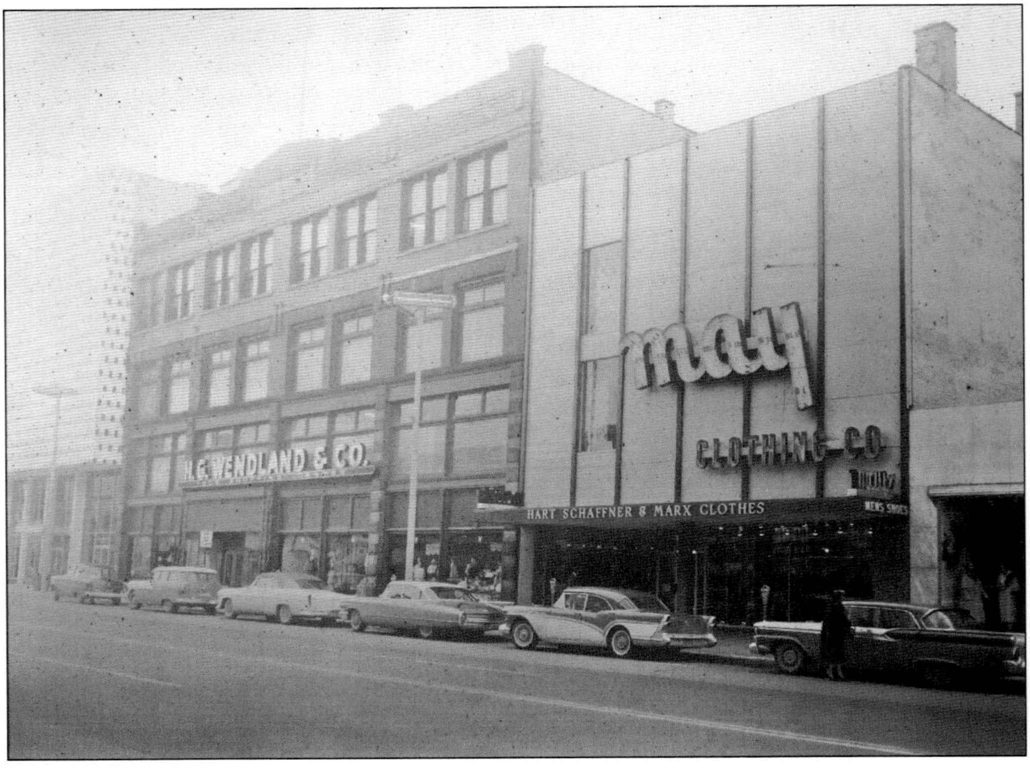

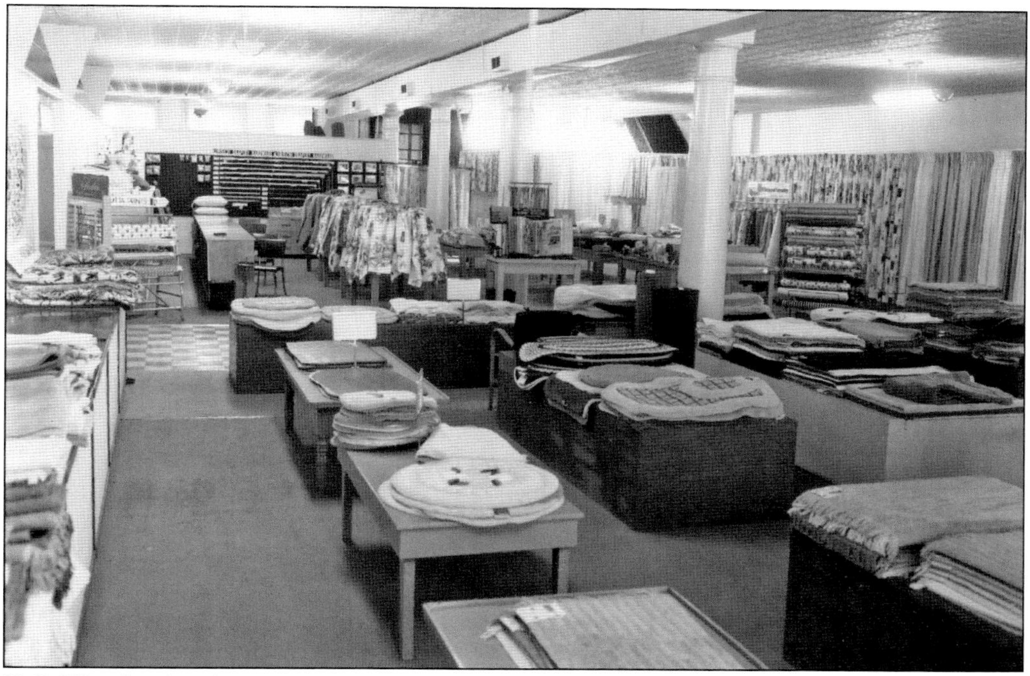

H.G. Wendland and Company was an anchor in the downtown area for more than 70 years. The store underwent its final large-scale renovation in 1961, two years after the founder, H.G Wendland, passed away. In addition to renovations to the interior, the exterior façade on Washington Avenue was given a modern treatment of aluminum panels with strong vertical lines. These photographs show some of the new interior sales spaces, including draperies (above) and infants (below). In August 1963, after a period of financial difficulty, the decision was made to close the store, which was subsequently sold.

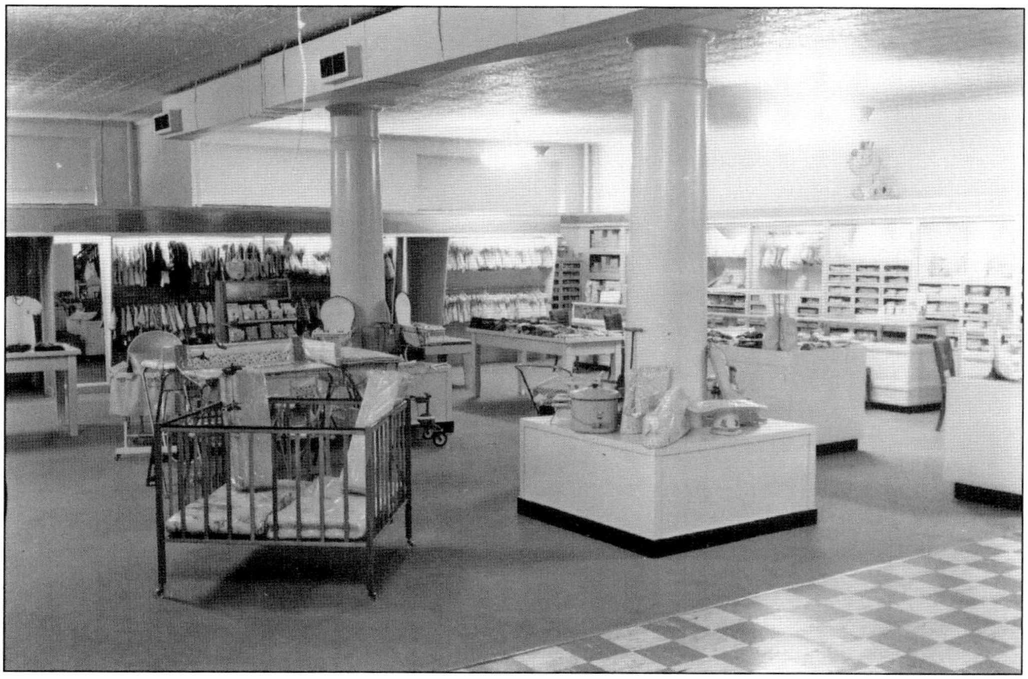

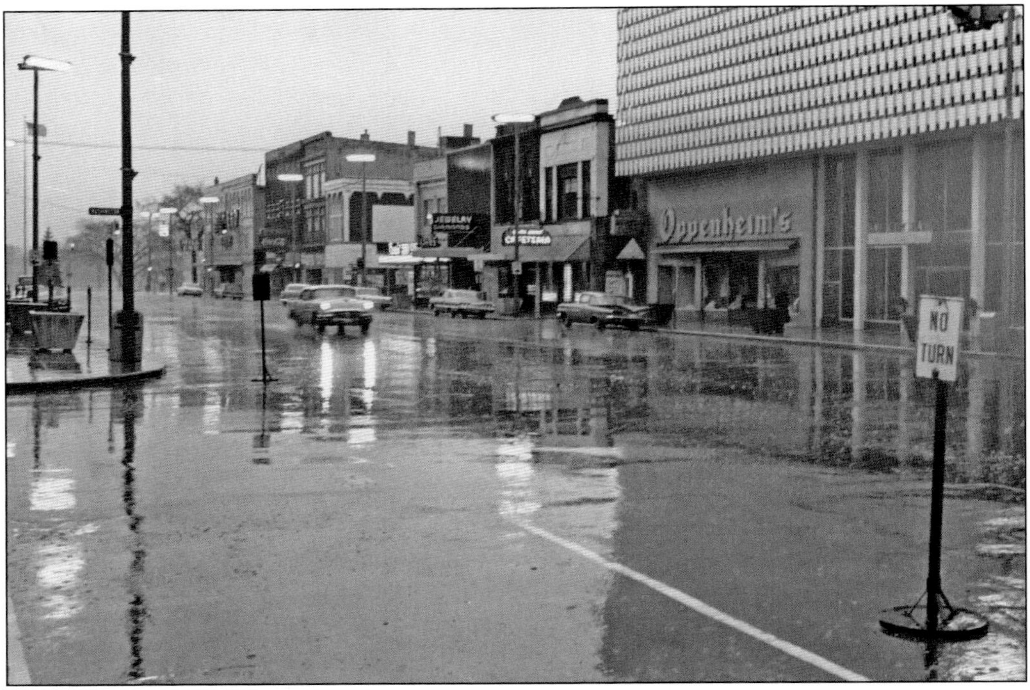

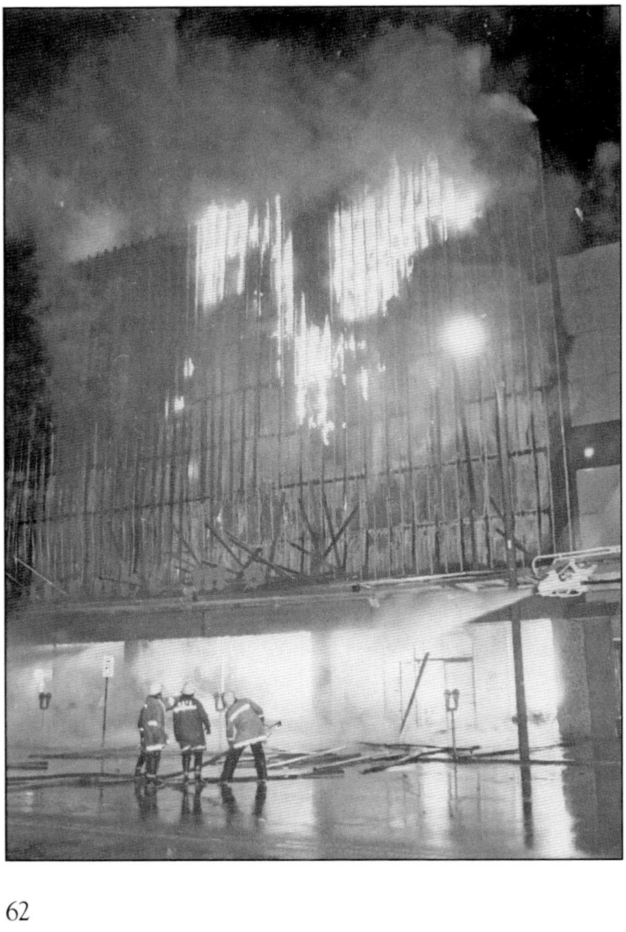

The L.E. Oppenheim and Company apparel company was originally started in 1882. For more than 50 years it was located in the Bay City Bank building (above) before moving to the former H.G. Wendland and Company location on Washington Avenue in 1964. For many years, Oppenheim's was one of the premier clothing stores downtown. On Christmas Eve 1979, police responding to an after-hours burglar alarm at the store found smoke. Soon, the structure was engulfed. Hundreds of residents watched as the building eventually collapsed due to the severity of the fire. Surrounding buildings, including the bank building to the south, were not severely damaged; however, Oppenheim's was a total loss, estimated at over $1 million in damages. To this day, the site is still vacant.

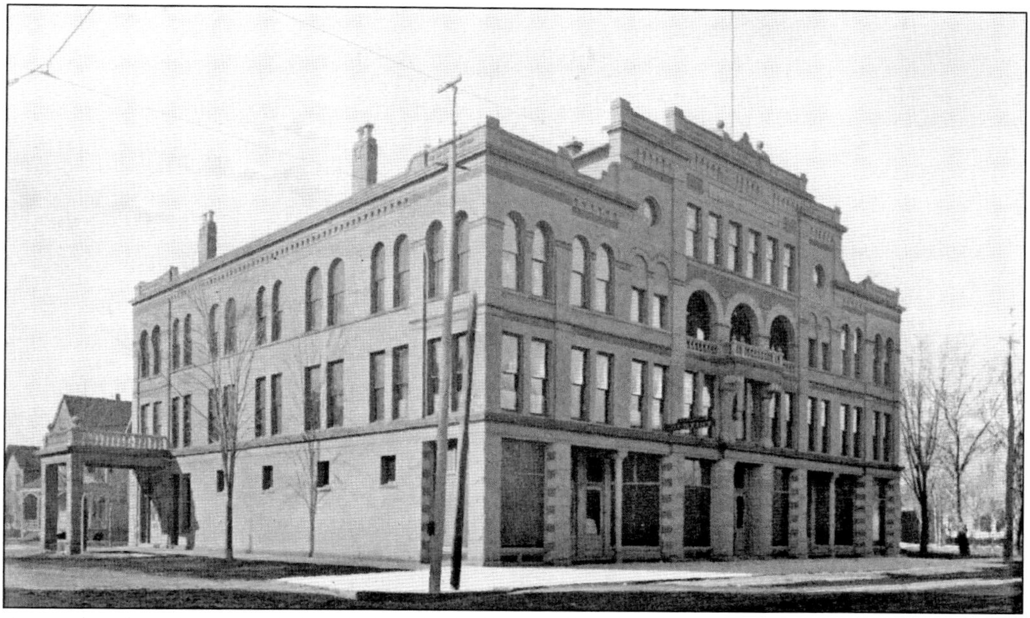

An early advertisement claimed that the Ridotto office building on the corner of Center and Madison Avenues was one of the finest in Bay City, built of Zanesville pressed brick and "practically fireproof." The building had large storage and office rooms, easy access through "commodious" stairways and elevators, and an "immense public assembly hall" on the third floor. Local architect Dillon Prosser Clark designed the Ridotto in 1890 for Frank and Fremont Chesbrough. It featured one of the largest halls in Michigan, with accommodations for 500 and a full orchestra. The Ridotto's many tenants included the Aladdin Homes Company (1912–1920) and Bay City Business College, which was in session on April 1, 1940, when fire broke out. Luckily, there was no loss of life; however, the building was a total loss. The site is now parking for the Alice and Jack Wirt Library.

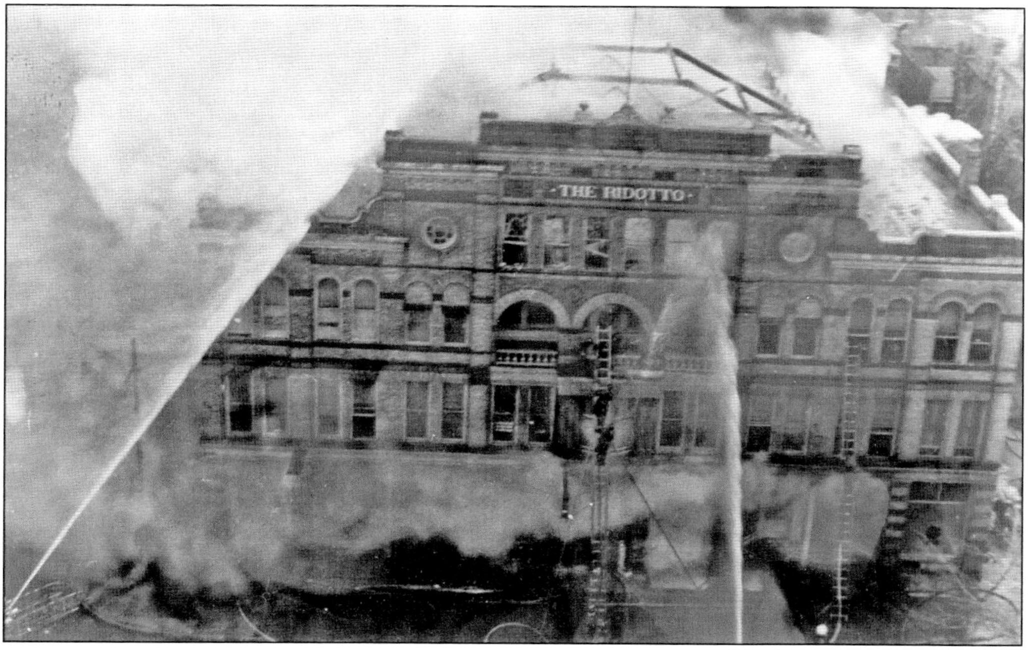

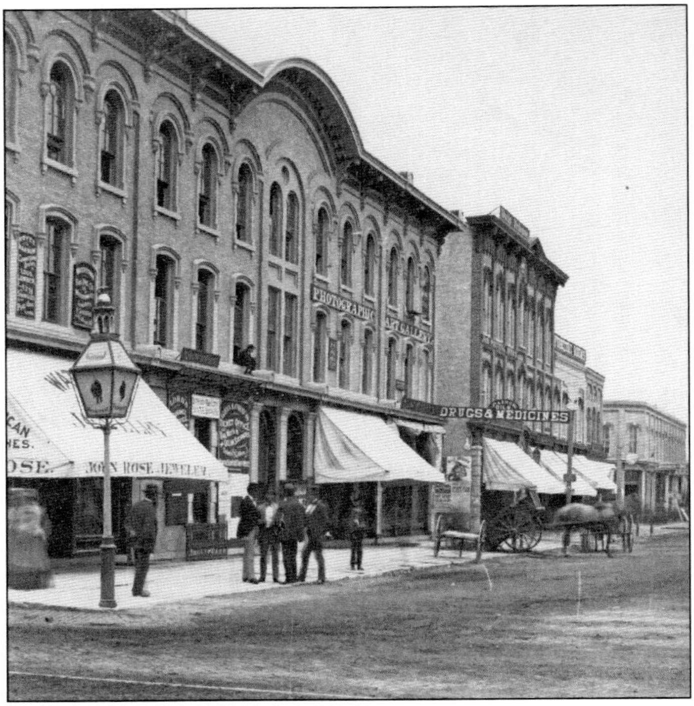

Noted local architect James Shearer built the first Shearer Block in 1867 at Center Avenue and Water Street, shortly after a devastating fire leveled parts of the downtown area. Located across Center Avenue from the Fraser House, this new brick building met new building codes. One longstanding tenant was jeweler John Rose, who welcomed a young Herman Hiss into his business. Hiss eventually moved the business to Washington Avenue in 1910.

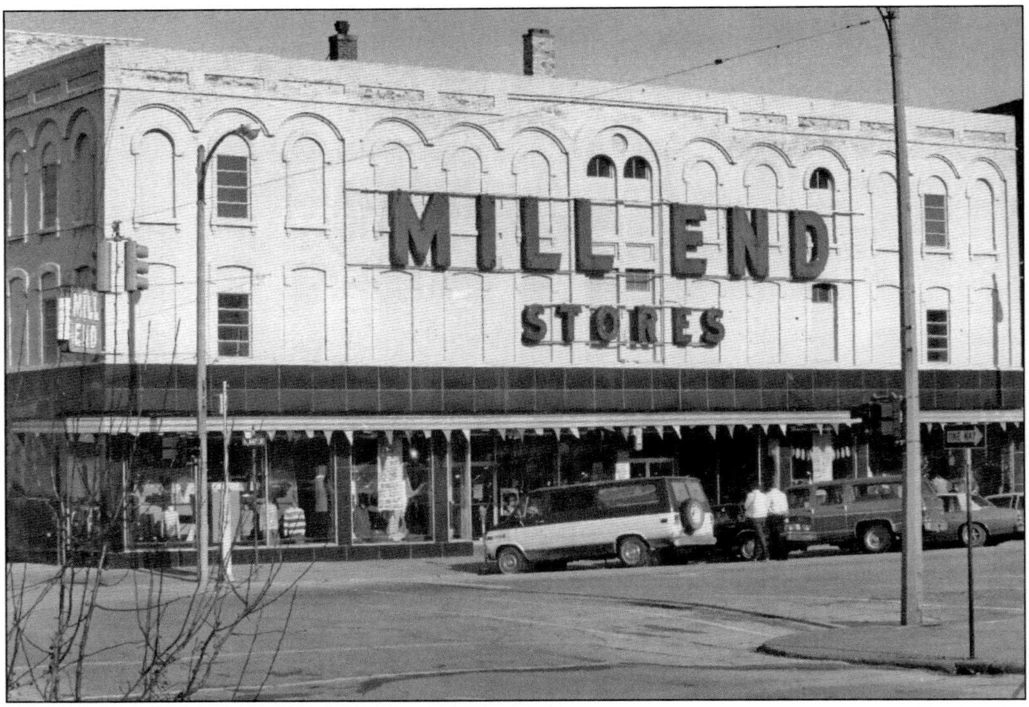

Shearer's first block is best known for the store that occupied it for over 65 years. Dubbed "The World's Most Unusual Store," Mill End was started in 1940 as a women's clothing store. It eventually became known as the place to find almost anything; inventory was purchased from bankruptcies and fire sales. Mill End closed in 2005, and the dilapidated building was razed in 2012 to make way for Mill End Lofts.

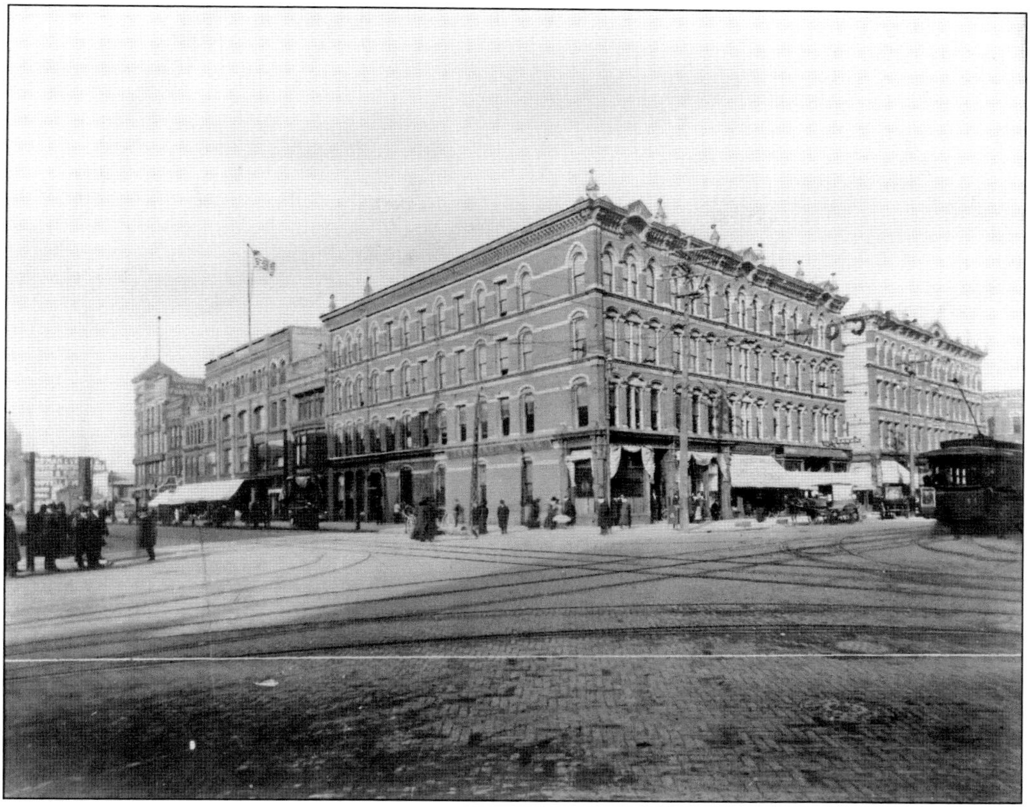

Twin Shearer Blocks are unmistakable landmarks at the northeast corner of Center and Washington Avenues in the photograph above taken around 1900. James Shearer and his brother George built the Central Block on the corner in 1880 and the Shearer Brothers Block to the east in 1886. Both blocks were built as commercial space and quickly became one of the most desirable locations in Bay City. In 1940, the Central Block was razed, and a new building with curved frontage on the corner was built to house the S.S. Kresge and Company store. The image below captures that building under construction. Kresge was a five-and-dime store that featured a lunch counter. It was later turned into retail space and renamed Landmark Plaza. The Shearer Brothers Block was renovated some years ago by a local developer and now houses condominiums.

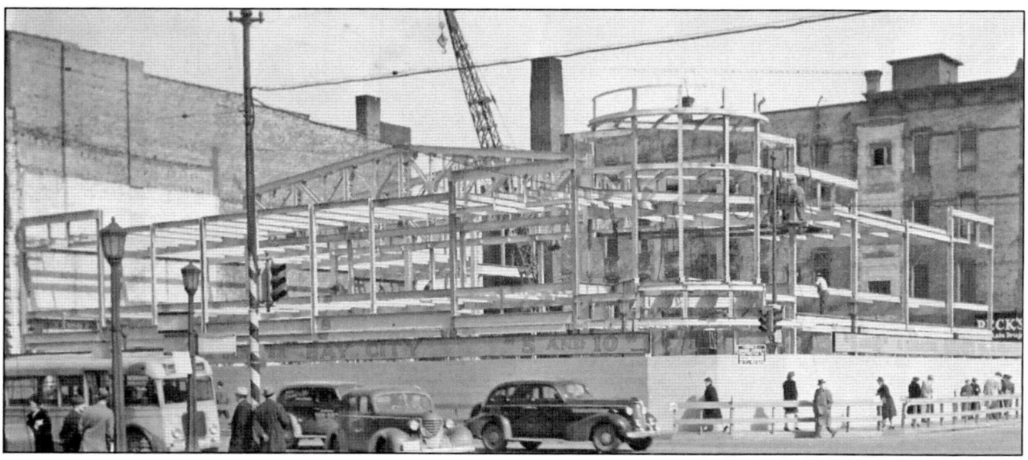

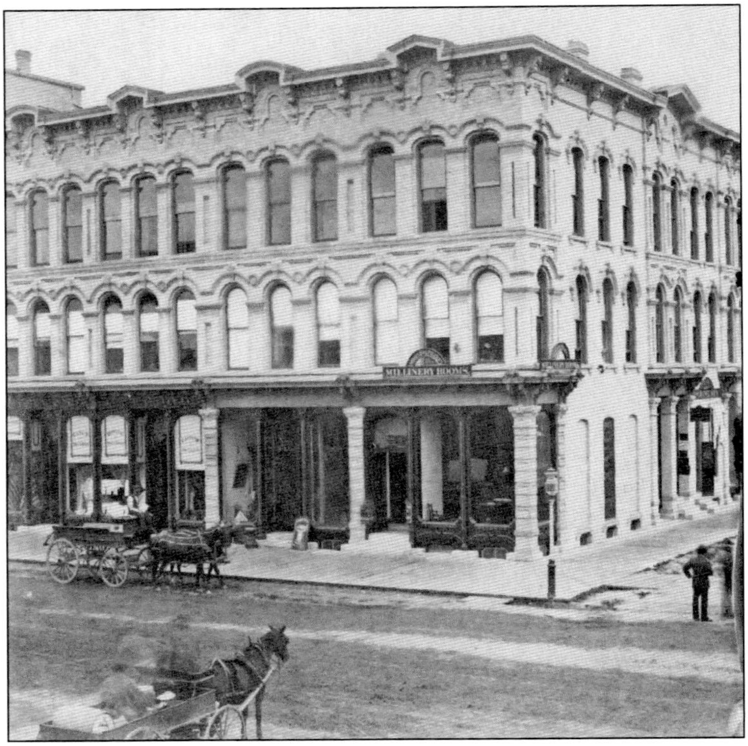

Algernon Munger and his brother Curtis (an early pioneer of Bay City) built the Munger Block on the southeast corner of Center Avenue and Saginaw Street in 1873. The Victorian business block originally housed their dry goods company, which was eventually succeeded by Cooke and Company, reputed to be the oldest dry goods company in Bay City, dating to 1848. The building later had many tenants, including Grow Brothers clothiers, Lewis Drug Company, and other offices for construction companies, music studios, milliners, lumber inspectors, chiropractors, and doctors. One of the longstanding tenants was Mason and Beach Druggists. In 1893, the building was sold and became known as the Fay Block.

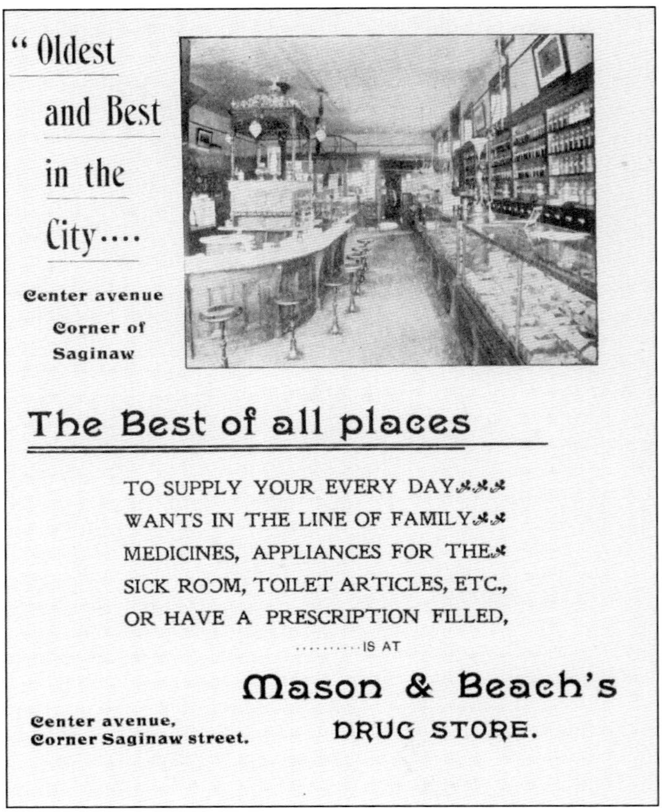

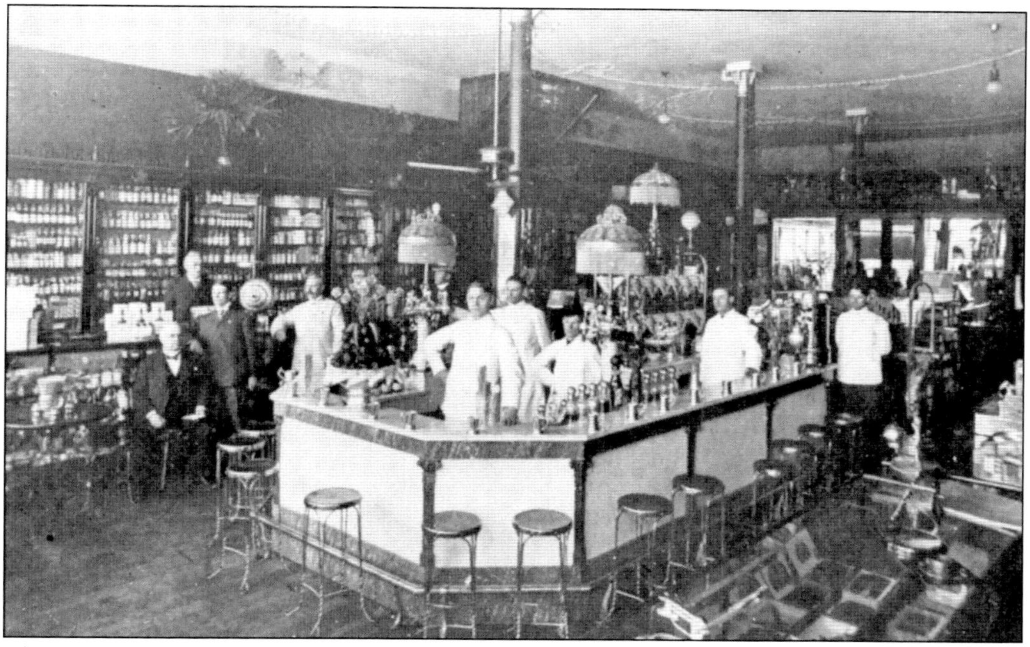

This 1905 interior view of the Mason and Beach drugstore in the Munger/Fay Block included the following information: "The modern and leading drug store of Bay City. They carry the largest stock of genuine drugs, have the handsomest soda fount, and the largest line of sundries in the city. They have been thirty years in the business and have adopted every modern method."

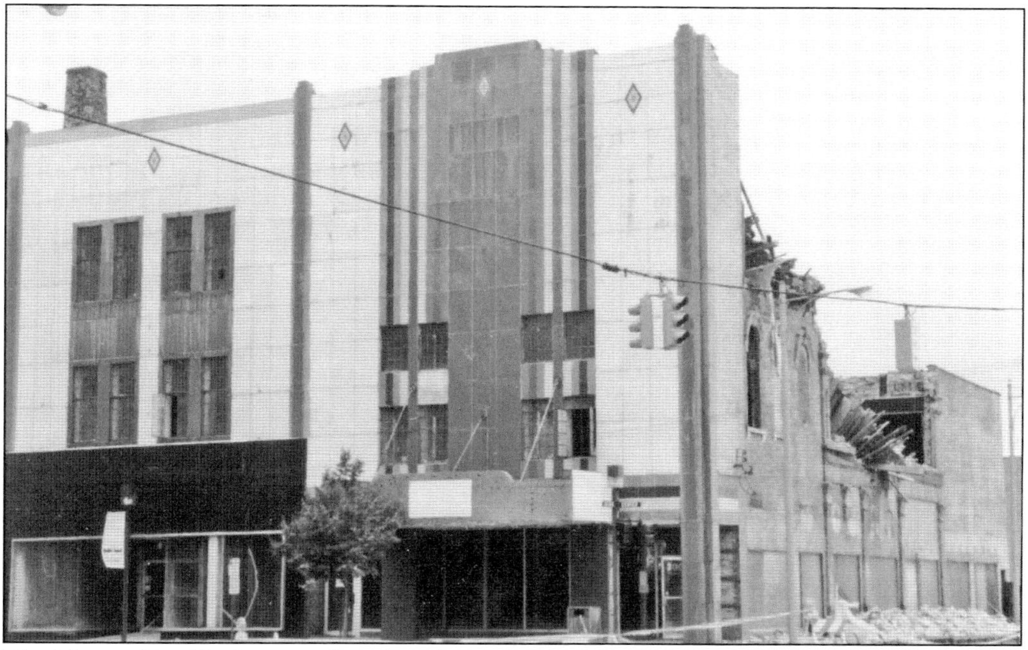

The Munger/Fay Block was perhaps best known as the Center Theatre, which opened in 1936. It was owned by Butterfield Theatres Inc., which also owned the Regent, Bay, and State Theatres. A new façade was added in an attempt to modernize the look. In 1989, the building collapsed while being renovated into apartments. The site was cleared, sat vacant for well over a decade, and eventually became home to a new restaurant building.

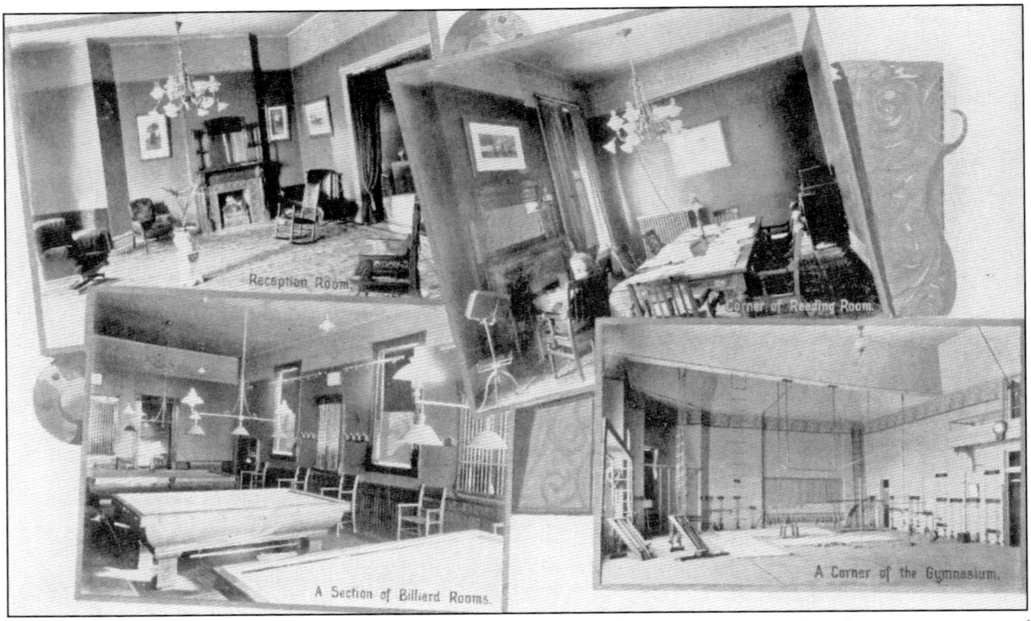

The Bay City Club was organized in 1886 as a club for gentlemen to gather for an evening of socializing. They originally met in rented rooms within Woods Opera House (shown in this montage), until it was destroyed by fire. They then commissioned a club building from local architects Clark and Munger, which was completed in 1904. The Bay City Club became a popular place to hold wedding receptions and other festive events.

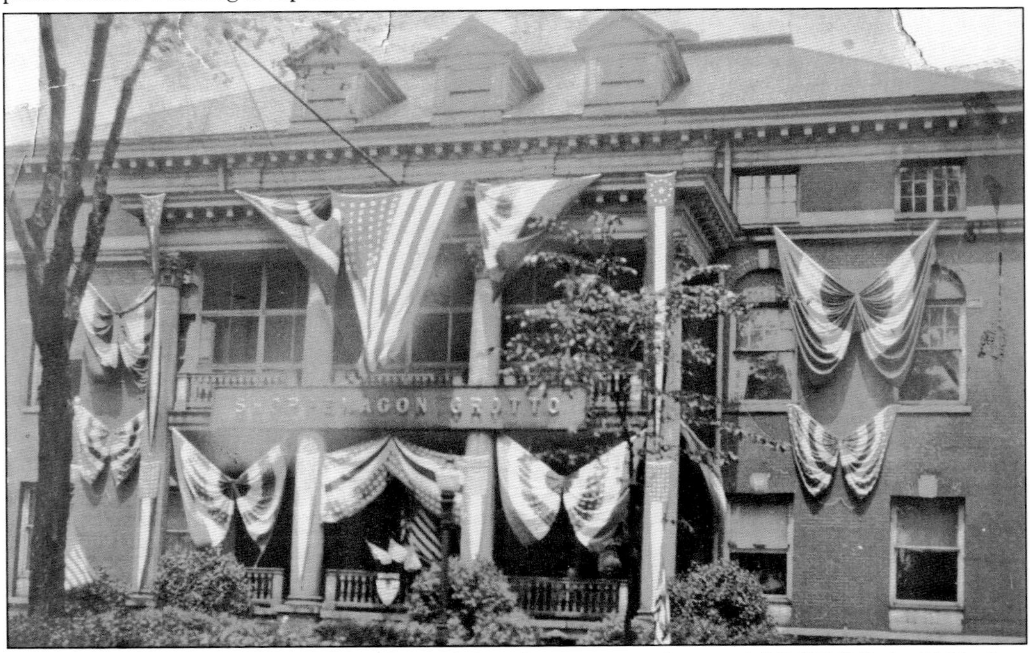

Just prior to 1920, Bay City Masons formed the Shoppenagon Grotto, M.O.V.P.E.R. In 1920, they held their first grand ceremonial at the Washington Theatre. J. Harry Nelson (mayor of Bay City from 1925 to 1936) was the monarch of the grotto that year. By 1924, the group was meeting at the Shoppenagon Grotto Club at Center Avenue and Jefferson Street, previously the Bay City Club. Shoppenagon Grotto disbanded in the mid-1930s, and the building was razed in 1940.

Five

Traces of Transportation

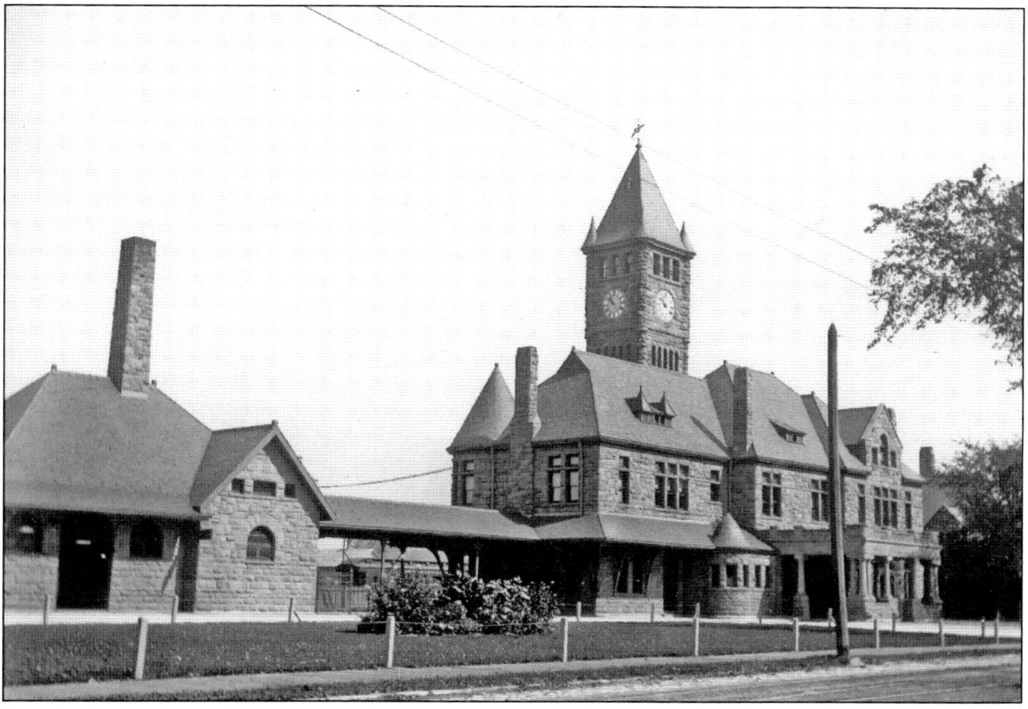

In today's mobile world of automobiles, freeways, and high-speed rail and air travel, the entire world is accessible in a relatively short time. However, it has taken many generations and innovations to get to this point. Each successive advance brought a change in culture, and when it ran its course and was lost, it left traces on the landscape and in the collective memories of the country. Pictured here is the Michigan Central depot around 1895.

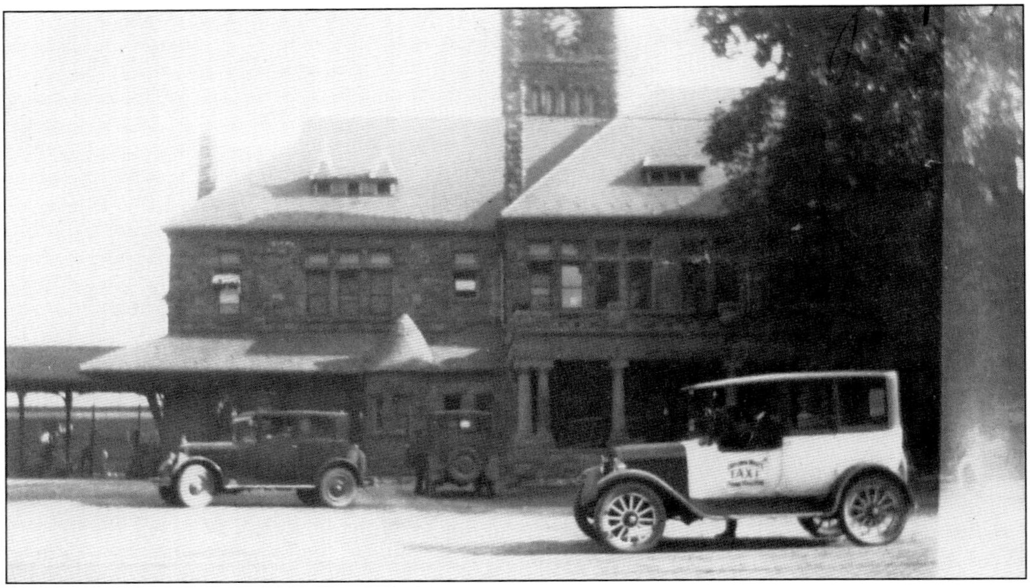

The first railroad in Bay County ran between Bay City and East Saginaw, over swampy ground on a system engineered by A.S. Munger. The line was opened with much acclaim in late 1867 and declared a triumph of engineering skill. The first line to service the west side was the Jackson, Lansing & Saginaw, which started runs to Wenona in 1868. Mergers and new railroad lines would eventually link Bay County with passenger and freight lines throughout the Midwest. The coming of the railroads marked a significant change in the commerce of Bay County. Lumber, salt, and other commodities could be distributed by overland routes instead of relying solely on the traditional water system routes, which were more unpredictable and could not run year-round.

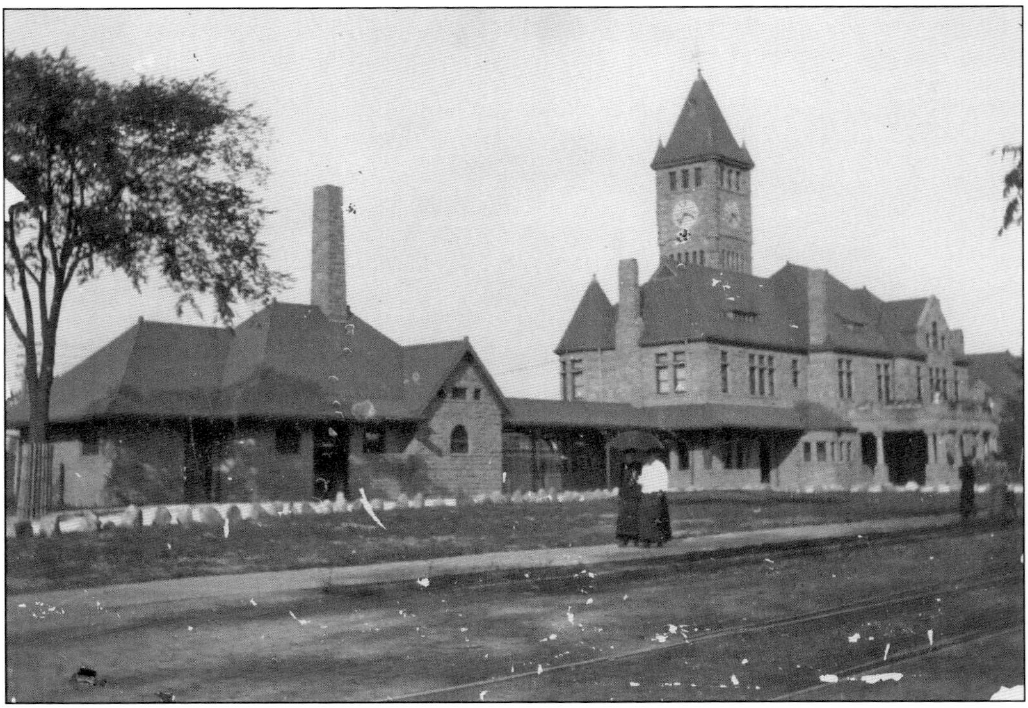

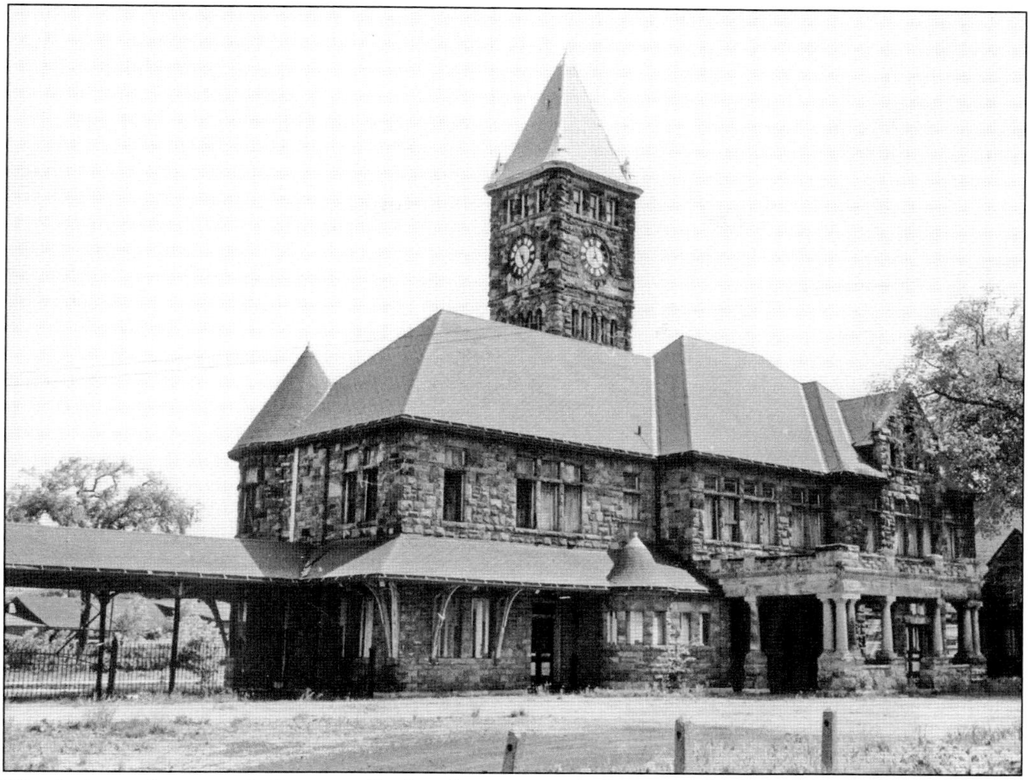

The Jackson, Lansing & Saginaw Railroad became the Michigan Central Rail Road (MCRR) in 1871 and later the New York Central. The Michigan Central built a station in Bay City in 1887 that was located at First and Jackson Streets and served the northern area of Bay City. It seems that no detail was spared, and this depot quickly became one of the jewels of rail travel in the entire area. The photographs on the preceding pages show the depot shortly after it was built and in the 1920s. A post–World War II decline in passenger and freight service merited the shuttering of the depot in 1958, and the rundown building was razed in 1964 (right). The baggage building is all that remains on the site today.

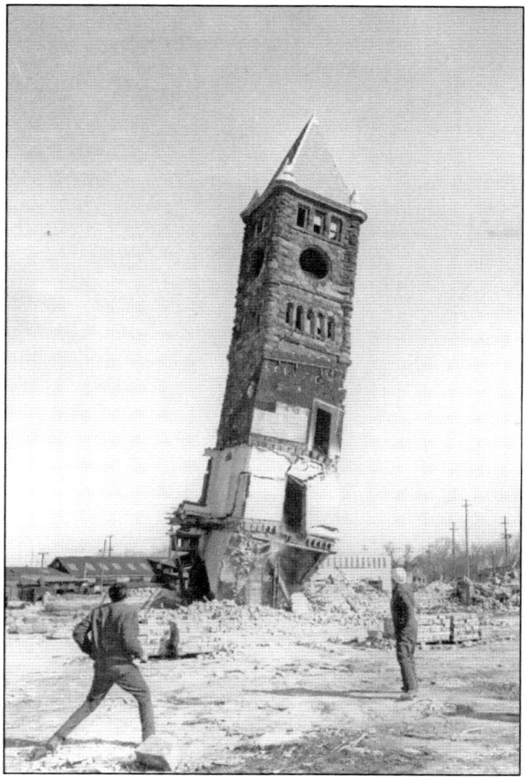

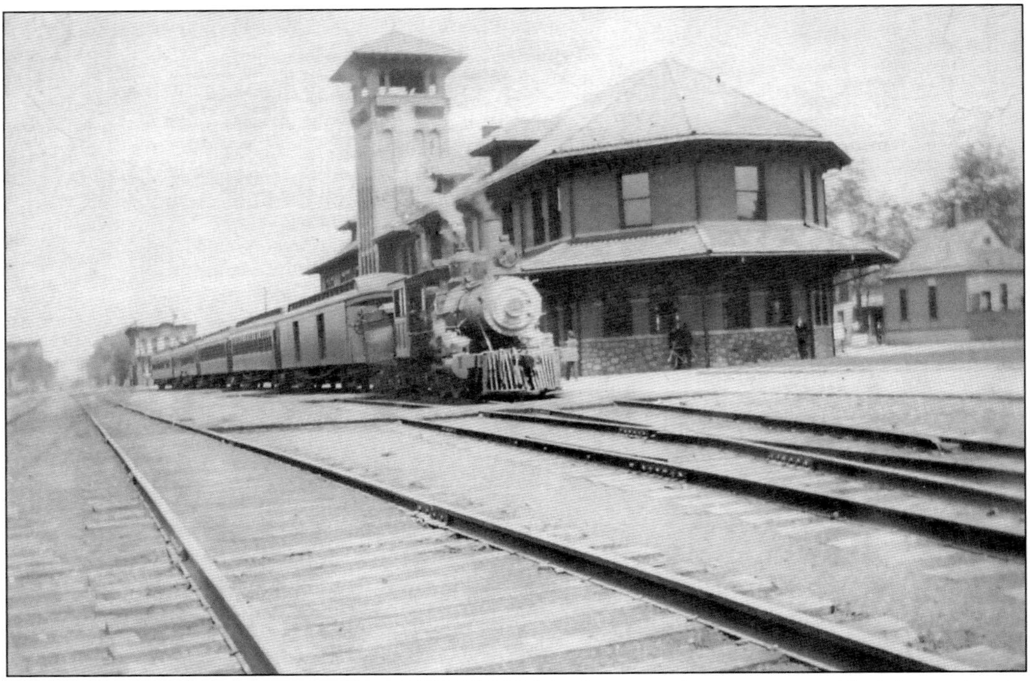

The Flint & Pere Marquette Railroad (F&PMRR) built a grand passenger and freight station in Bay City in 1904. The Arts and Crafts depot was located between Adams and Jefferson Streets two blocks north of Battery Park. The simple lines of the building belied the opulent interior, which was finished in oak, with marble wainscoting and mosaic tile floors. The above image was captured around 1908. Below, around 1915, railcars are lined up on the tracks, and the freight shed is at the left, with the corner of the depot at right. As passenger service dwindled in the days of highways and automobiles, many stations were abandoned. This station later became a Greyhound bus terminal, sat abandoned for many years, and was eventually painstakingly restored by the Great Lakes Center Foundation to house offices and meeting facilities.

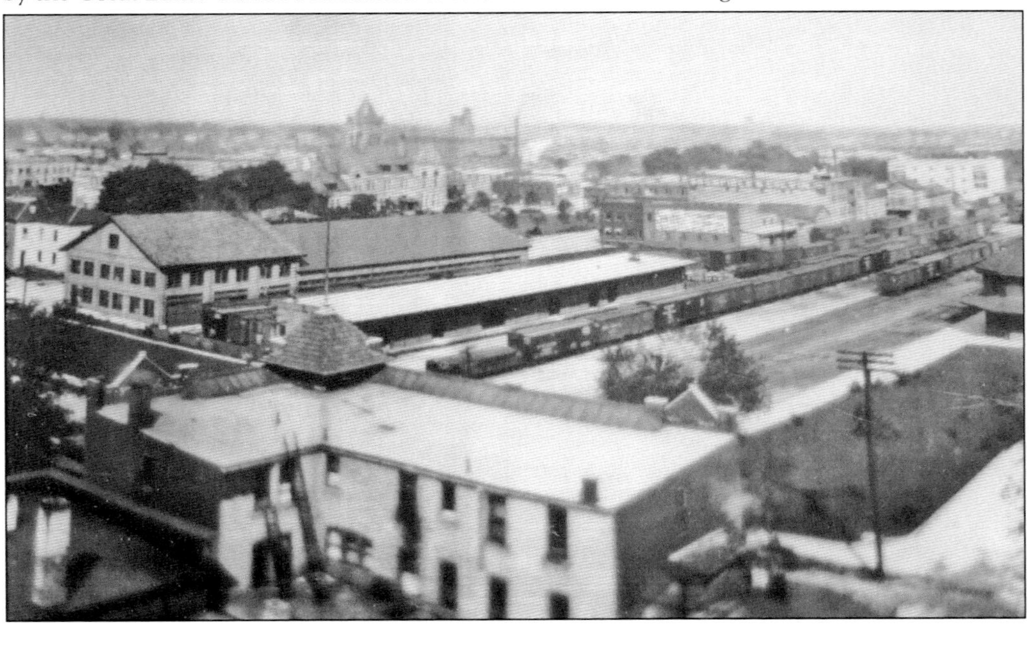

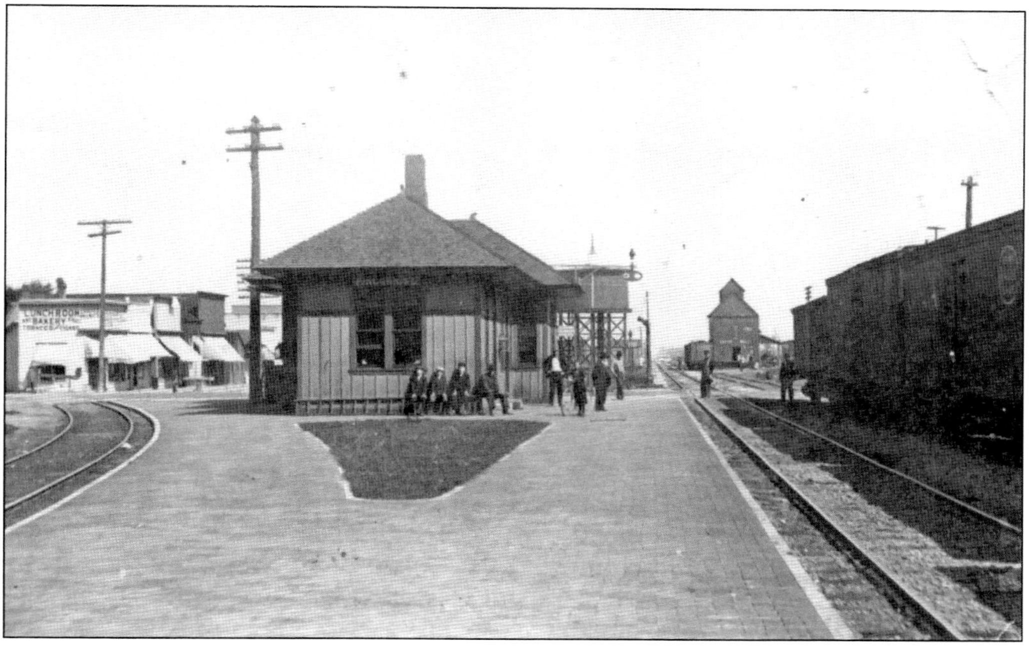

As railroads spread throughout the area, it was necessary to have infrastructure to move freight and passengers to and from the railway. A series of depots emerged in locations where they made sense. Many small towns on the rail line had their own depots, and some even developed around (and because of) access to rail lines. The above photograph shows the Pinconning Depot in northern Bay County, which was located on Manitou Street between Third and Fourth Streets. As a result of the availability of rail access, people and freight could move rather quickly between the larger cities and small villages. Some of these depots were fairly small, simple buildings with a platform, waiting area, and a small office, much like the one below. Many of these buildings were abandoned after they were no longer needed.

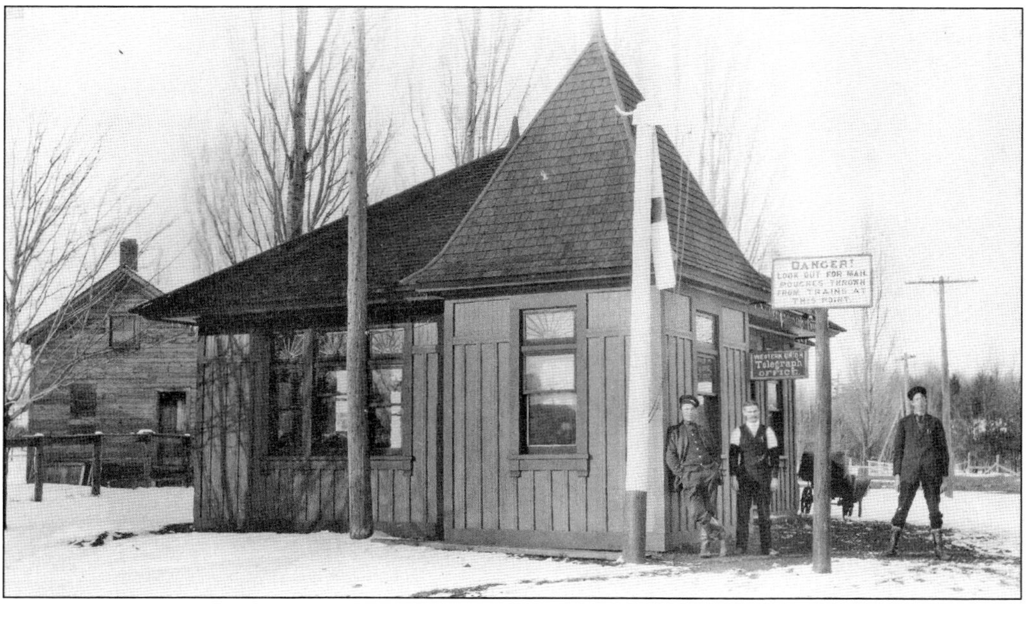

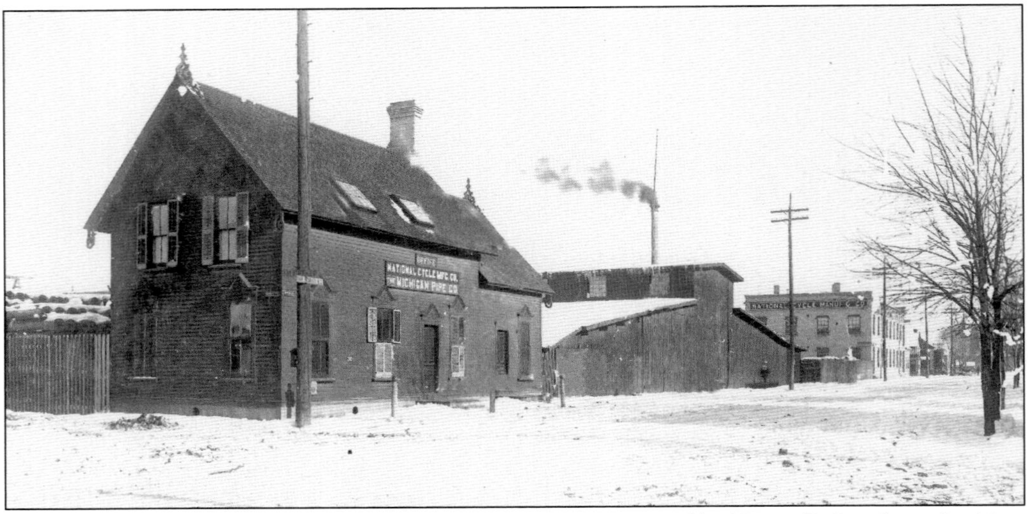

In 1892, the National Cycle Manufacturing Company was started by Henry B. Smith, and sold its bicycles all over the United States, with the slogan, "A National Rider Never Changes His Mount." The catalogs offered bicycles with new and patented designs. Several models were chainless, or driven by a gear shaft, and most had shock absorbers to dampen a rough ride. Features like these were considered futuristic to the cycle world of the time; however, they still used wooden rims instead of metal. The tandem National pictured below is from the 1898 National catalog. By 1916, the Chevrolet Motor Company needed a parts plant, and the National Cycle buildings fit the bill. In 1916, the deal was finalized and brought the first automobile plant to Bay City. The National plant became part of what is now Bay City Powertrain.

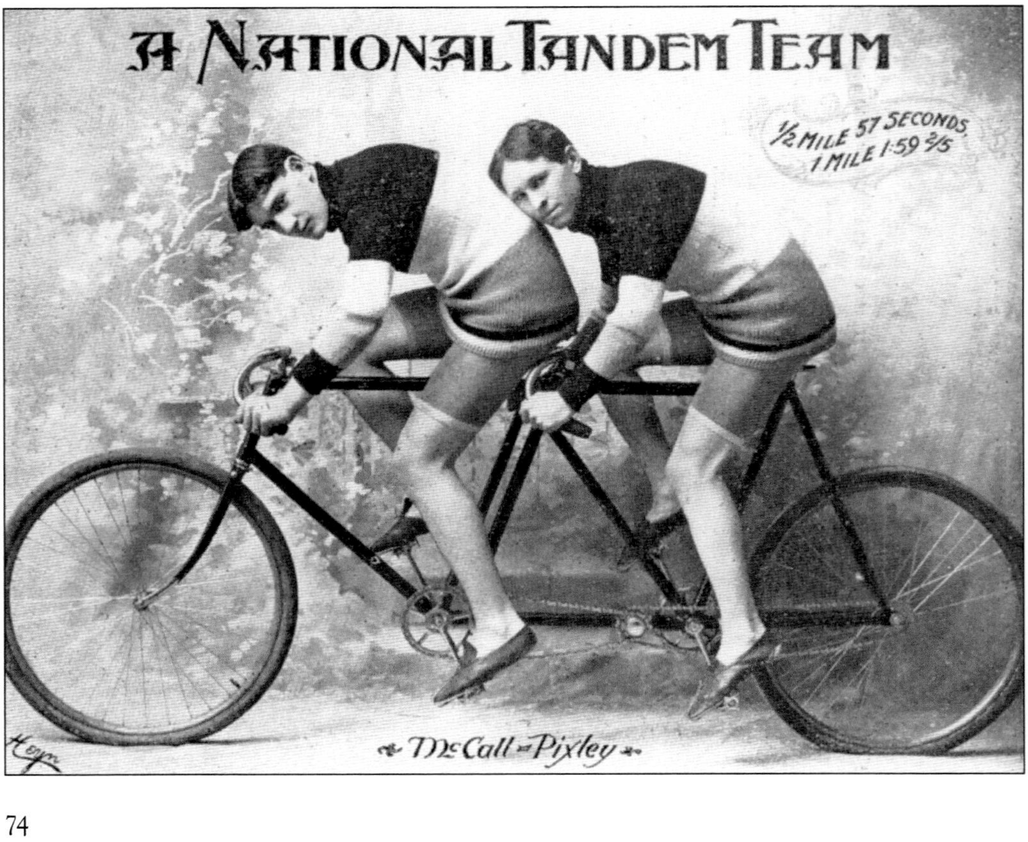

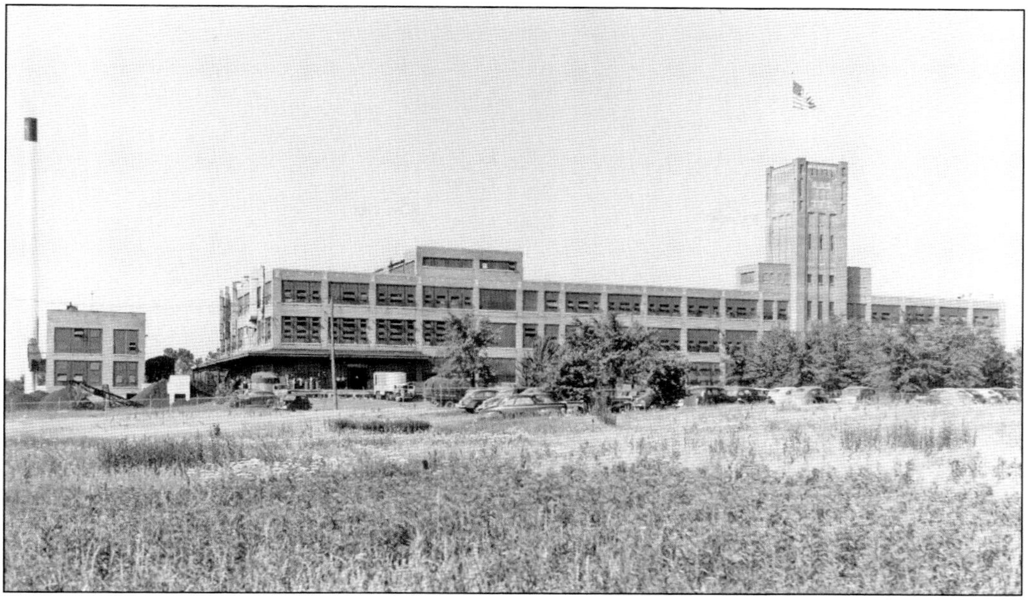

Built in 1922, the failed Wildman Rubber auto tire plant at the foot of Morton Street became Electric Auto-Lite's Bay City division when its 1,300 employees took up residency and began manufacturing automobile parts in 1936. In 1957, they added a lamp division. In 1963, Electric Auto-Lite became Prestolite and was now manufacturing a host of automotive parts. In later years, the company produced parts for the Army's Humvee vehicle; however, the facility was closed by 1989.

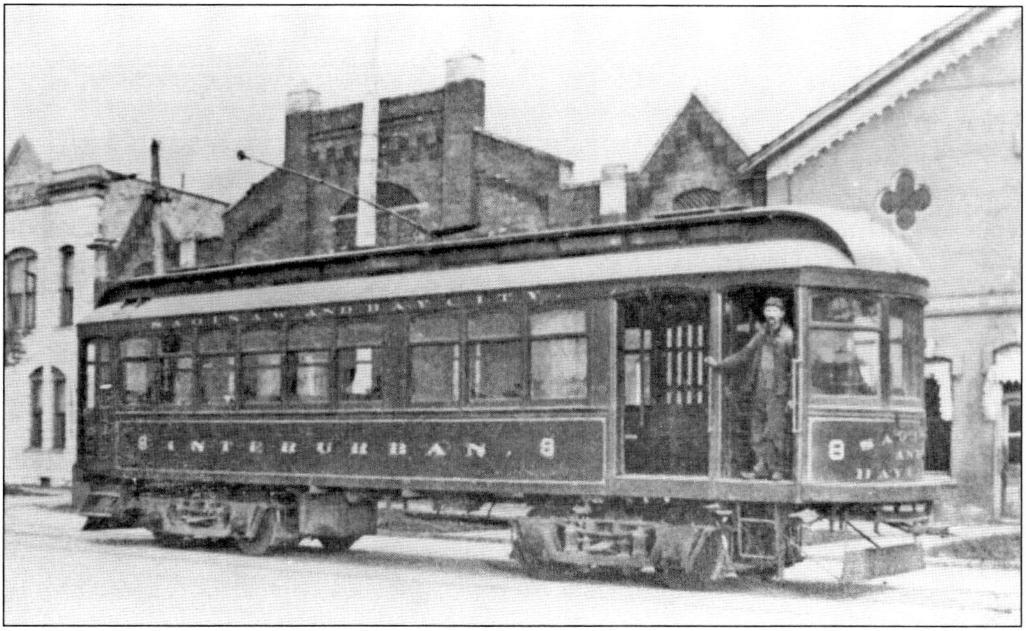

The interurban was an electric trolley line that ran between Bay City, Saginaw, Flint, Detroit, and as far south as Cleveland, Ohio. Started in 1895, its cars could reportedly reach speeds of 80 miles per hour. The Bay City–Saginaw route followed the Saginaw River south on the east side and crossed to the west side south of the city. The interurban was in business until 1929, slightly longer than conventional streetcars.

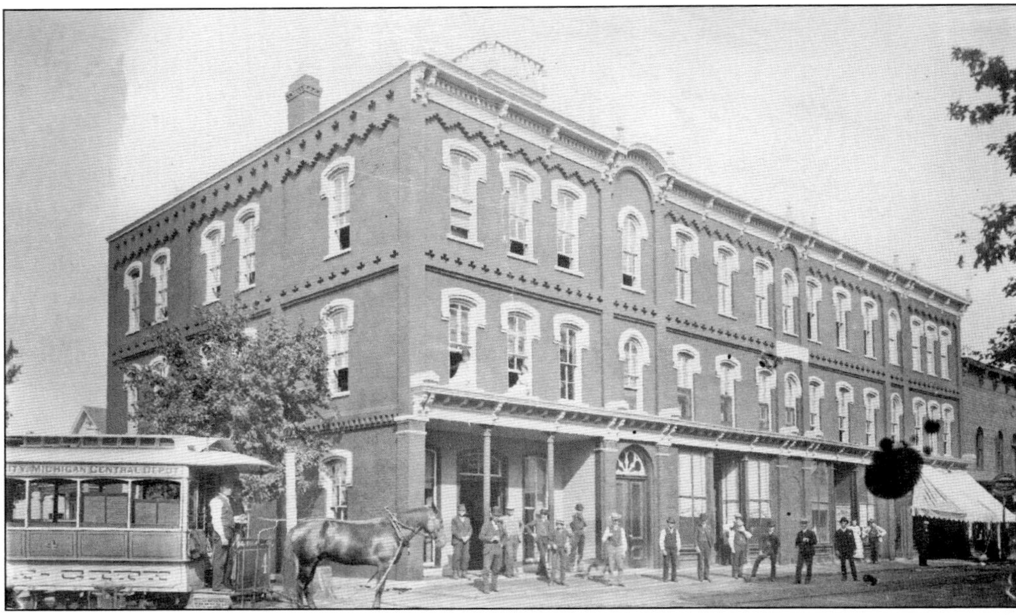

The first streetcar system in Bay City started around 1865 with cars pulled by horses. Tracks were placed on the streets of the most-traveled routes and horse-car barns were erected. In the photograph, a horse-drawn streetcar sits outside the Astor House Hotel at Harrison Street and Cass Avenue (South End) in 1887. Note the tracks that run away to the right, near where the dog is seated.

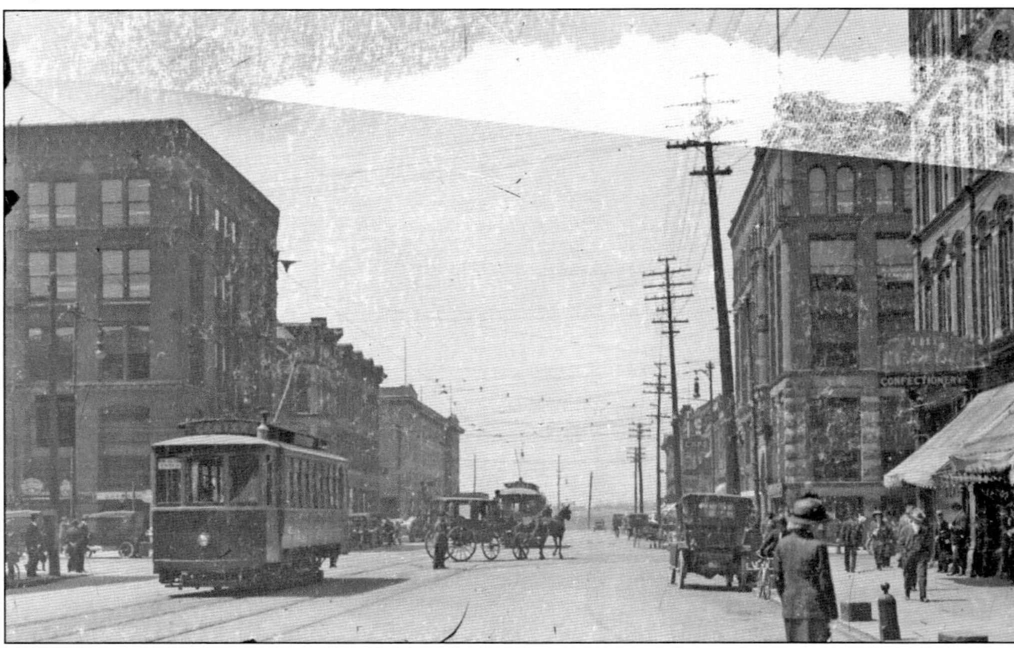

The electric streetcar made its first run in 1889, from the Third Street Bridge through West Bay City. By 1893, a line also ran down Center and Washington Avenues and Third Street on the east side. The streetcar was the only public transit within the city limits from the 1860s until the early 1920s. Looking west down Center Avenue around 1912, this photograph shows both the Center Avenue and Banks trolleys.

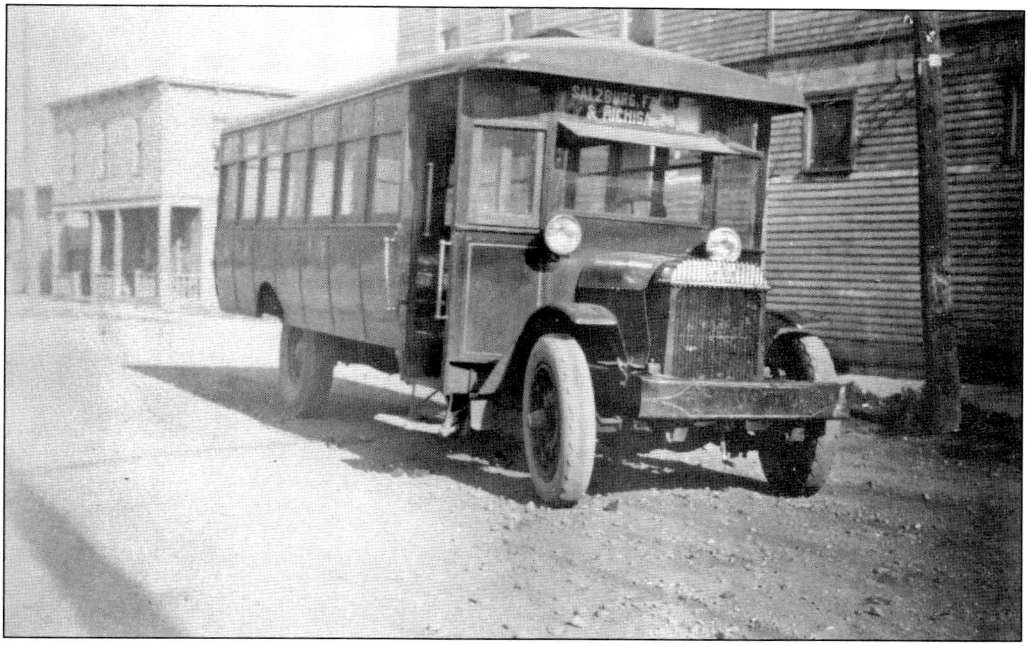

Bus service first was offered early in the 1920s by several companies. The Balcer Brothers Motor Coach Company started its jitney bus line in the 1920s. By the mid-1930s, it was the only line operating in Bay City. The Balcer bus of the mid-1920s pictured above was made from a Bay City–built Union Truck chassis. The image below features a Balcer Brothers Motor Coach Company bus from the early 1940s. By the late 1950s, with the rise in ownership of automobiles, bus service was operating at a loss, despite increases in fares. In 1957, historian George Butterfield remarked that Bay City faced a problem of how to prevent the loss of all bus service.

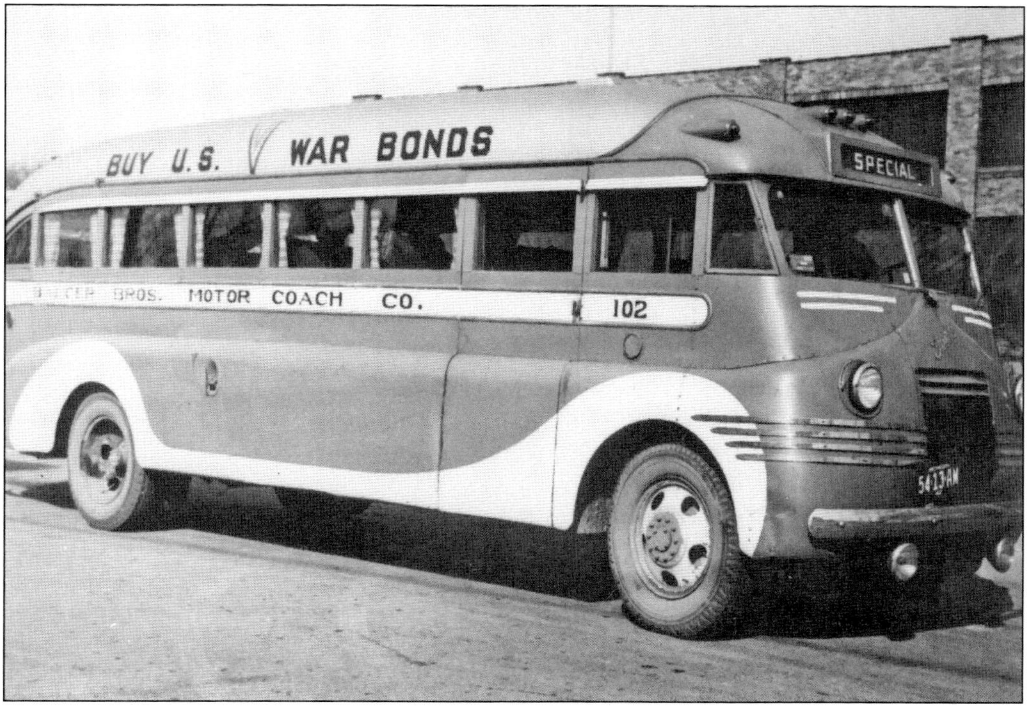

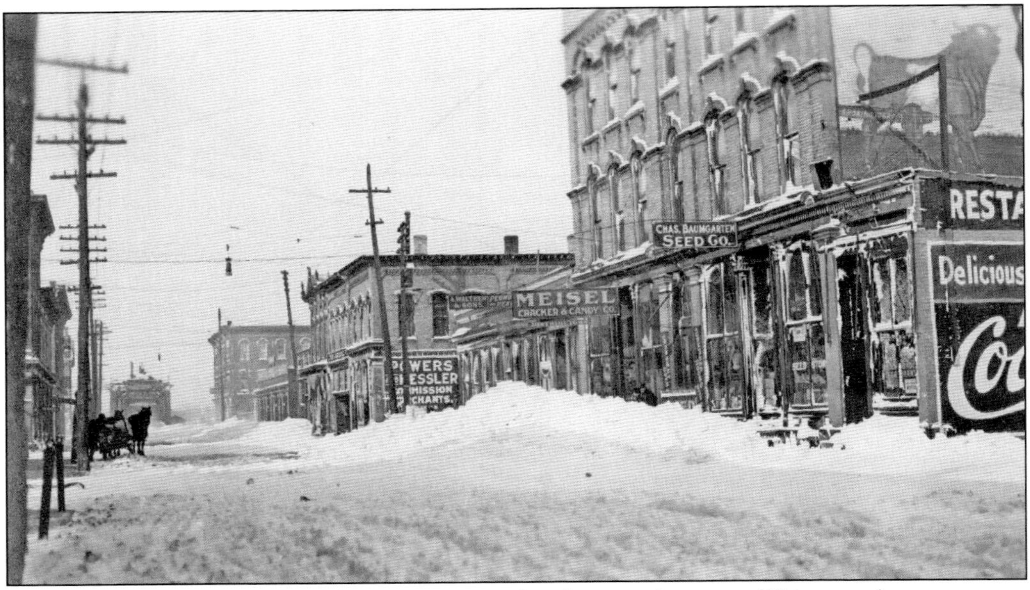

This view of Third Street looking west was a familiar site for years. This was the gateway to the Third Street Bridge and thus to the west side. Bay City's first bridge, the original wooden span was erected in 1865 as a toll bridge. It was replaced by a steel structure and purchased by Bay County in 1883, when the toll was discontinued. The swing-span bridge was once again reconstructed in 1889.

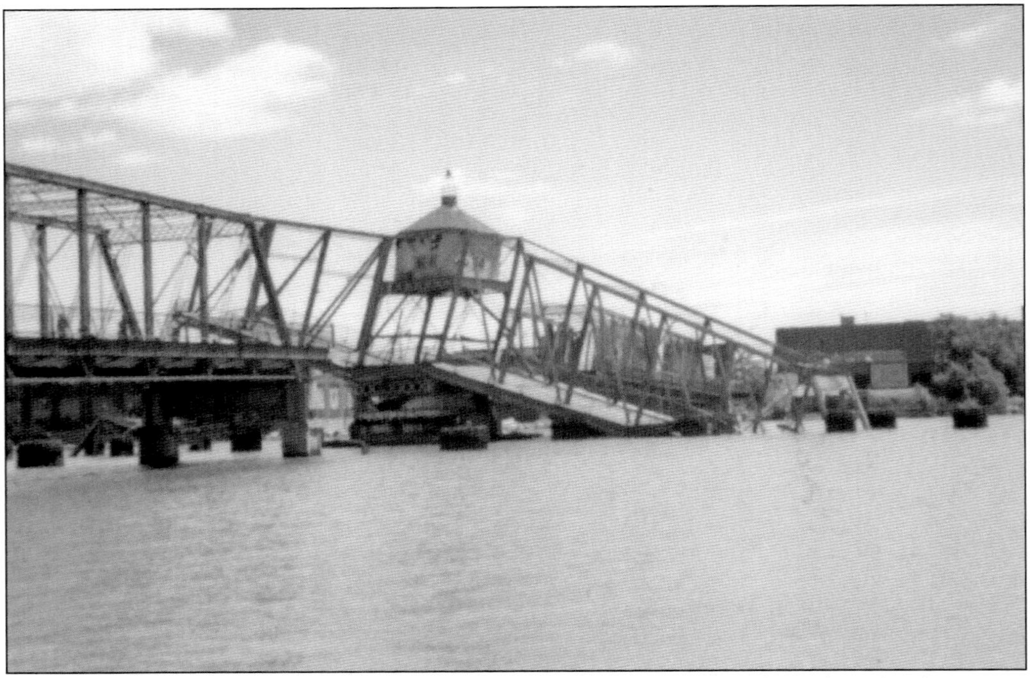
The last major renovation of the bridge was in 1919, and from 1927 through 1958, there were no major repairs made to the aging structure. Several incidents in the ensuing years took their toll on the bridge, and on June 18, 1976, the Third Street Bridge collapsed as it was opening for a vessel. The event made national news, and a new bridge was not built until 1987, on a site several blocks north.

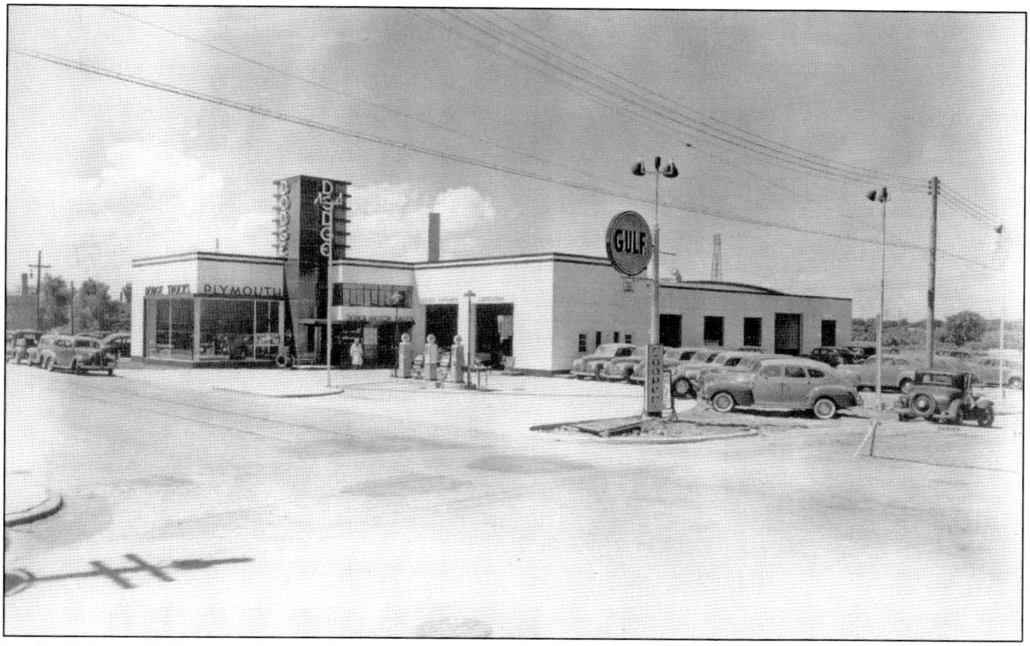

Zeder Motor Sales was located at 621 North Water Street between Sixth and Seventh Streets, on the west side of the street, where the Doubletree Hotel's conference center now sits. Henry D. Zeder built the dealership in 1949 to provide services that included "tires, batteries, greasing and lubricating, genuine Mopar parts and accessories for Dodge and Plymouth cars and trucks." By 1958, Zeder was deceased, and the building sold to Reed Draper Chevrolet, which operated there from 1959 to 1966. Bromm and Ray were on the site from 1967 to 1971, while Mel Smith Lincoln Mercury occupied the dealership from 1972 to 1973. After a few vacant years, Bay Metro Transit used the building from 1977 until around 1982. The Bay City Rollers mural in chapter two was painted on the back of this building.

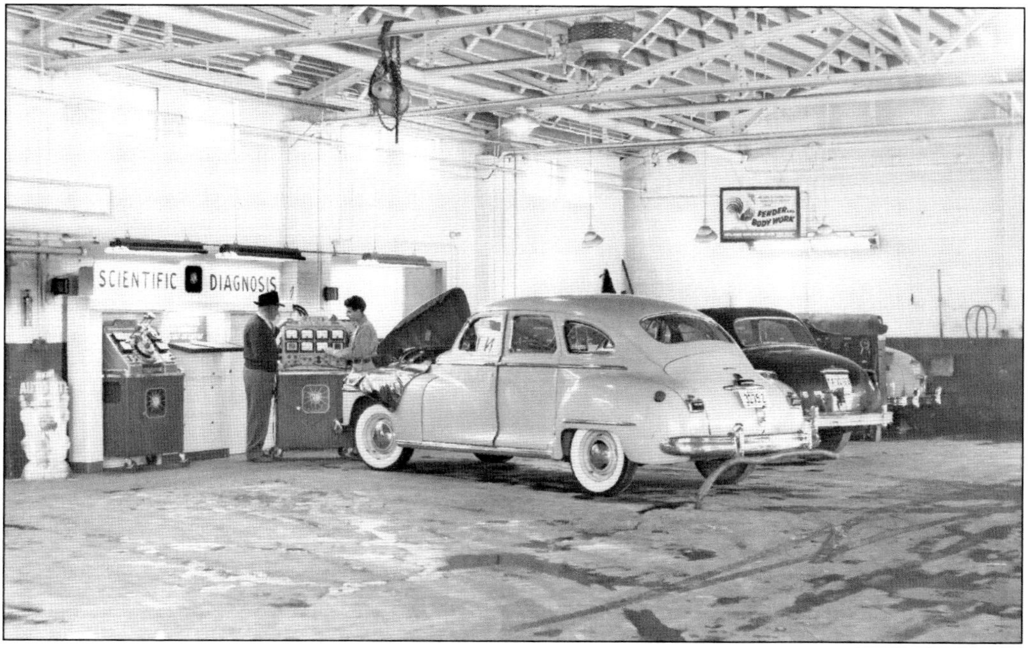

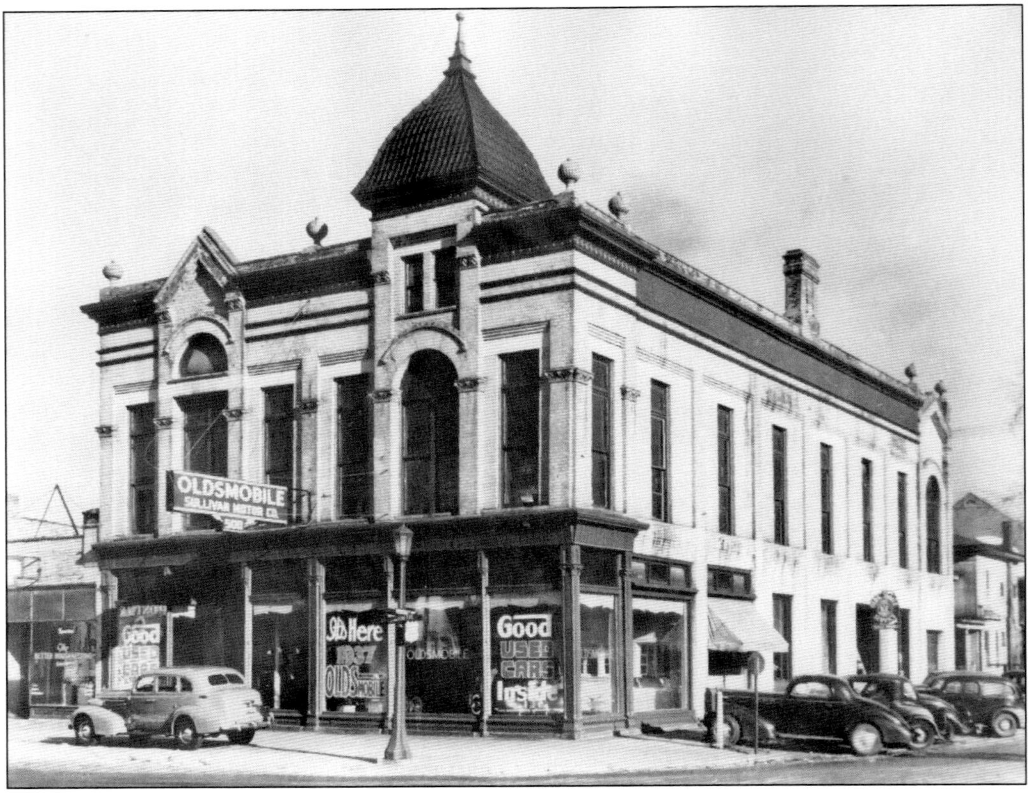

The distinctive tower cap of Sullivan Motor Company's Oldsmobile dealership made it an easily recognizable building at 500 Washington Avenue from the mid-1930s through the mid-1940s. Standing on the northeast corner of Washington Avenue and McKinley Street, the building later became Atlas Furniture and unfortunately lost its distinctive cap. It did, however, gain five important murals for a time in the 1970s before being torn down around 1983 (see page 31).

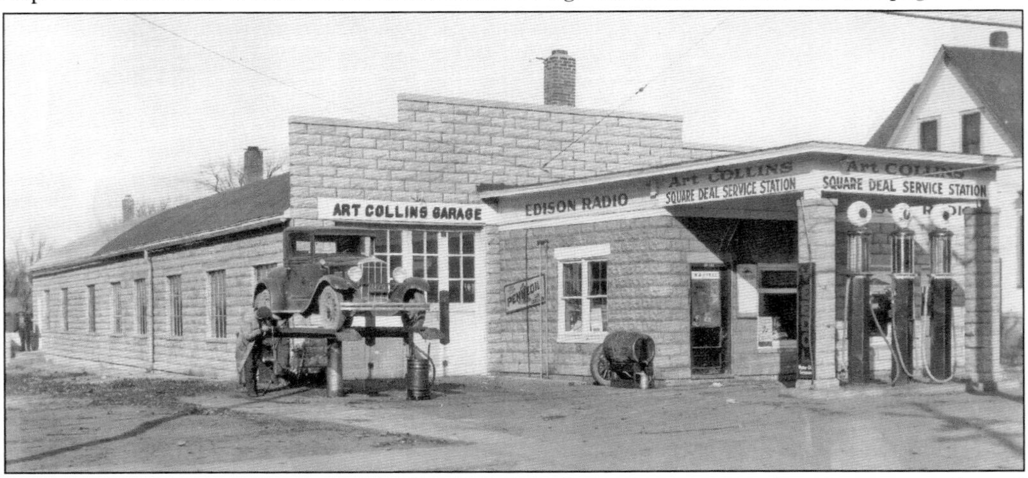

The automobile was introduced in the first decade of the 20th century, and production accelerated at an unbelievable pace through the 1920s. By the late 1920s, there were over 23 million cars on the road. An entire industry sprang up almost overnight to provide support for owners. Arthur Collins's automobile garage on Woodside Lane (in 1928) was one of many such garages that sprang up throughout the area to repair automobiles.

Six

The Magnificent Wenonah

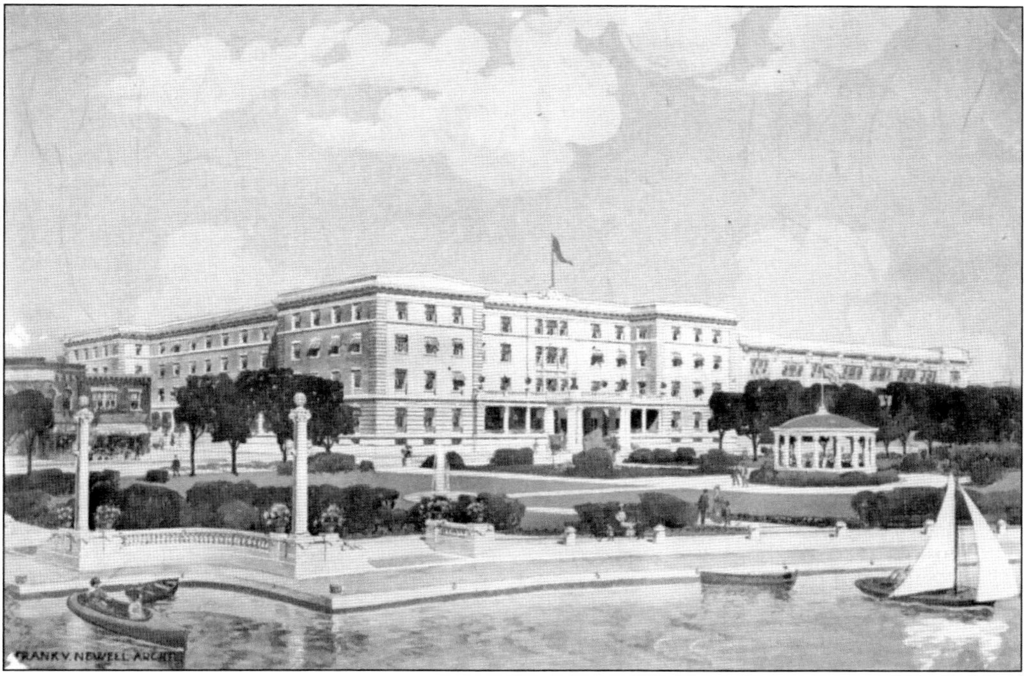

On the southeast corner of Center Avenue and Water Street sits 100 Center Avenue. This site has always been in the heart of the downtown, near the river, and at one end of what many consider Bay City's main thoroughfare. It is fitting that this site anchors Center Avenue, which travels east through what were once the workplaces and residences of some of the most influential players in Bay City's history. Pictured here is an artist's rendering of the Wenonah Hotel around 1925.

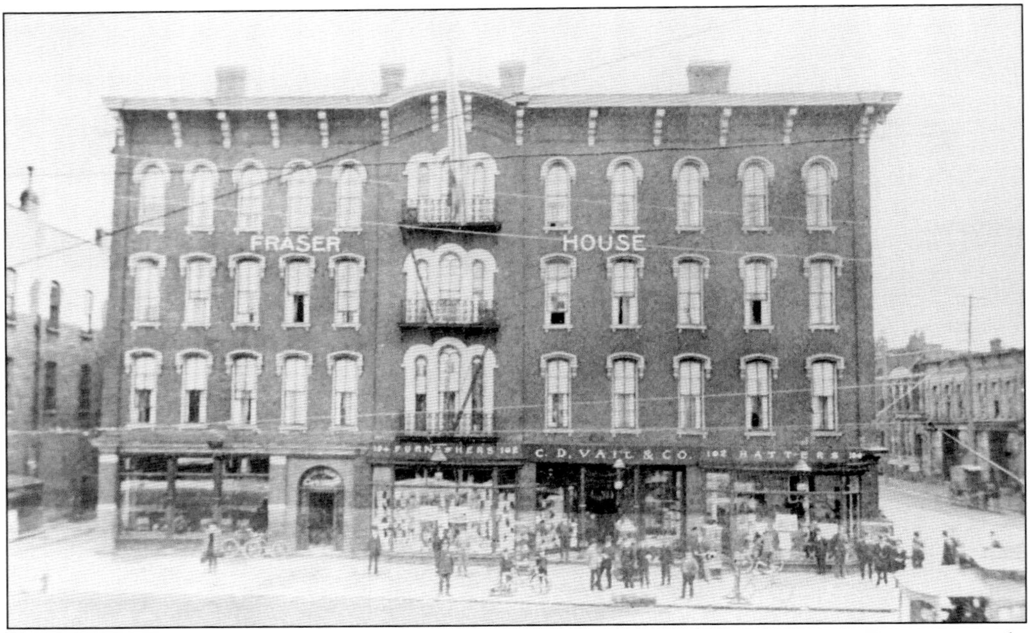

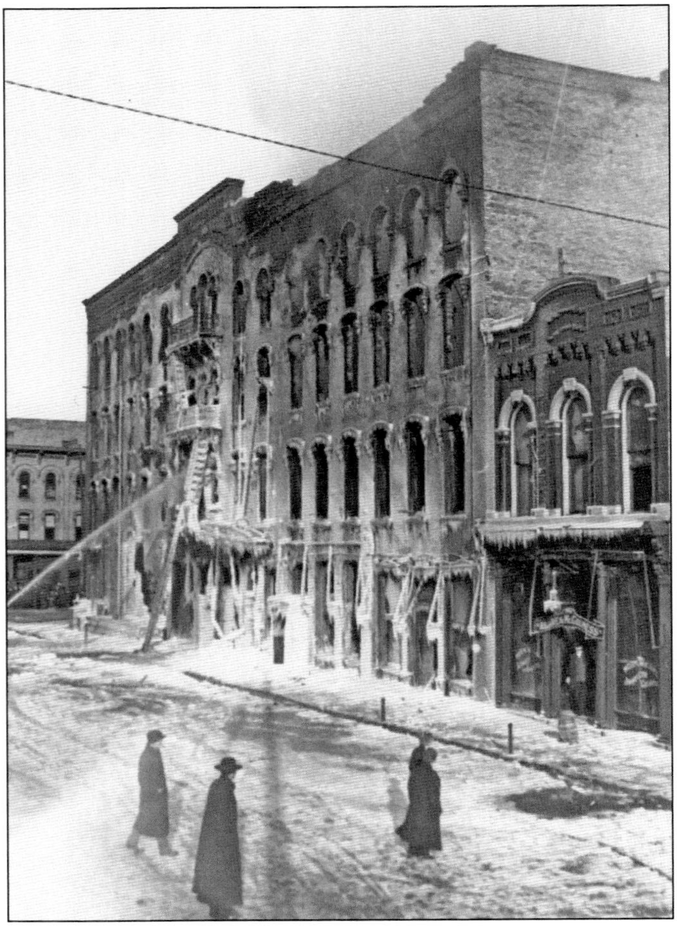

In 1865, James Fraser, an early settler of Bay City, built the Fraser House hotel at the corner of Center Avenue and Water Street, but died before it was completed. It served the burgeoning community as one of the major public houses for many years. The first professional theatrical performances presented in Bay City were produced by Saville and Lindley's Theatrical Company in the hall at Fraser House in 1867. A 1904 promotional booklet said of the Fraser, "It is a solid brick structure with seventy-five guest chambers, well planned sample rooms, electric lights, bell service, elevator, steam heat, private baths, spacious office and lobby, cozy parlors and a magnificent dining room." The lower level of the Fraser House also housed numerous businesses typical of the time, notably C.D. Vail and Company, which sold men's furnishings, including hats.

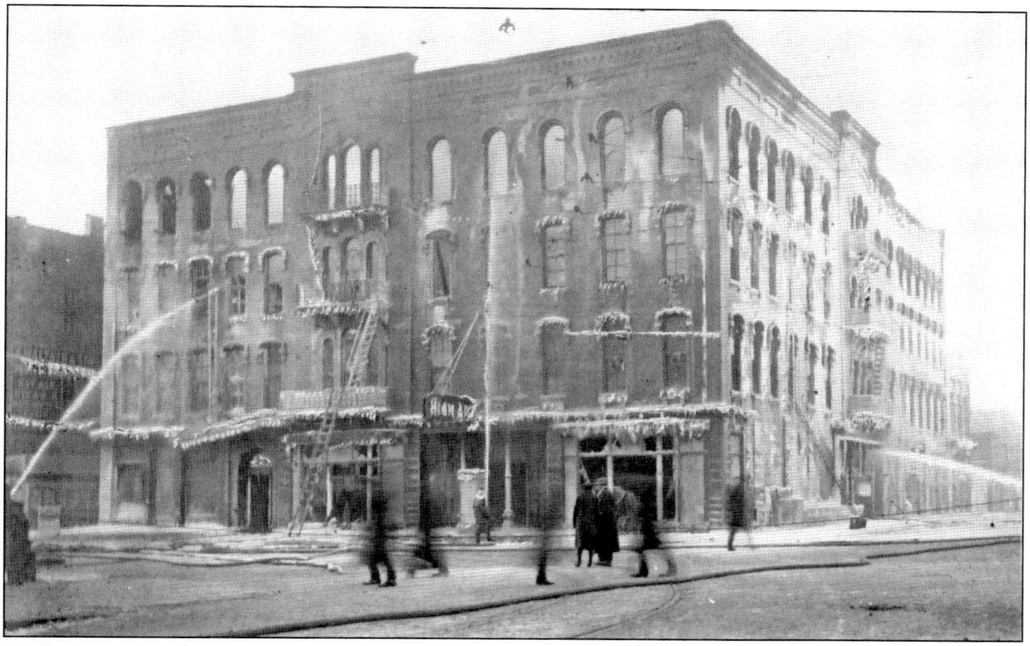

Unfortunately, the Fraser House became a casualty of fire on December 23, 1906. A fire that started in the annex across the alley spread quickly and eventually engulfed the building. The fire department responded in the early hours of the morning and quickly called for reinforcements. Several guests had to be rescued, as did eight girls who had been sleeping in the annex. One person died, and one of the girls was badly burned. Firefighters did not have ladders tall enough to reach the top of the four-story building, forcing one man to jump from an upper floor, only sustaining a cut arm as he grabbed for a telephone cable. At the time of the fire, the temperature was around zero degrees, making it one of the department's toughest fires to date. A total loss, the Fraser was later demolished.

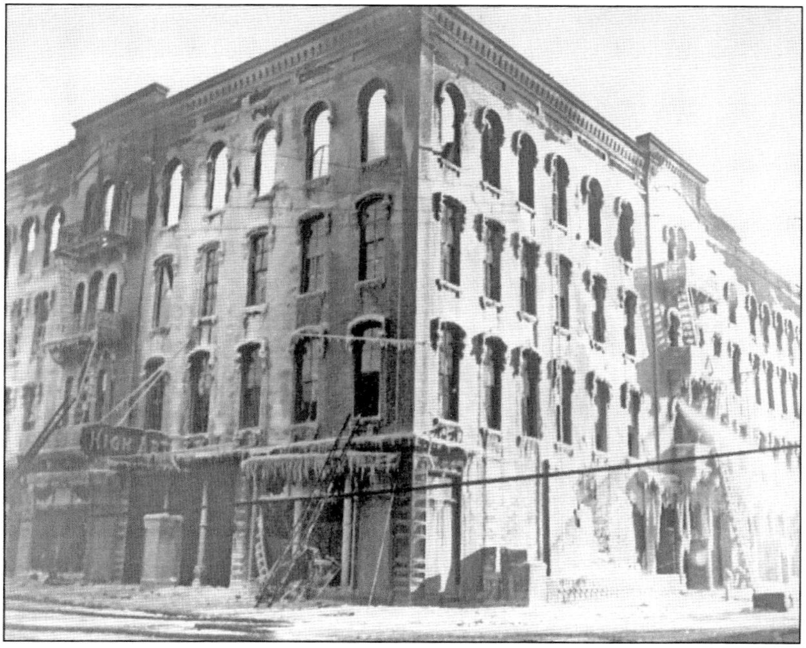

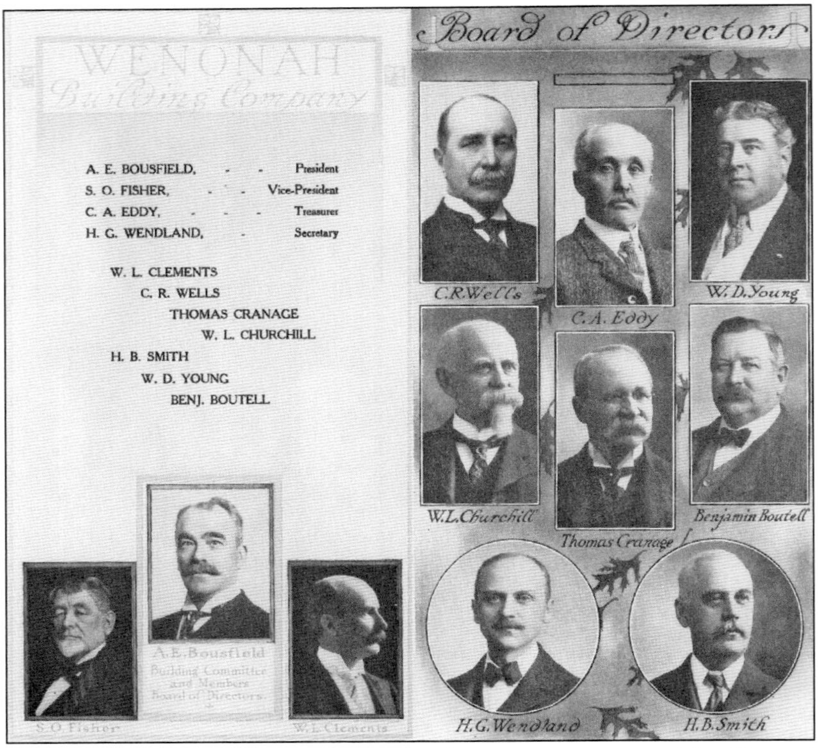

A board of directors that featured prominent Bay City businessmen organized the Wenonah Building Company shortly after the fire. They purchased the site where the Fraser House once stood and commissioned Chicago architect Frank Newell to design a modern hotel, the Wenonah. The four-story building, named for the Indian maiden in Longfellow's epic poem *The Song of Hiawatha*, was designed as fire-resistant with an interior steel frame and brick exterior. The Wenonah opened to rave reviews on November 9, 1908, and was immediately acclaimed the most luxurious hotel north of Detroit. The photograph below was taken during construction.

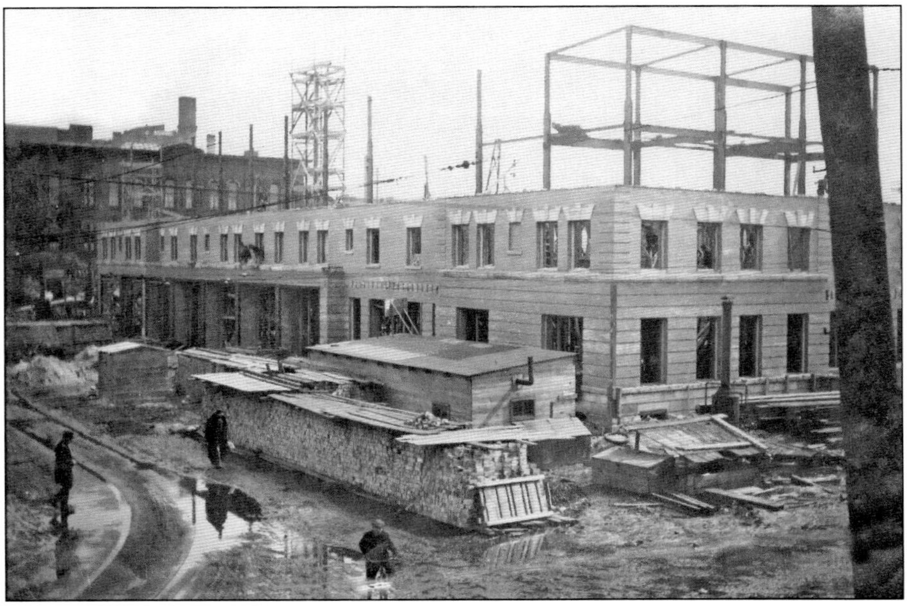

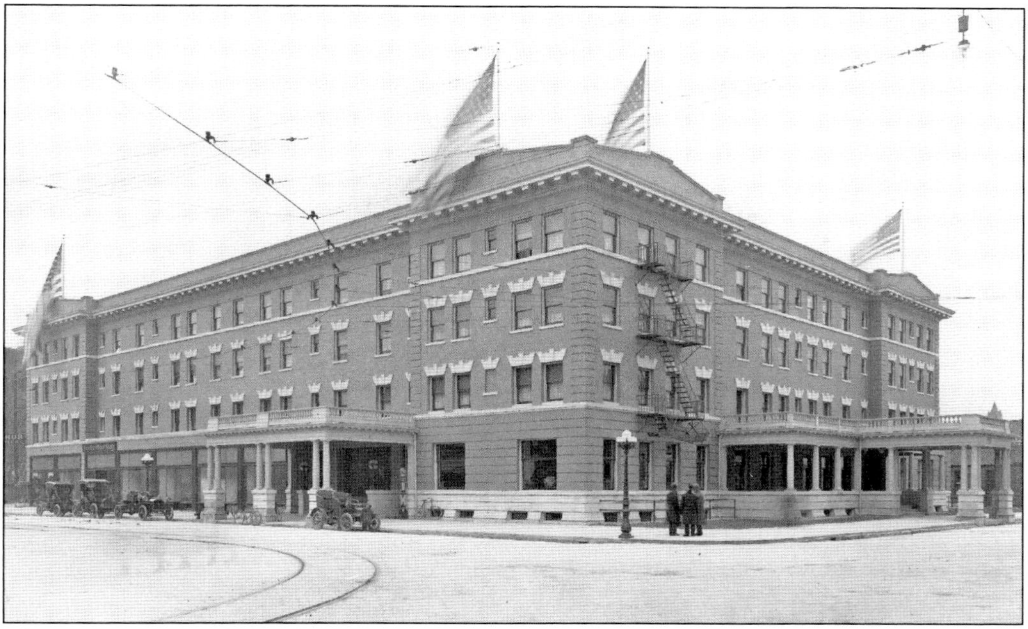

The Beaux Arts–style hotel featured an exterior of buff-colored brick with limestone trim. Two porte cocheres accented the Saginaw and Water Street entries, and the lobby featured a central two-story octagonal rotunda. The columns, walls, and registration desk were wainscoted in veined white Italian marble. The lobby floor was ceramic tile, with the inlaid patterns reflecting the paneled ceiling. In front of the elevators was a mosaic panel of Princess Wenonah, a memorable centerpiece of the hotel's decor. The elevators and stairs rose to the second floor of the rotunda where there were several small parlors. The remainder of the second and all of the third and fourth floors were guest rooms. The dining room was on the first floor, and the basement housed a barber shop, tailor, wine cellar, Turkish bath, and other services for guests.

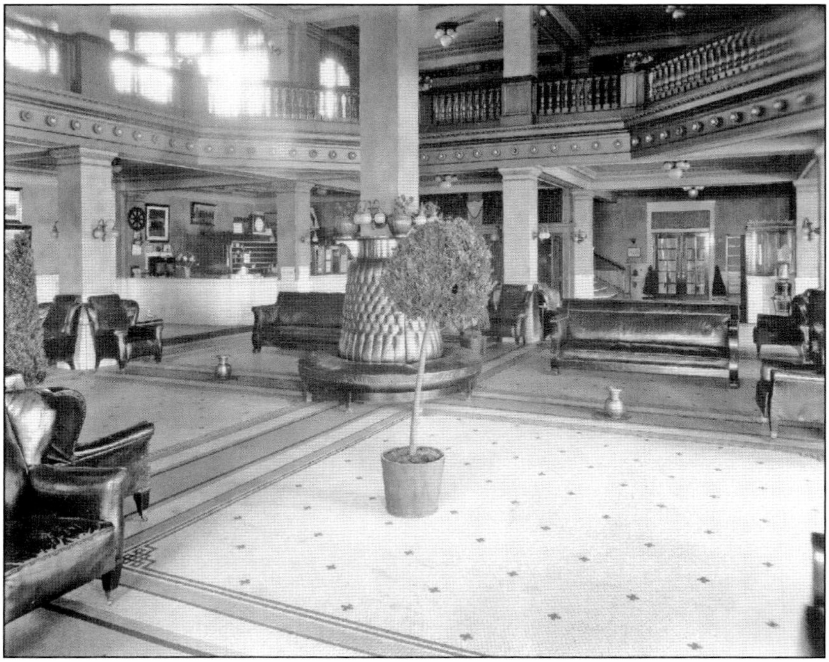

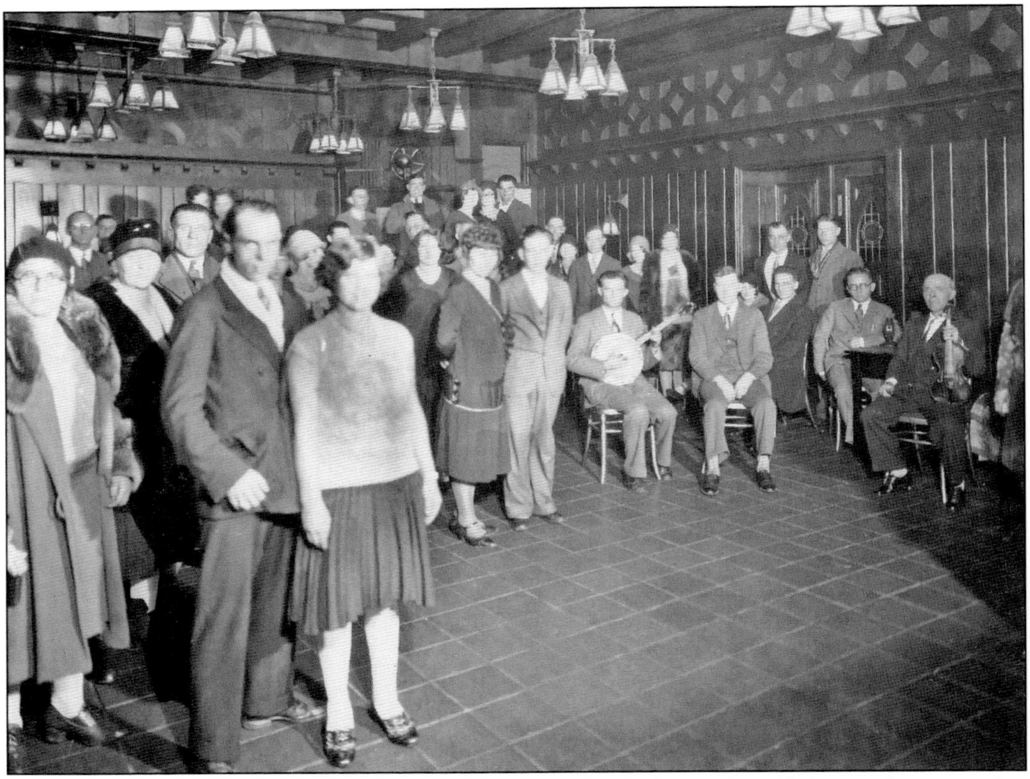

A function was held, complete with a band, in the Wenonah Hotel Grill Room, shown in this photograph taken around 1911. According to management, "On the first floor are the lobby, dining, grill, ladies' reception and writing rooms, telephone booths and buffet. All woodwork is of mahogany finish. Tile floors in basement and first stories, ceramic mosaic predominating."

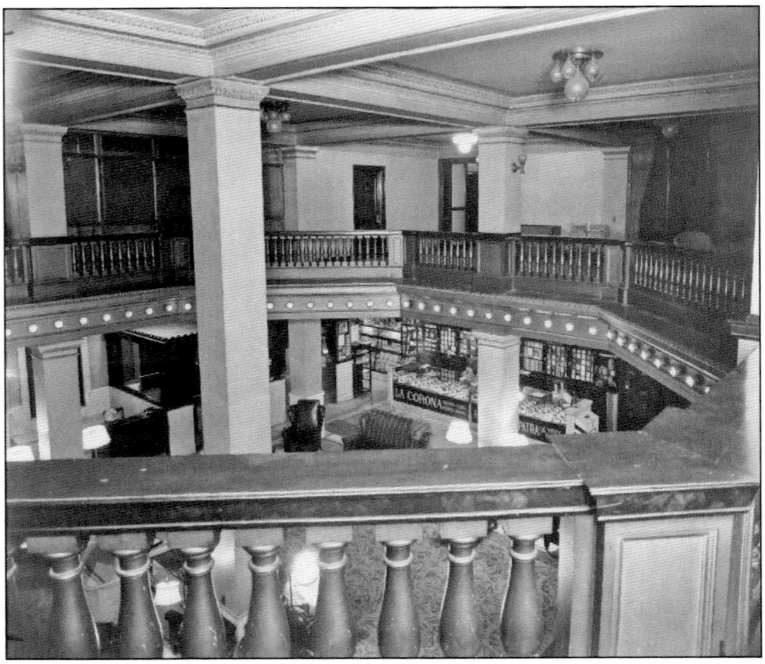

According to the first proprietor, P.A. Shares, when first built, the Wenonah featured 2,500 electric lamps, 250 radiators, two miles of water piping, 395 tons of steel, 2,875,000 bricks, 30,500 yards of plaster, 83,000 square feet of fireproof partitions, 97,500 square feet of floor area, 23,500 feet of tile floors, two passenger elevators, one writing room off the lobby, and 200 guest rooms. Of these 200 rooms, 100 had private baths, and 50 had toilets.

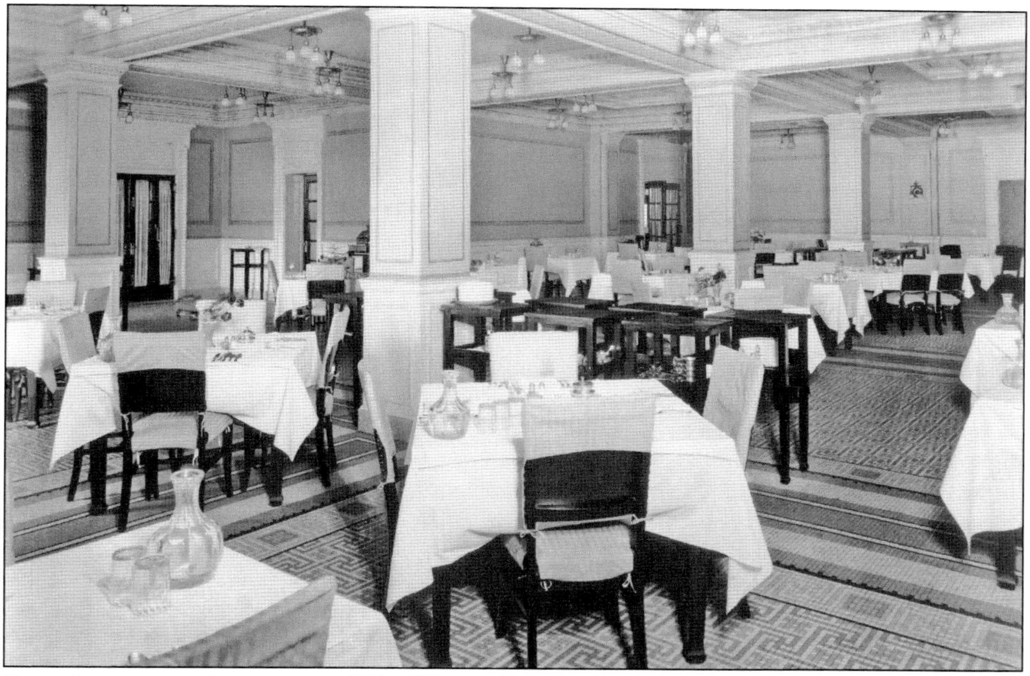

From the opening day program: "The Wenonah is absolutely fire-proof. The one-quarter of one percent of inflammable material that has entered into its construction is seen in the wood work of the doors and windows. Everything else is stone, brick, cement, steel and glass." Pictured here is the formal dining room of the Wenonah, at the ready for guests.

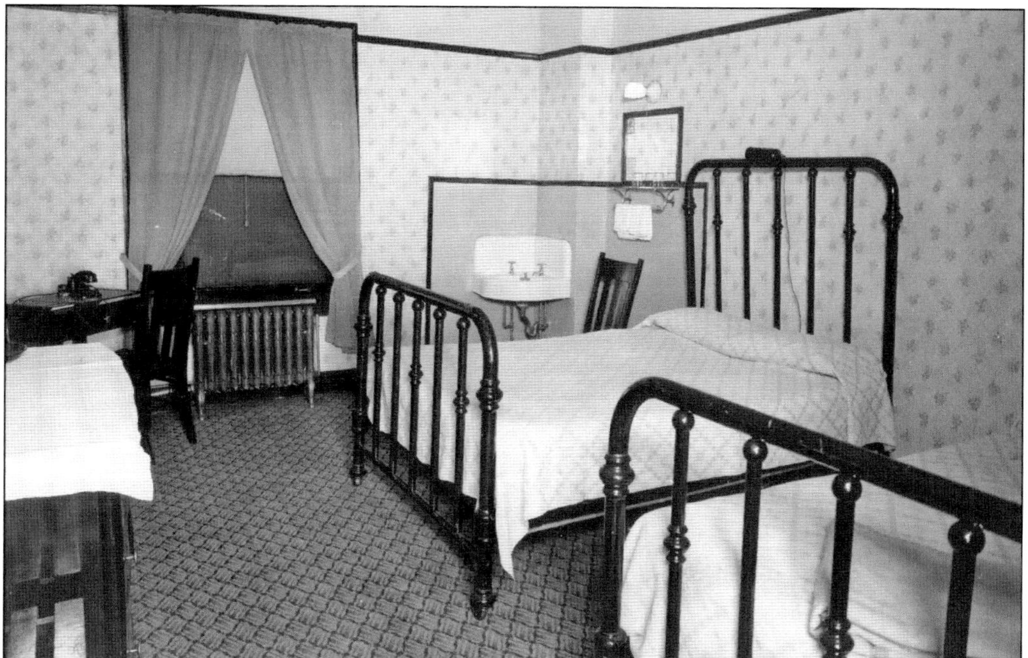

The Wenonah had 72 rooms with private baths, plus a public bath and lavatory on every floor. Every room had a lavatory, hot and cold running water, gas, electric light, and telephone. The smallest guest room was 12 by 14 feet, and the largest was 16 by 22 feet.

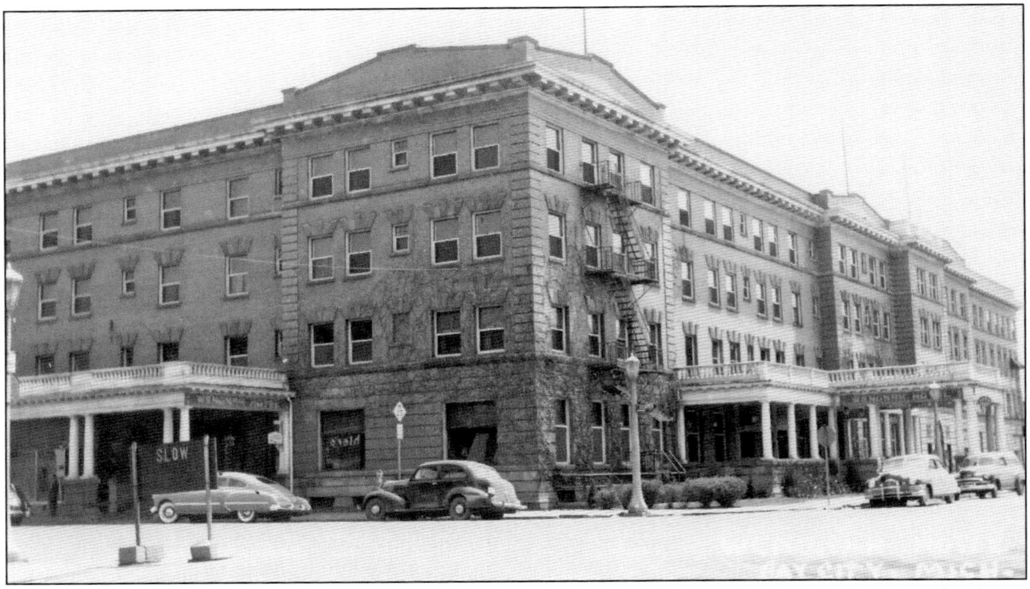

In 1925, the Wenonah Hotel was enlarged to accommodate 100 more guest rooms and a large ballroom. This ushered in an era of increased prosperity for the Wenonah, which was well known for its excellent hospitality and service.

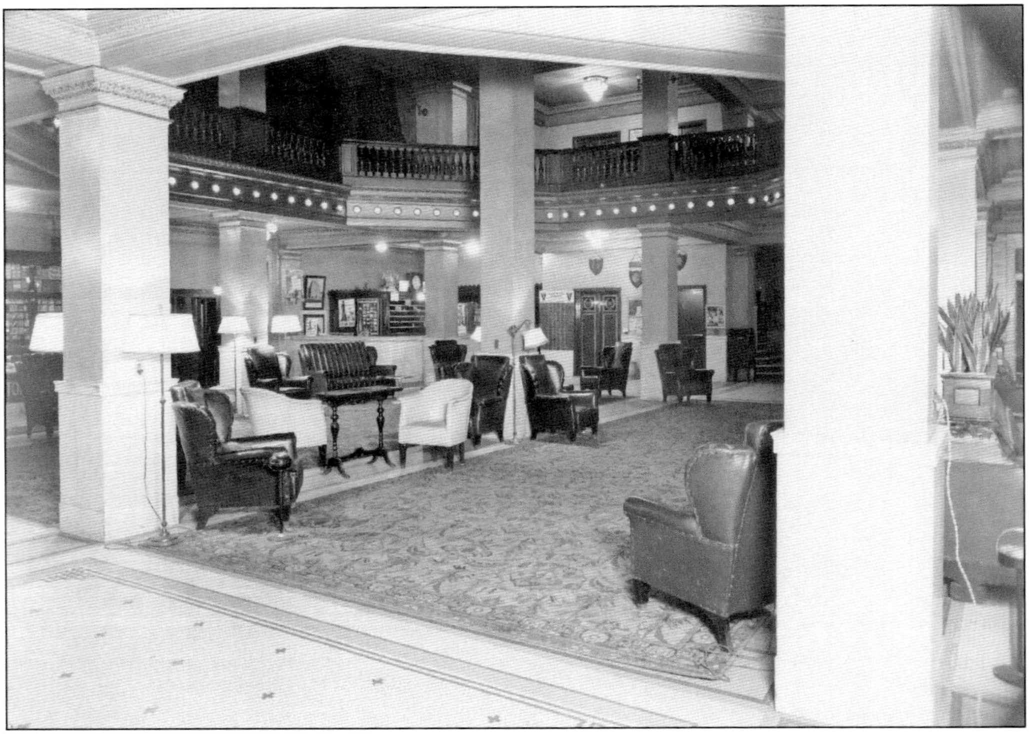

This photograph was taken in 1943, looking through the lobby toward the reception desk and elevators. The decor has changed to reflect the new trends; however, much of the original hotel appointments still stand. On the walls by the elevator doors are plaques denoting the hotel as the meeting place of local service clubs, including Kiwanis and Lions. The Bay City Rotary Club also called the hotel home for many years.

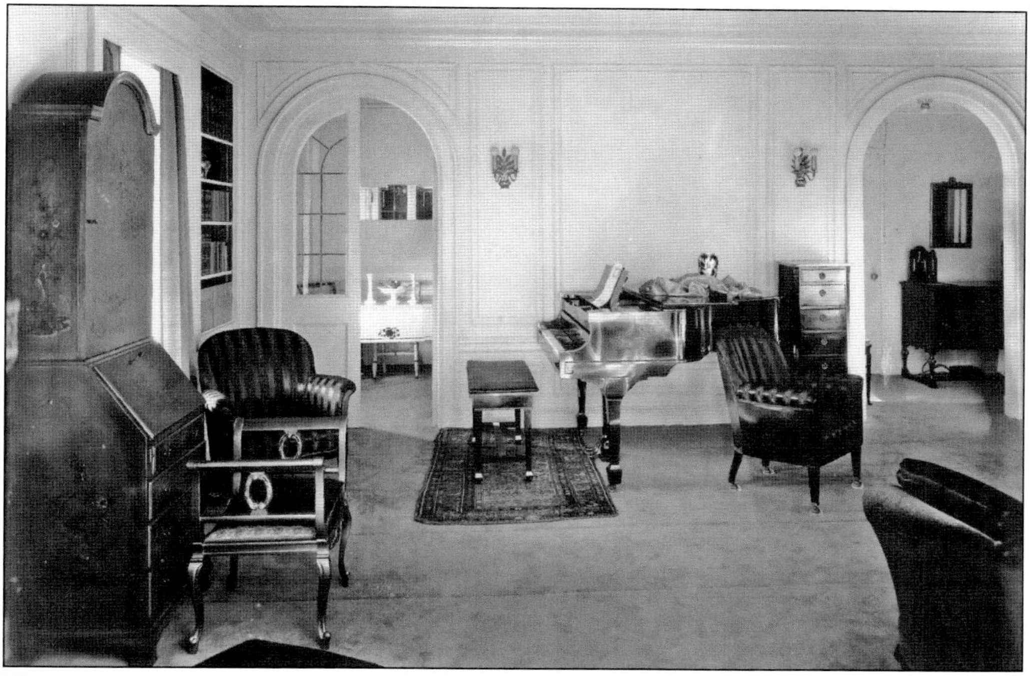

The owner's suite of the hotel was located in the 1925 addition and included appointments like arched doors with leaded-glass windows. These doors still existed (though painted) years later when the hotel was dismantled after the fire. They were salvaged and eventually donated to the Bay County Historical Society, where they reside alongside other pieces of the Wenonah.

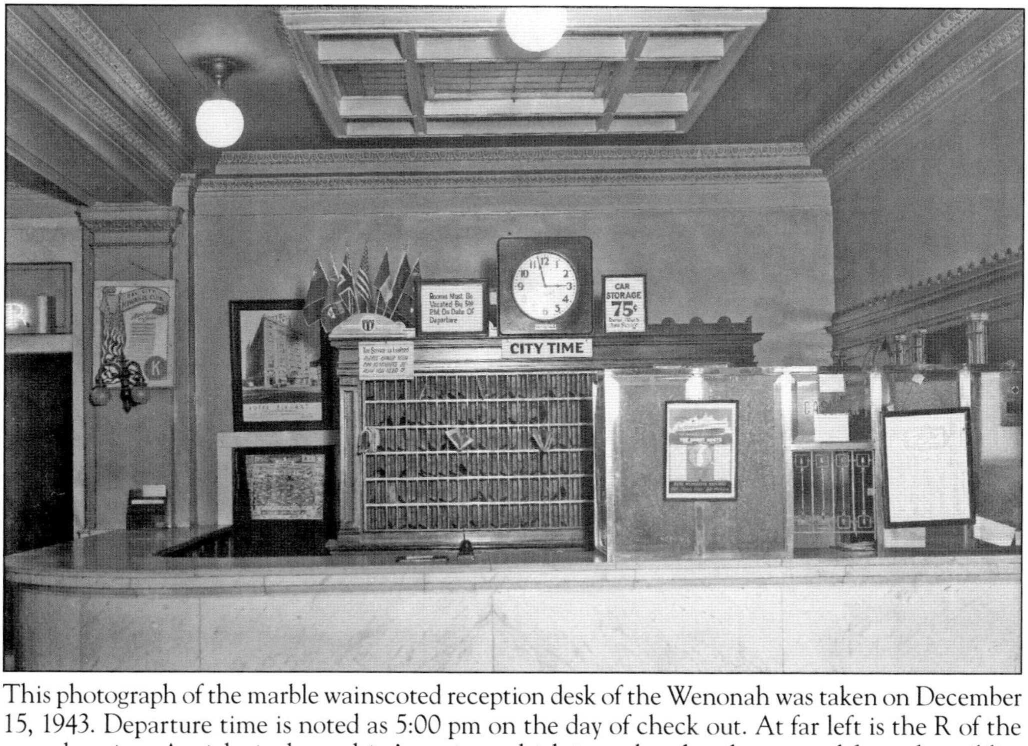

This photograph of the marble wainscoted reception desk of the Wenonah was taken on December 15, 1943. Departure time is noted as 5:00 pm on the day of check out. At far left is the R of the neon bar sign. At right is the cashier's station, which is enclosed and separated from the public.

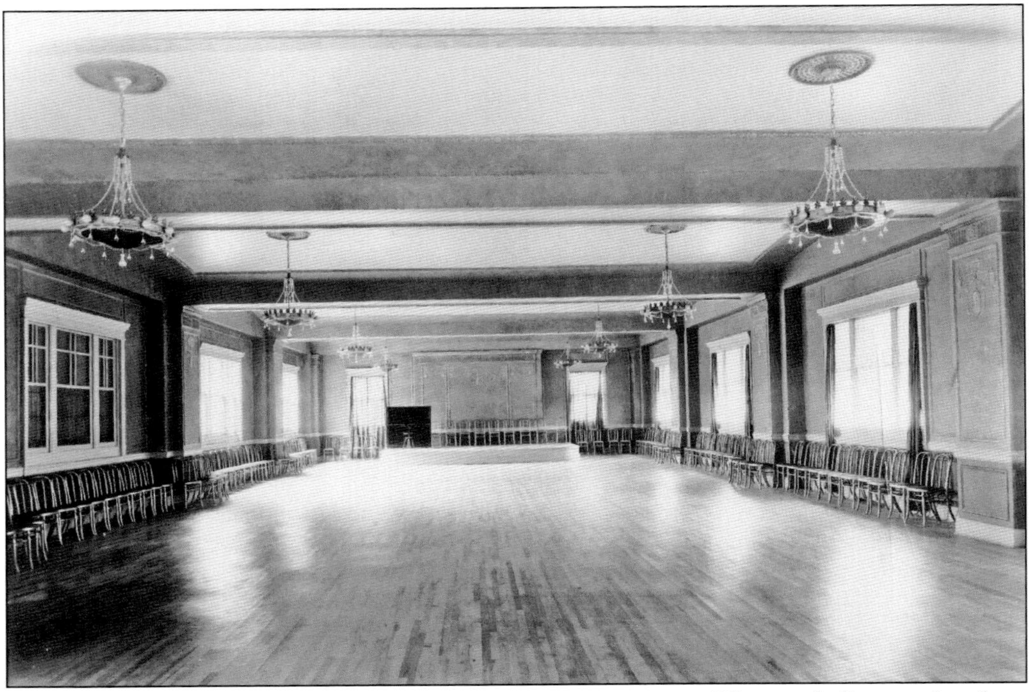

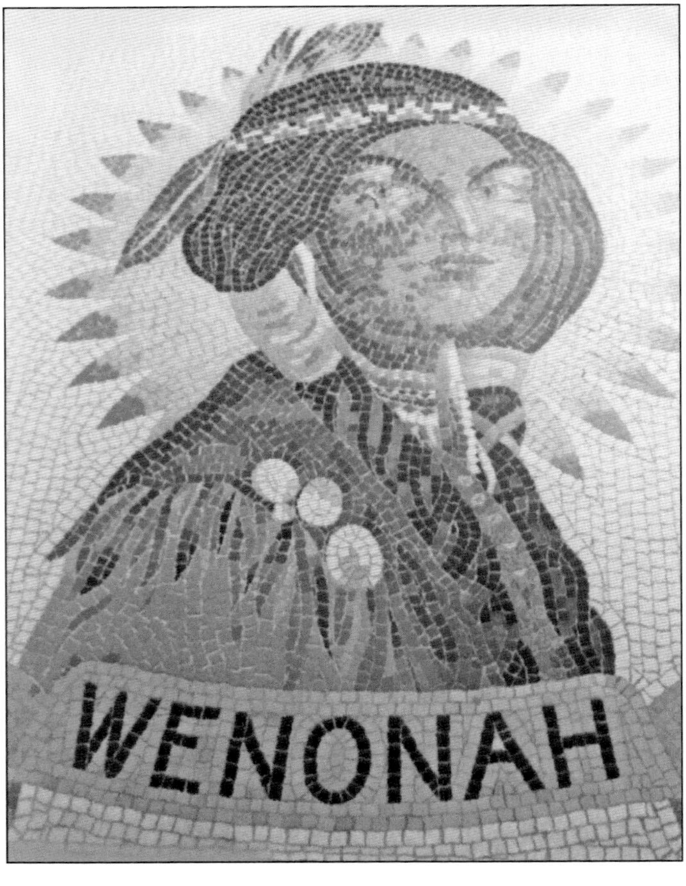

The new ballroom played host to weddings, political events, fundraisers, banquets, and school proms. Among the more notable guests were former presidents Richard Nixon and Dwight D. Eisenhower, and actor Charlton Heston.

The Princess Wenonah tile mosaic once graced the floor of the lobby of the Wenonah. The mosaic was salvaged and ended up for a short time in a cow pasture in Pinconning, Michigan. Wenonah owner John Rapanos reclaimed the mosaic and returned it to Bay City. After some time in city hall, it was placed on exhibit with other pieces of the hotel at the historical museum in 2005.

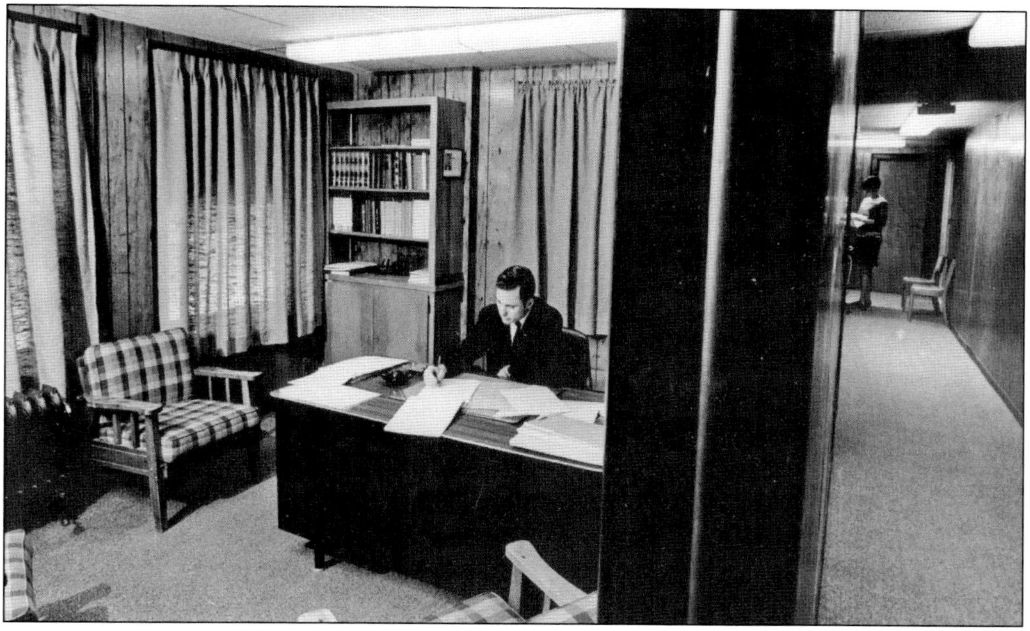

A decade of declining patronage forced the Wenonah's owner into bankruptcy in 1964. But, in 1968, John A. Rapanos of Midland acquired the hotel and extensively remodeled the structure into the Wenonah Park Building, a mixture of retail space and apartments. In 1969, the Wenonah Park Building won the Business of the Year award from Downtown Bay City Inc. for its contribution to the local business economy and job market.

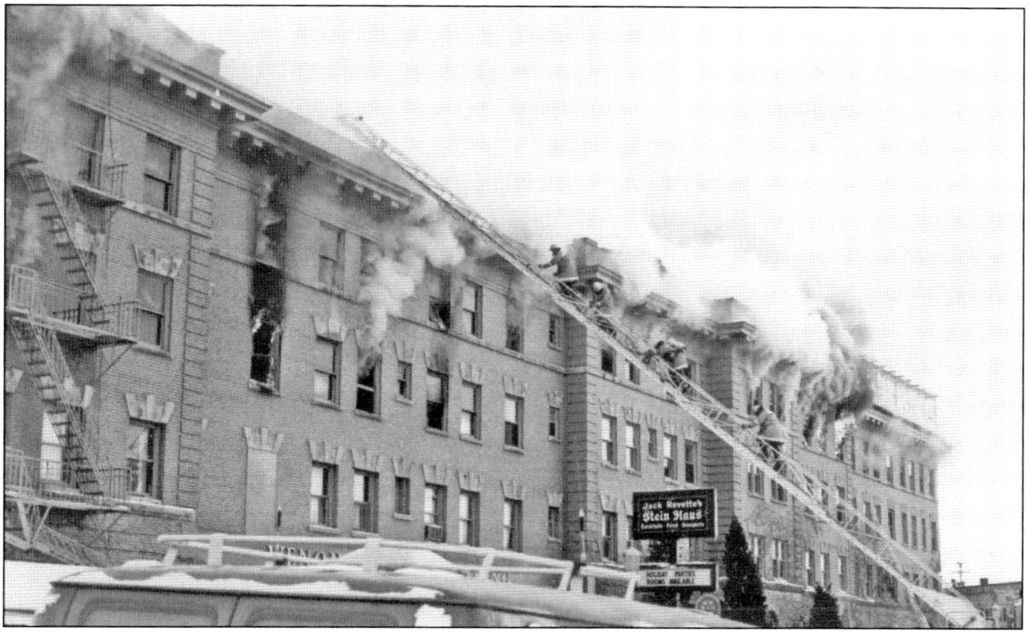

On December 10, 1977, reminiscent of the Fraser House 71 years earlier, fire engulfed the Wenonah Park Building. Fire crews from Bay City, Bangor, Essexville, Midland, and Saginaw battled the stubborn blaze on a day when temperatures hovered around 10 degrees, and ice caused hazardous conditions. The fire was under control by nightfall; however, several hot spots kept firefighters on standby through the night.

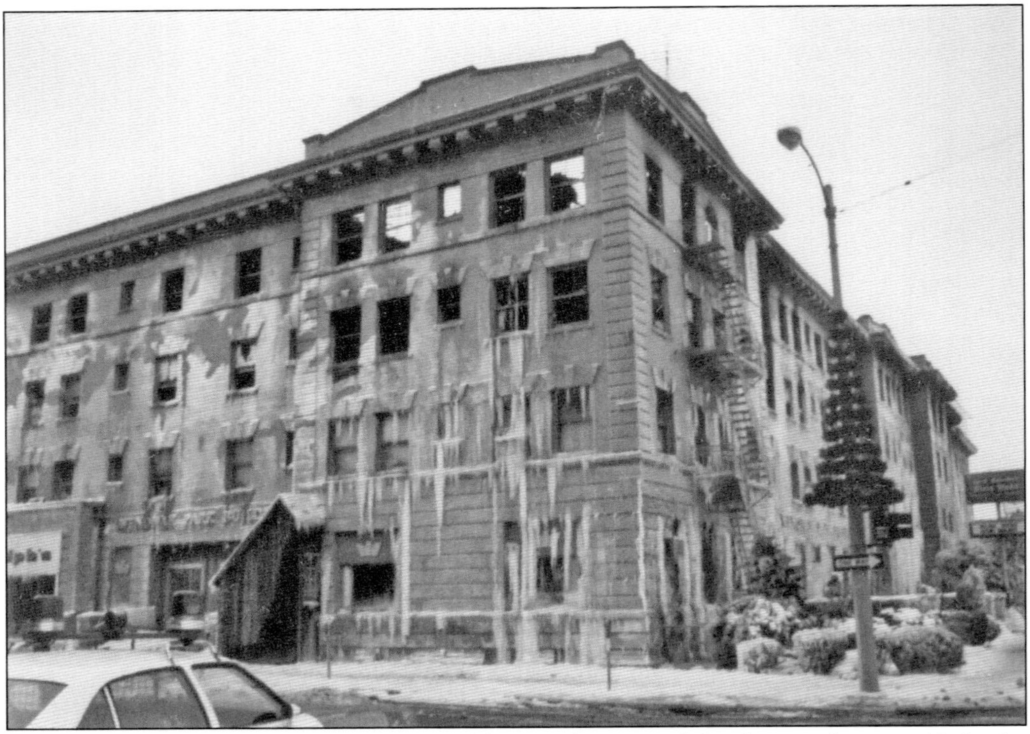

Approximately 160 people were in the building at the time of the fire, resulting in 10 deaths and more than 40 injuries. Many had to leap several stories to nearby roofs to escape the blaze. The fire left the former residents homeless and displaced local businesses from the main floor, including the WGER-FM radio station, which was on the air when the fire started, and Jack Revette's Wenonah Catering and Tavern. It was later determined that the fire was caused by a malfunctioning lighting fixture in the third-floor corridor. The building was demolished, with many pieces finding their way into the hands of local residents who were eager to purchase mementos of the former landmark. The site was used as a parking lot (below) until Delta College purchased the site and built a planetarium, which opened in 1997.

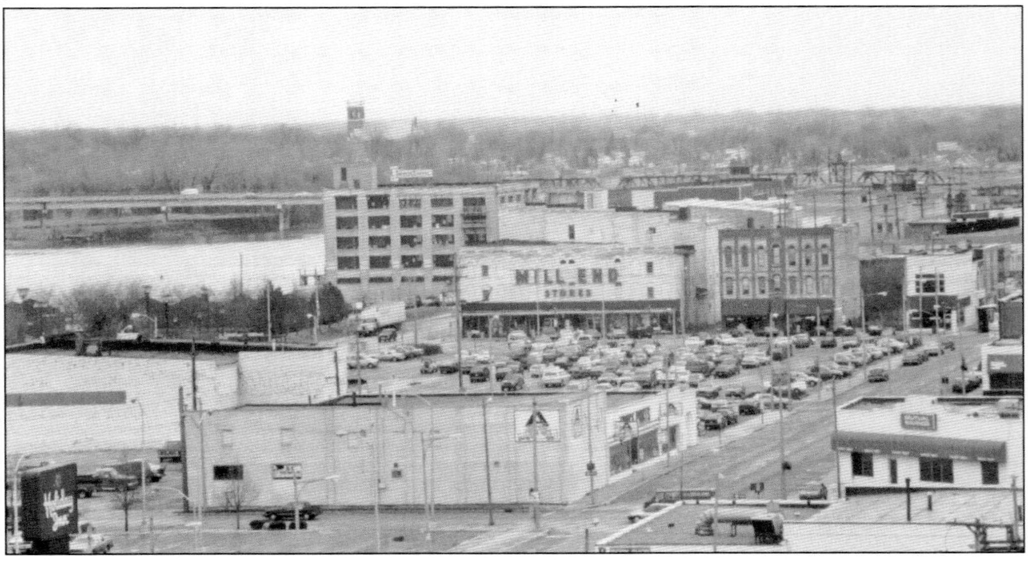

Seven

Residences

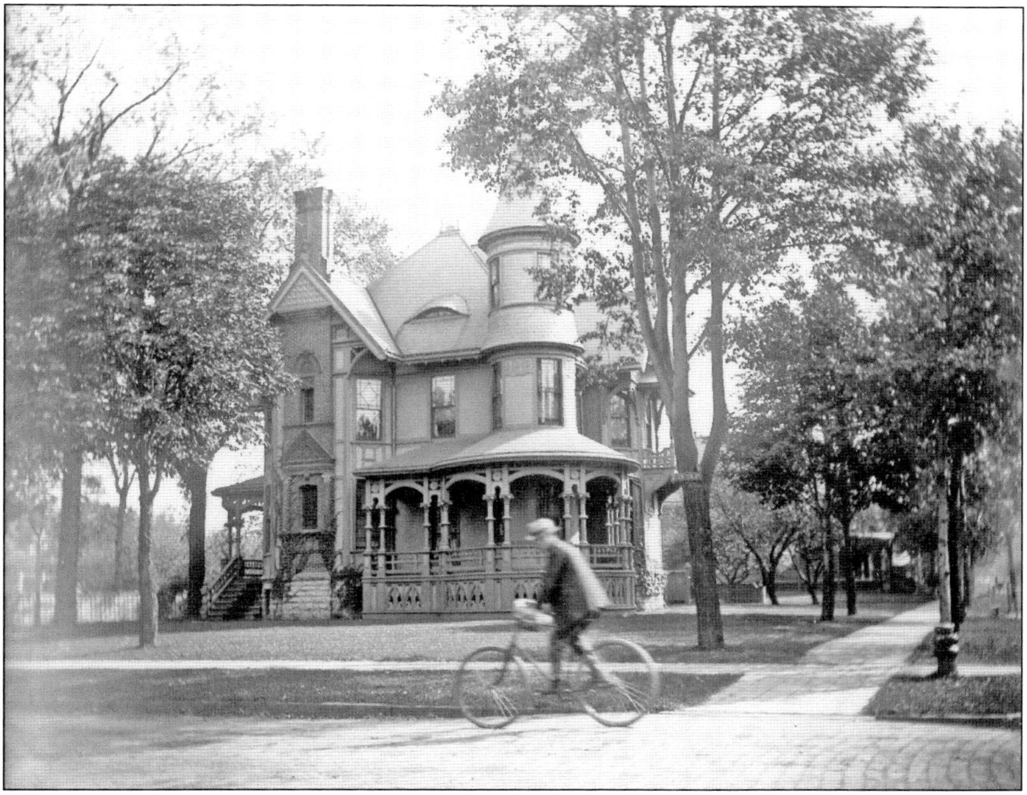

Since the river was considered a workplace during the lumbering era, it was not a good place to build a residence. Those of means purchased a plot of land away from the noise, stench, and pollution of the busy riverfront. Many built residences along Center Avenue and adjoining streets, some of which have been lost to the ravages of time. Pictured is an unidentified Bay City residence photographed by the Boutell family around 1890.

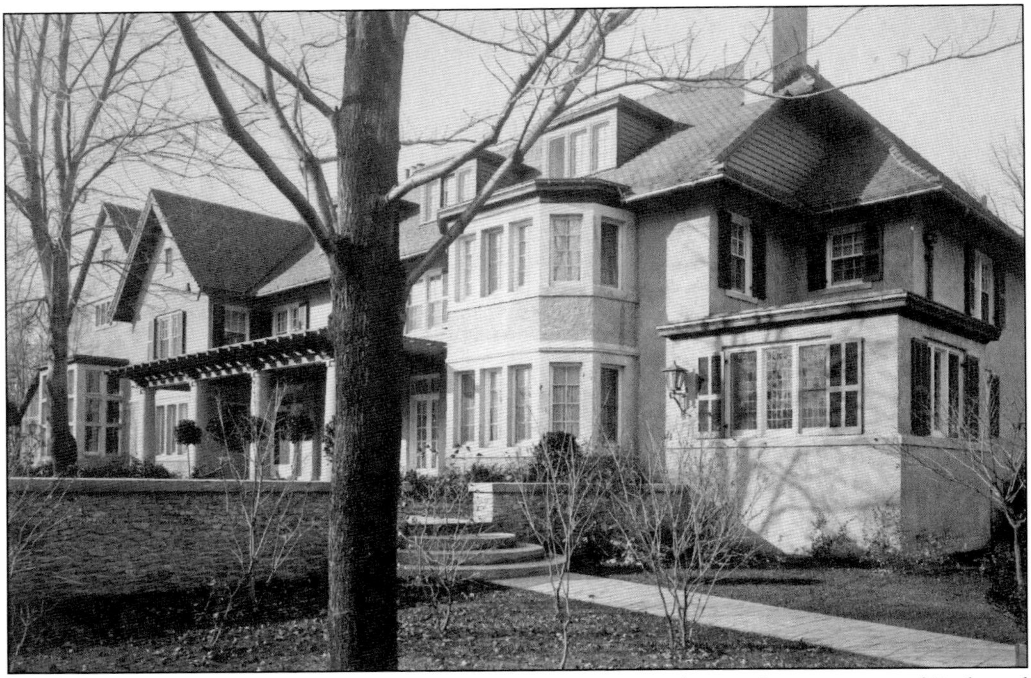

Industrialist William L. Clements built this stately home on the northeast corner of Park and Center Avenues in 1910. Clements joined the staff of his father's company, Industrial Works (IW), as chief mechanical engineer in 1882. He had a background in engineering from the University of Michigan, and would become one of the major figures in shaping the future of IW and Bay City.

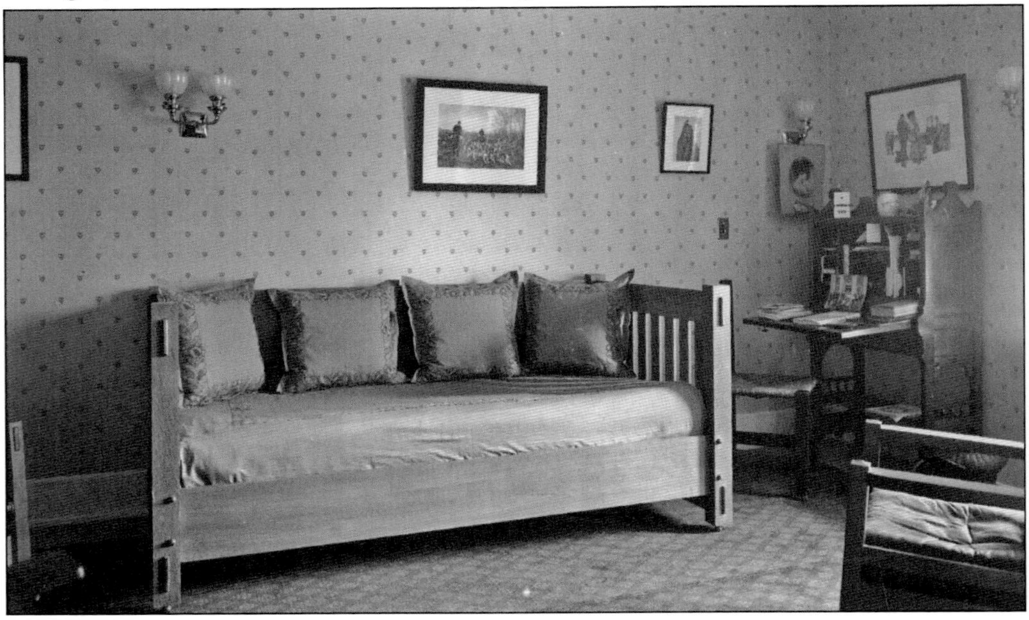

The house was designed with Arts and Crafts features, with an interior that was not ostentatious, unlike the grand Victorian mansions of the previous decades. Clements had previously owned a Pratt and Koeppe shingle-style Victorian at 1712 Center Avenue since 1887, from which he and his first wife, Jessie, moved to this new residence. Pictured here are some of the Mission furnishings that were well at home in the Clements home.

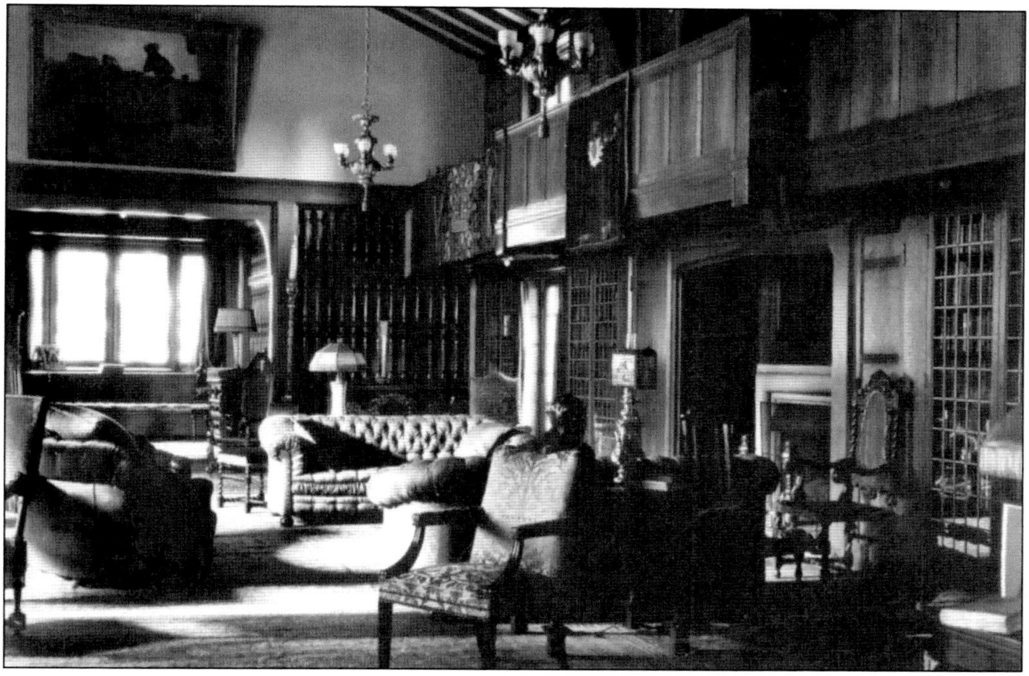

Clements commissioned noted Detroit architect Albert Kahn to build the residence with instructions to design a large library within the 20-room structure. Much of Clements's fortune had been spent amassing a large collection of historical papers, books, and maps, which would eventually become the foundation for the renowned Clements Library on the campus of the University of Michigan. Pictured here is one corner of the massive library.

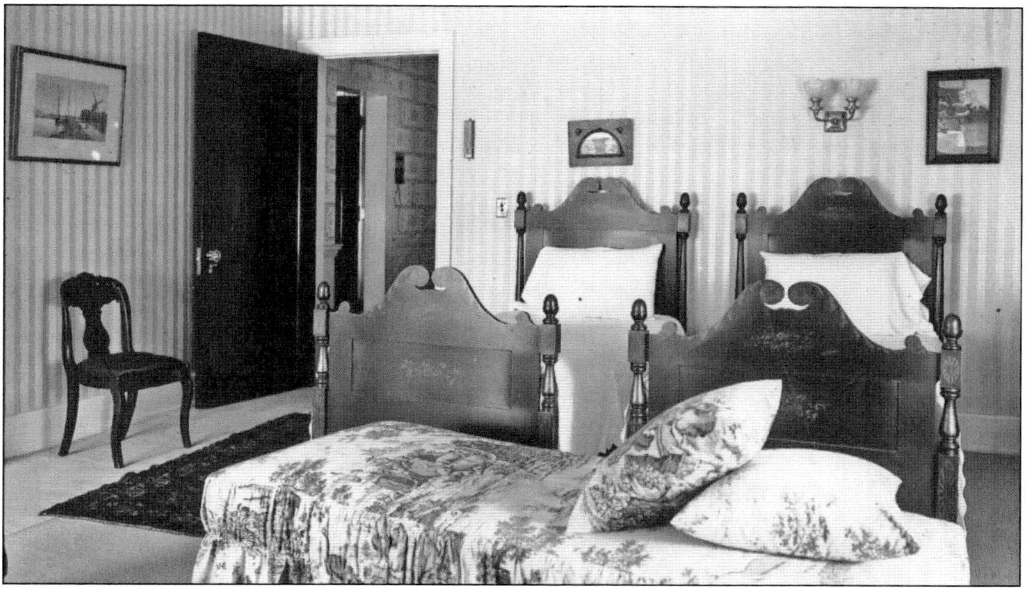

Clements donated the land for the James Clements Airport in honor of his son James Renville, who gave his life serving his country during World War I while in the US Army Signal Corps. W.L. Clements was an active and well-respected member of the Bay City community until his death in 1934. Pictured here is one of the bedrooms, featuring pieces from Clements's large antique collection.

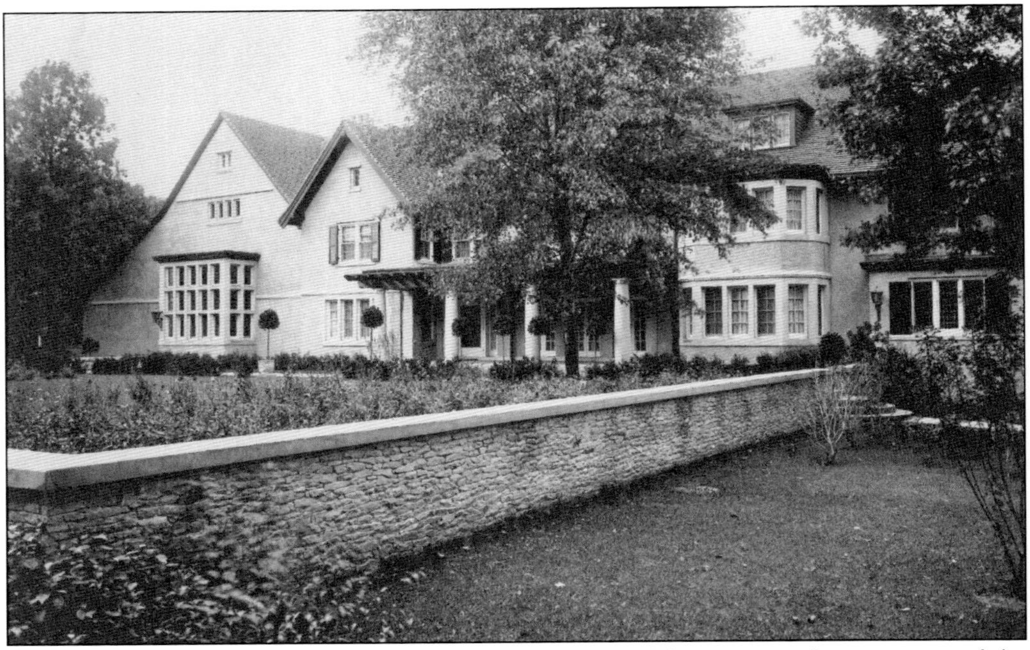

Architectural historian Dale P. Wollicki wrote, "The careful massing and proportions of the front façade provided for a quiet house that stood proudly in the open amid the spacious yard, recalling the great baronial estates of medieval times. The rambling plan with its large rooms provided for a picturesque composition of flowing roofs, prominent chimneys, bay windows and trellises." He goes on to say, "The interior of the house . . . was finished with a simplicity much like the exterior, providing a pleasant background to the Clements' exquisite antique furniture, much of it acquired on trips to Europe." Pictured below is the dining room, featuring some of the Clements family's antique furniture collection.

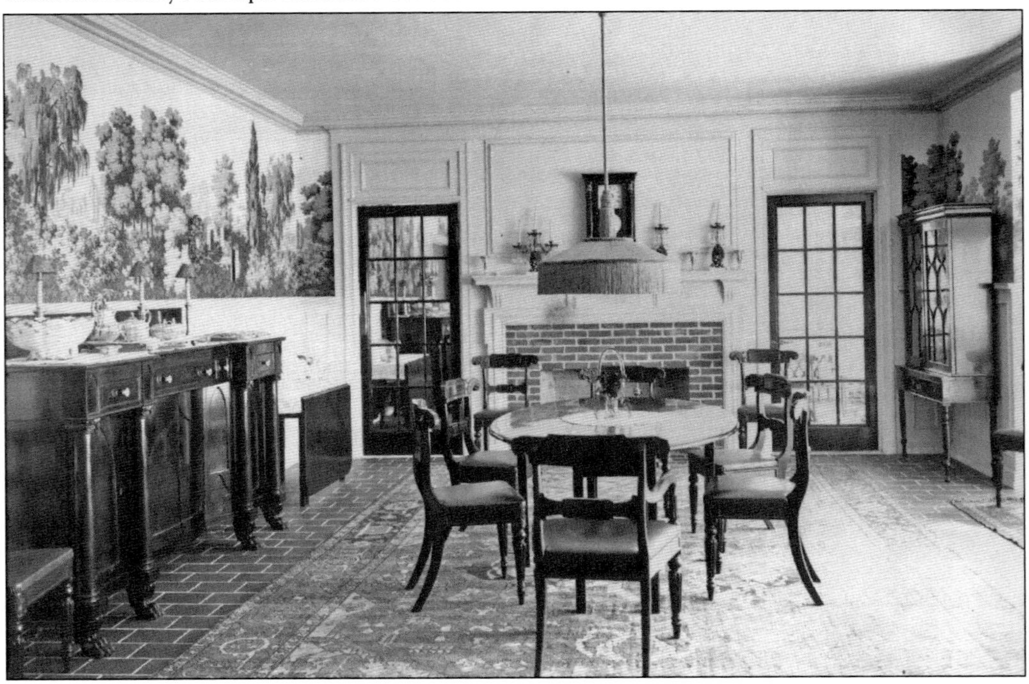

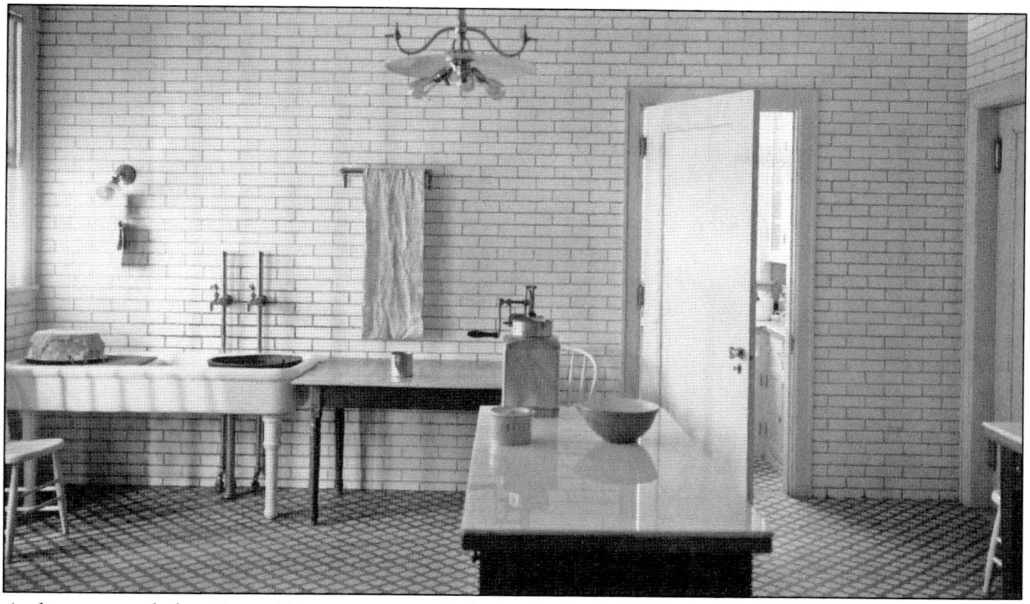

A divorce and the Great Depression severely hampered W.L. Clements' ability to collect more books. The First National Bank, of which Clements was president, failed, and he took personal losses in the process. In fact, he was forced to sell his remaining book collection to the University of Michigan. In November 1934, he died. His widow, Katherine Fisher Clements (he had remarried after his divorce), lived in the house for many years. In January 1952 the house was razed, all except for the original stable, which is located on Parkwood Court. In place of the sprawling estate currently stands a cluster of smaller residences built later. A photograph album is the only other reminder; these images are from that collection.

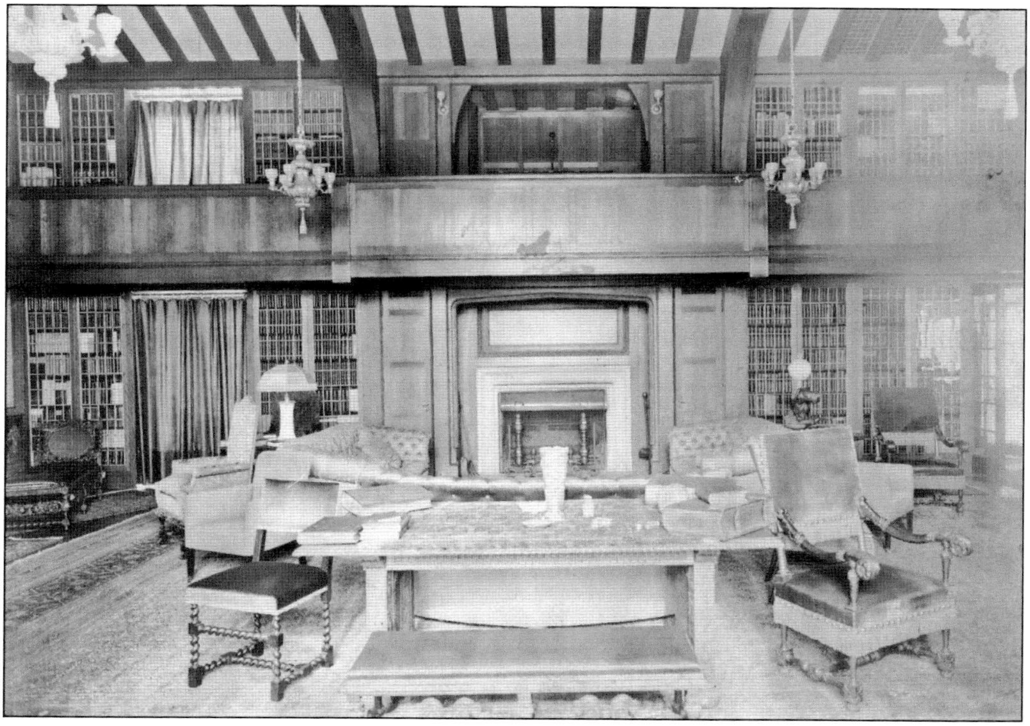

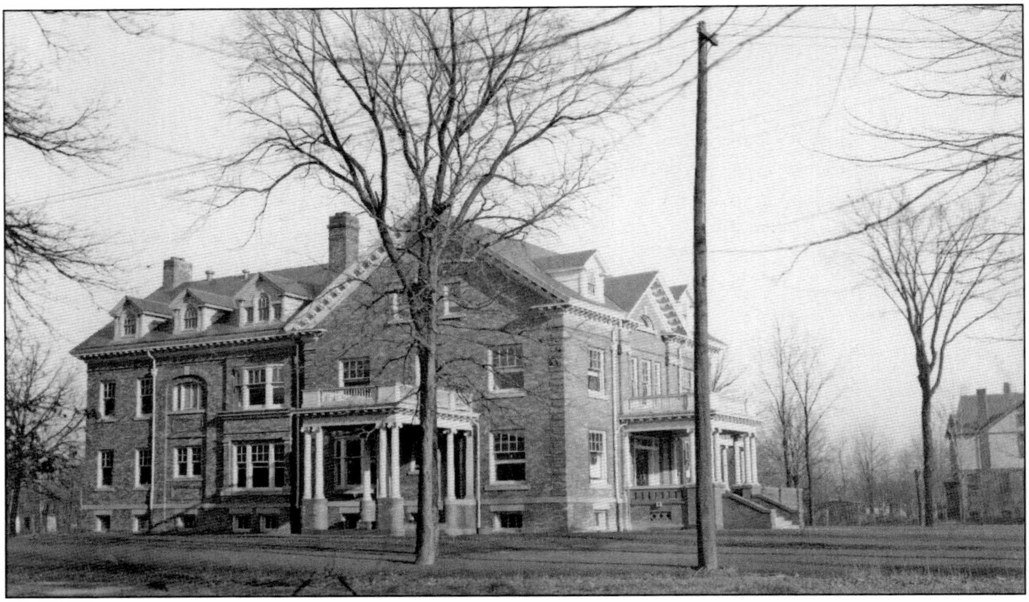

One of W.L. Clements's neighbors along Center Avenue was Charles R. Wells. A coworker of Clements, Wells started with Industrial Works in 1873 as secretary and in 1882 assumed the duties of treasurer upon the passing of his father, Ebenezer Wells. He continued with IW for 51 years, until 1924. In addition to IW, Wells was involved in local enterprises such as the Gas Light Company, the Bay City Street Railway Company, the First National Bank, and the Bay County Savings Bank. He built a spacious home at 2229 Center Avenue in 1905 (pictured here), where he was living when he died in 1928 at age 76. The 15-room mansion (between Park and Carroll Avenues) later passed to his son William and was torn down in 1948. The residences on Wells Court now grace this property.

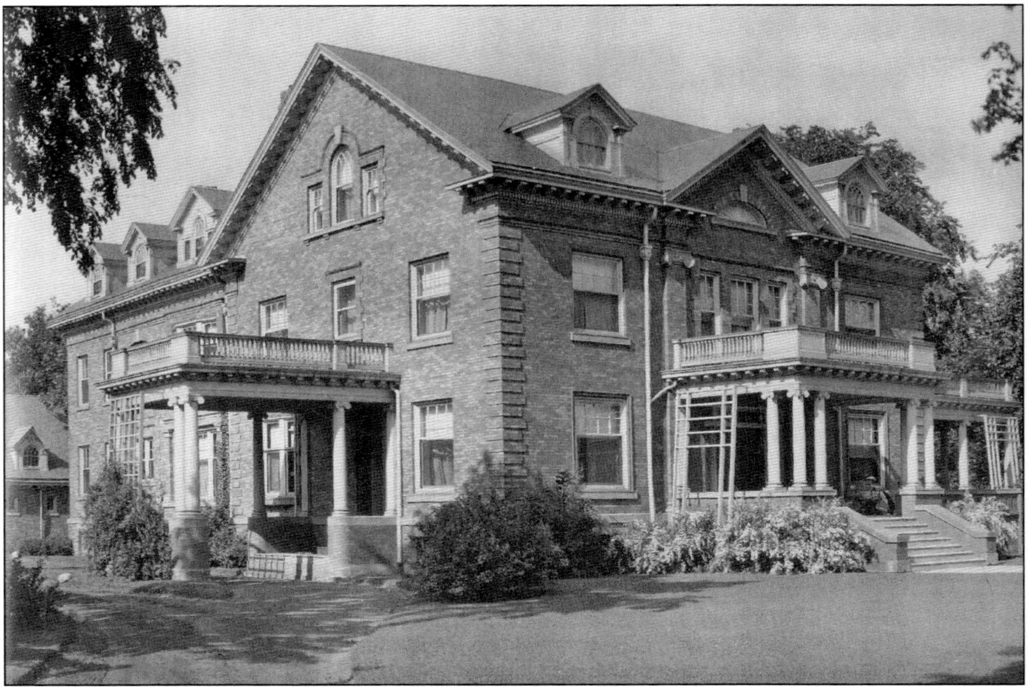

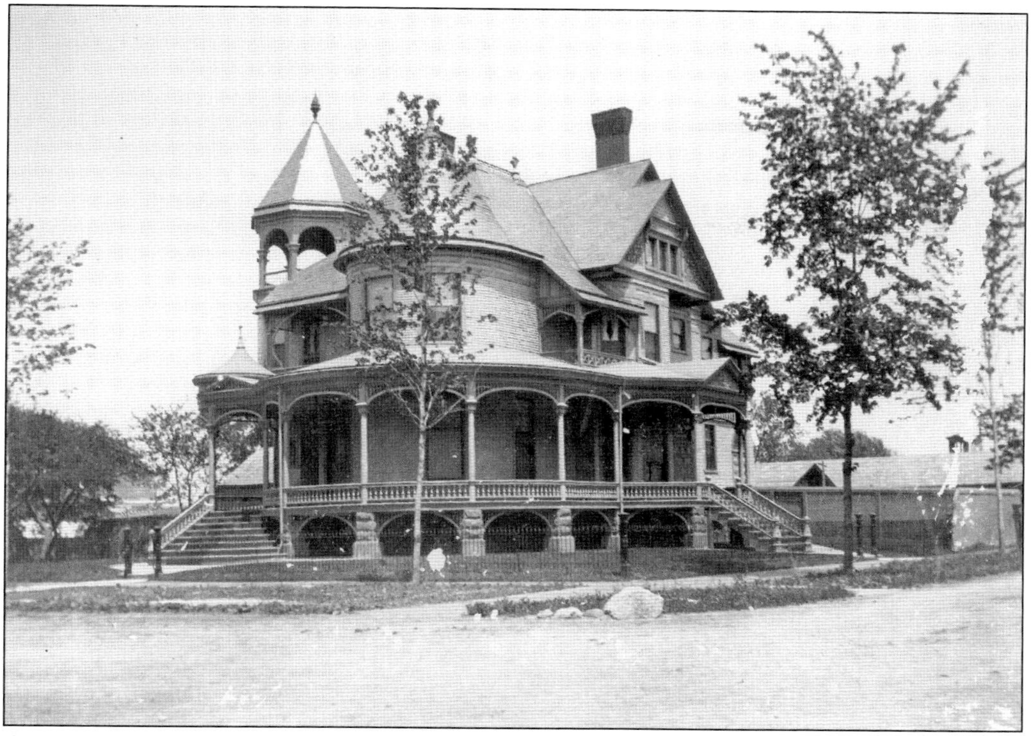

Capt. Benjamin Boutell built this mansion at 901 North Madison Avenue in 1892. Boutell was well known in the log-towing business and had amassed a large fortune with interests in towing and many other businesses, including sugar beets. After the family sold the home in 1928, it was owned by the H.A. Hardy family and later used as a juvenile detention center for 18 years before being razed in 1954.

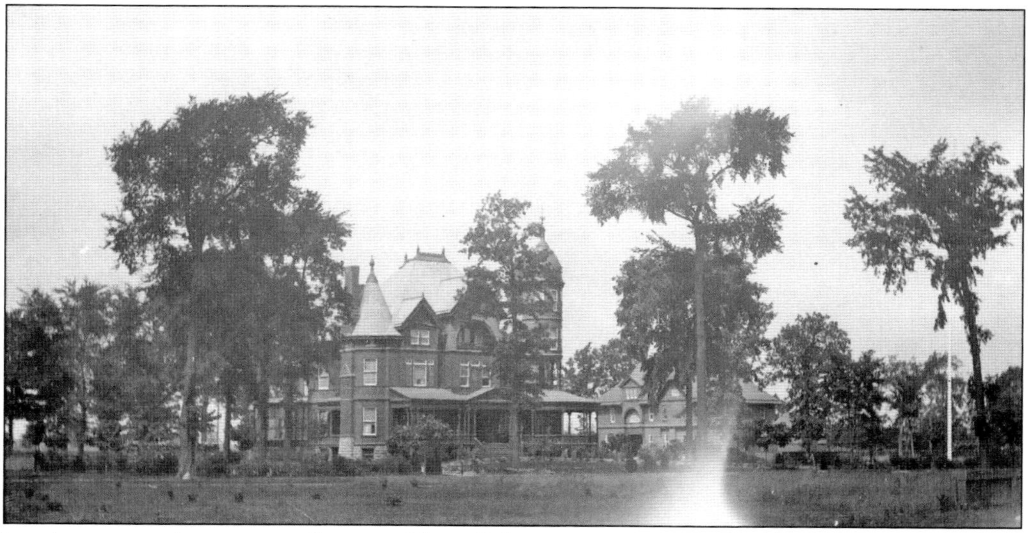

Lumberman and statesman Spencer Oliver Fisher commissioned Elm Place in 1887 from local firm Pratt and Koeppe. It was located at 205 North Mountain Street in West Bay City. The three-story Queen Anne residence with its 40 rooms, circular tower, enclosed observation deck, and 70 windows was considered one of the finest homes north of Detroit. When Fisher died in 1919, his wife sold the house, and it was razed in 1928.

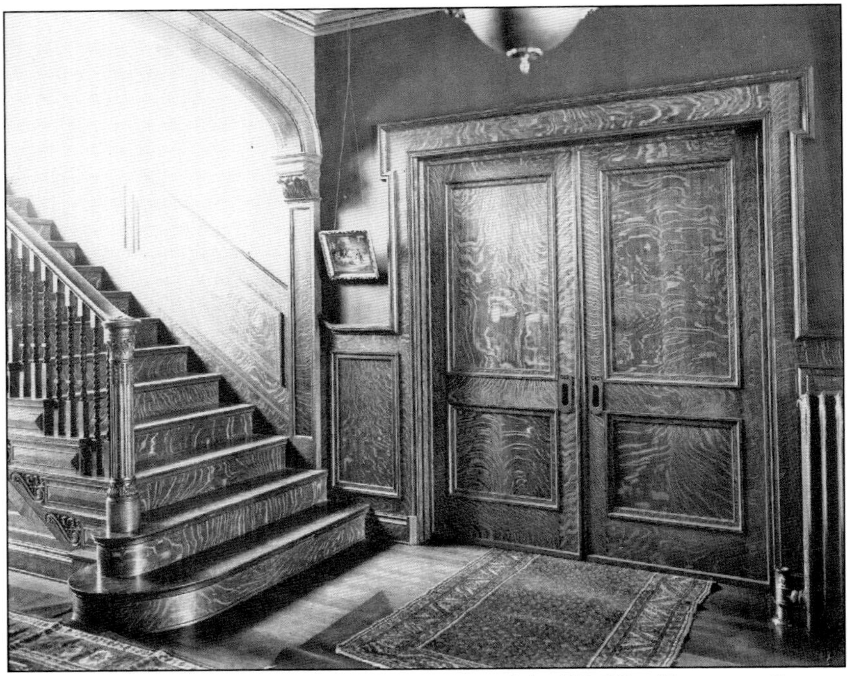

These two photographs are identified as interior views of the F.B. Ward home on Center Avenue. Franklin B. Ward was an owner of the Hanson-Ward Veneer Company in Bay City, and built a Colonial Revival–style home at 1417 Center Avenue (Center and Birney) around 1903. He was last listed in the home in 1931, with it being listed as vacant in 1935. It was likely torn down between 1935 and 1937; the land sat vacant until 1953, when a doctor's office was built on the site. All historians have is the donor's notations on the paperwork and the notes on the back of the photographs to go by, as well as some help from the city directories.

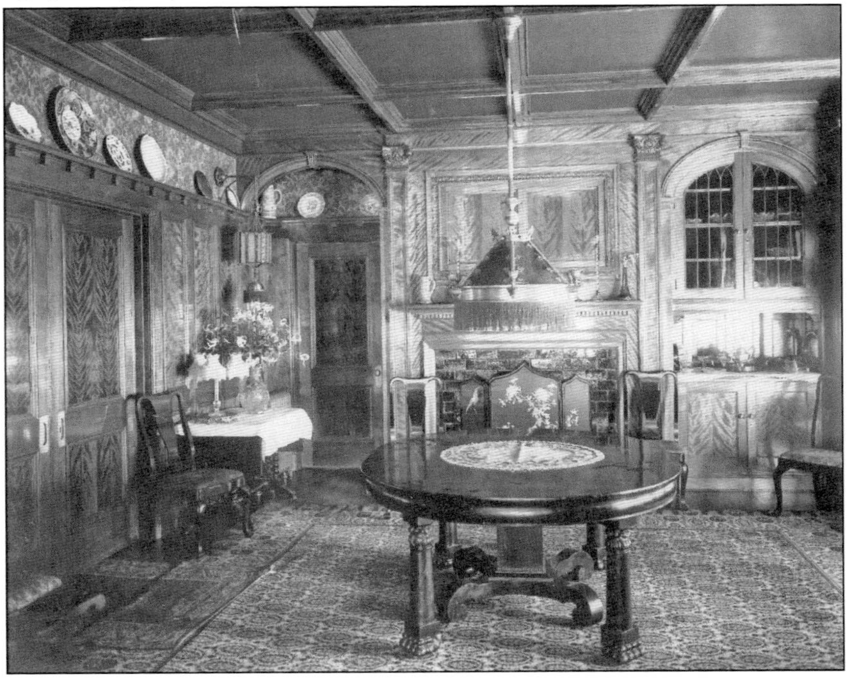

Eight

Entertainment, Recreation, and Fun

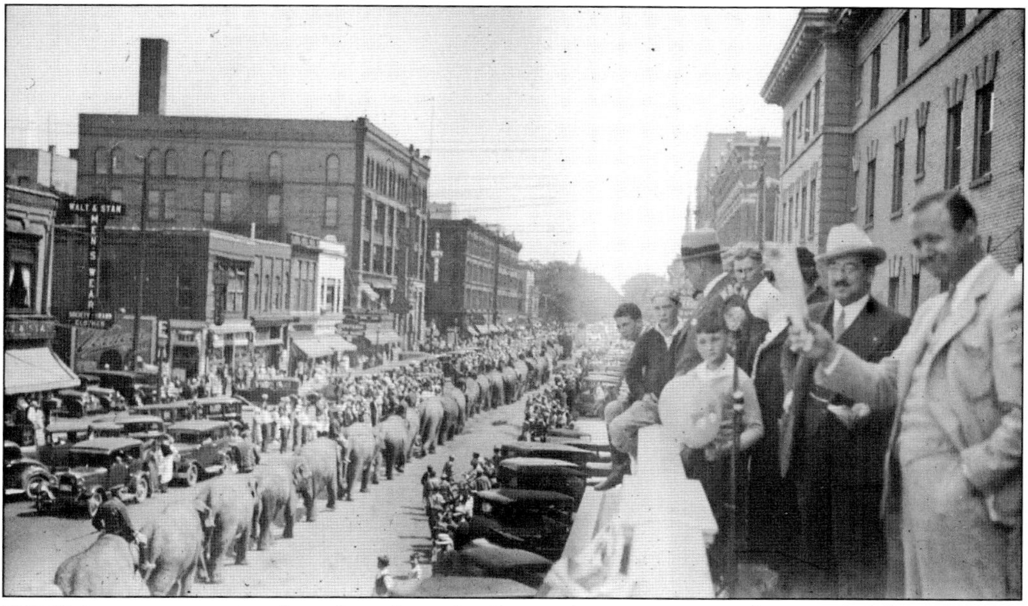

WBCM announcers often broadcast from the Center Avenue porte-cochere roof of the Wenonah Hotel during parades down Center Avenue. This parade was most likely in celebration of one of the traveling circuses that frequently came to town and was captured on film by Stanley Northcott Jr. around 1932. The photograph was taken looking east down Center Avenue.

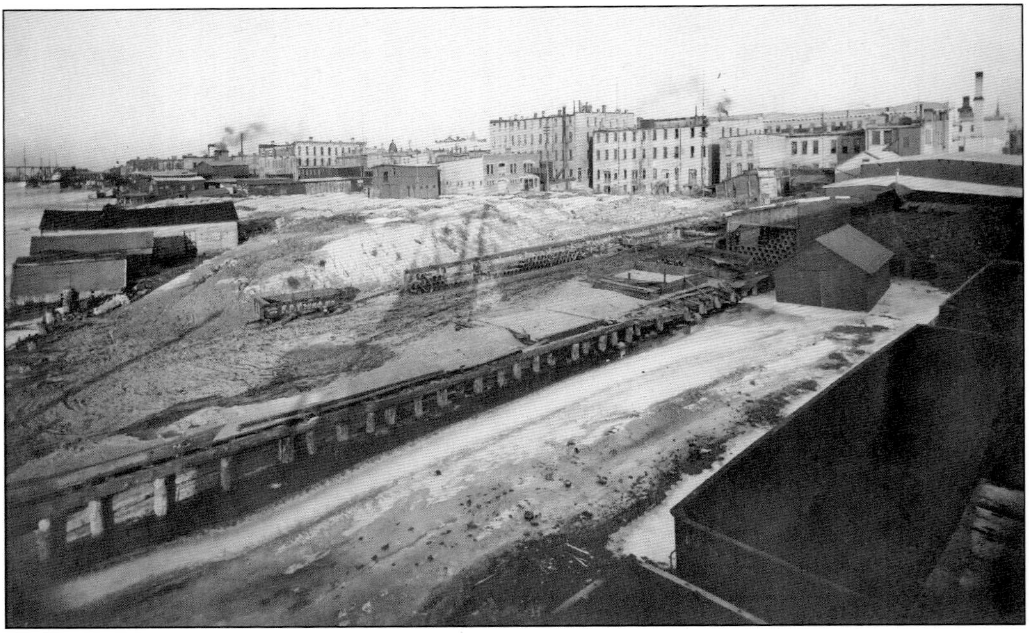

When the Wenonah Hotel was built, commercial buildings lined the west side of Water Street and blocked the view of the Saginaw River from the hotel. This was a good thing at the time since the riverfront was still an active area of lumber mills, docks, and commerce. The top of the hotel can be seen over the buildings in the above image, taken around 1907. In 1909, a fire destroyed the Watson Block at the foot of Center Avenue, and the remaining structures along that block of Water Street were razed for the creation of Wenonah Park. This provided the Wenonah with a commanding view of the riverfront. Below is an image of the newly landscaped Wenonah Park looking southeast, taken on April 25, 1911. Bay City Hall's clock tower can be seen in the distance.

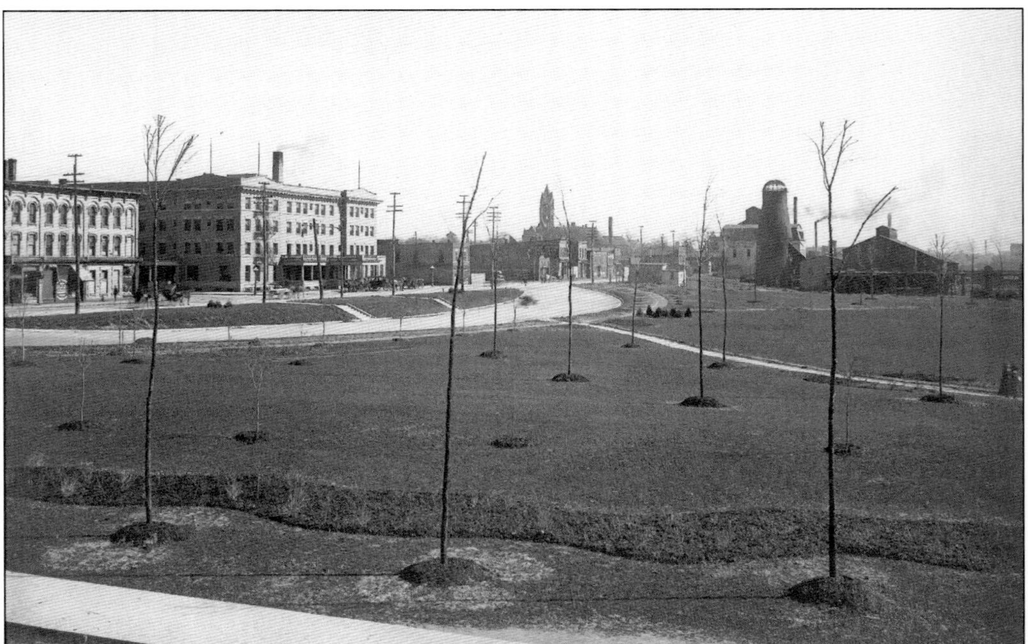

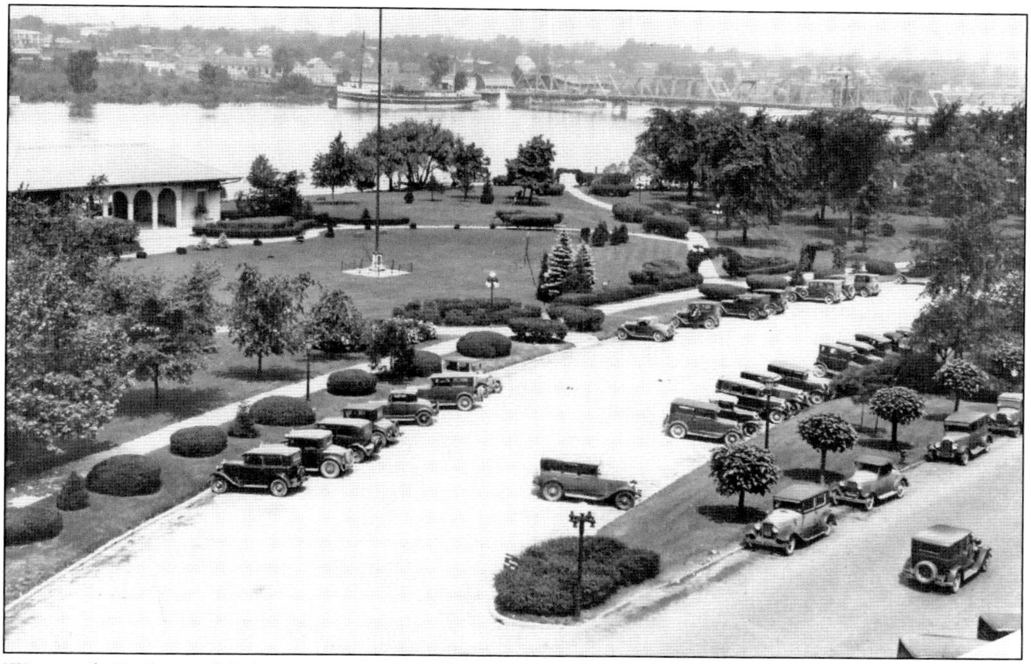

Wenonah Park quickly became a premier location for recreation and relaxation along Bay City's riverfront. Both of these photographs were taken within a decade after the park was built. The structure at left above is the Eddy Pavilion, which was a photogenic feature of the park for many years after it was built in 1915. It was eventually torn down in 1960 to make way for new park developments. In the 1940s and 1950s, parking was increased around the park, limiting the green space available. In 1976, the park was torn up for a sewage-retention basin. A renovated park was reopened in 1981, with a new band shell, followed by the *Ring of Friendship* sculpture and fountain. Much-needed improvements in recent years have vastly improved the park grounds.

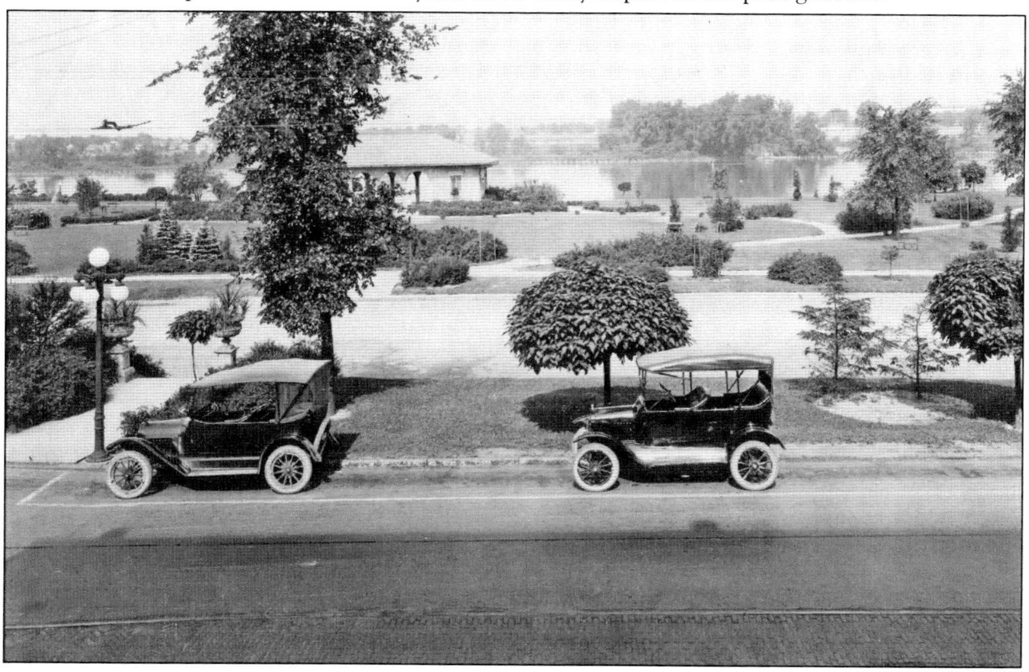

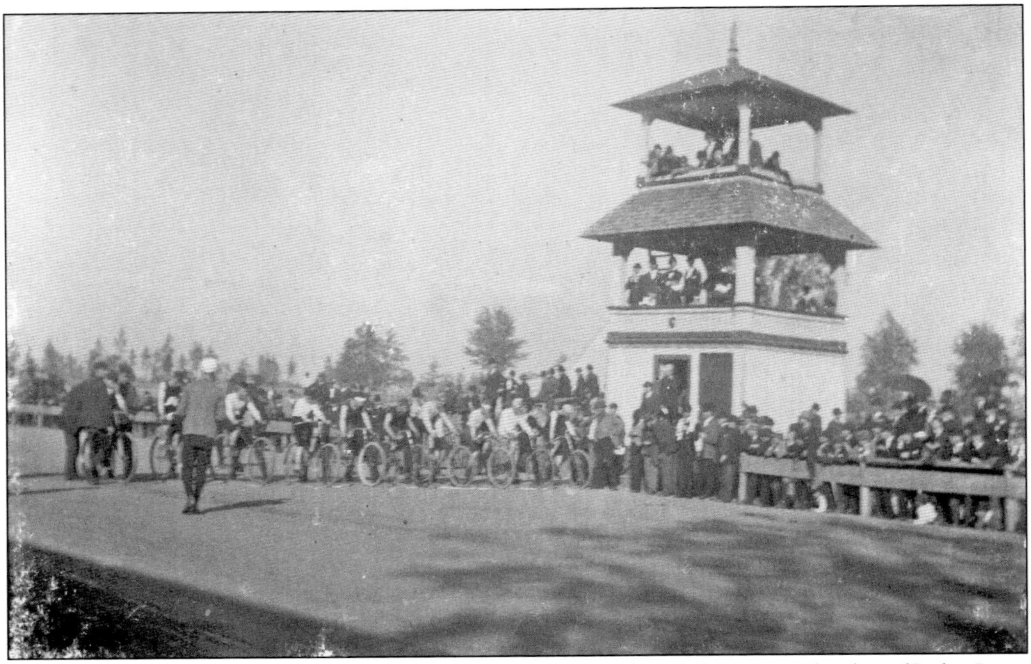

In 1905, Augustus Gansser wrote, "The Bay County Agricultural Society in the day of Judge Isaac Marston was a leader in Michigan. In late years it has acquired a most desirable Fair Grounds and a half-mile race track par excellence, on the eastern limits of Bay City, just north of the eastern limits of Center Avenue, and within easy reach of our oldest and most advanced townships." That racetrack was made of wood and featured a two-story observation and timing tower seen above. Bicycle races were spectacles of the day, and Bay City had one of the premier bicycle manufacturers in National Bicycle Company. Doubtless many of the riders pictured were using Nationals.

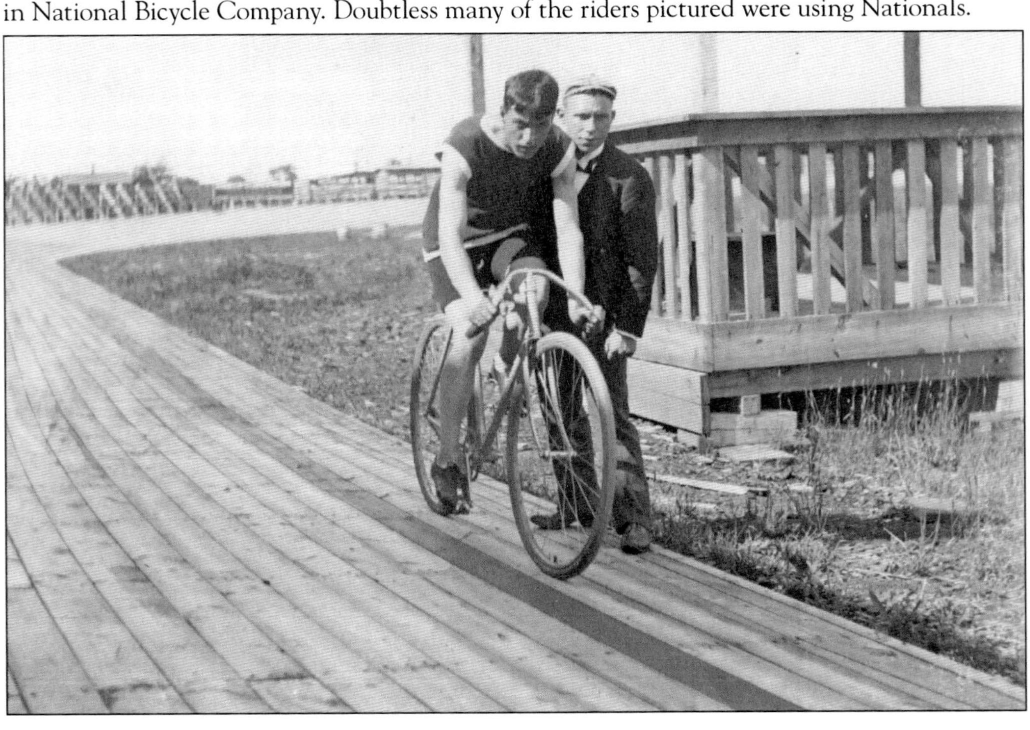

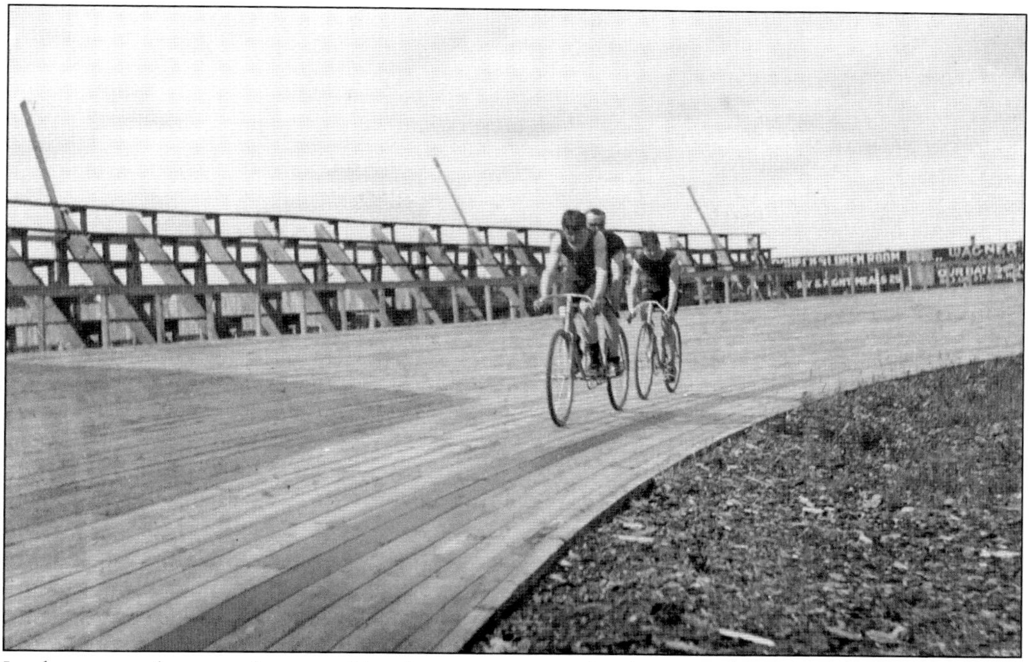

In these two photographs, more bicycles are racing at the fairgrounds track. Advertising on the fences of the track promote local businesses such as Rouech's Lunch Room. The Bay County Agricultural Society fairgrounds were located in the same general location as the present-day Bay County Fairgrounds, to the north of Center Avenue near the Essexville–Bay City line. In 1915, Bay County came to own the 45-acre fairground complex after the agricultural society went bankrupt. It sold the fairgrounds to the county for $1 in exchange for the elimination of a $106,000 debt owed by the society and the Northeastern Michigan Fair Association. The county has owned the fairgrounds ever since, though the wooden track has long since gone away.

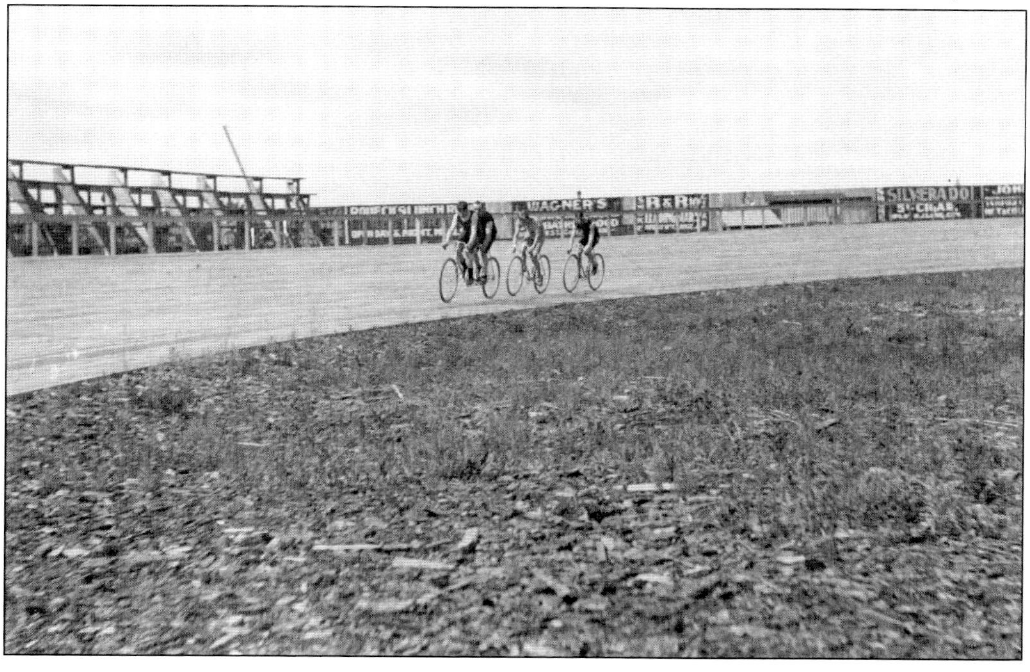

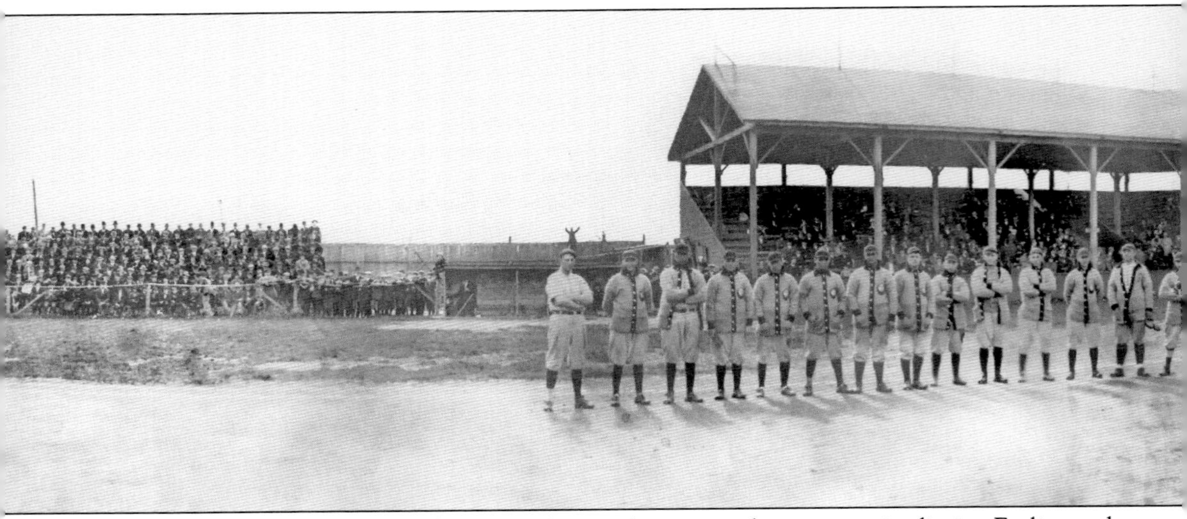

Bay City's official baseball park was on Center Avenue at the eastern city limits. Earlier parks were not officially named; however, in 1909, Clarkson Park was posthumously dedicated to John G. Clarkson, a former National League pitcher who played most notably with the Chicago White Stockings (1884–1887) and the Boston Beaneaters (1882–1894). Clarkson retired to a life of cigar manufacturing in Bay City after his National League days, but he still stayed active in promoting

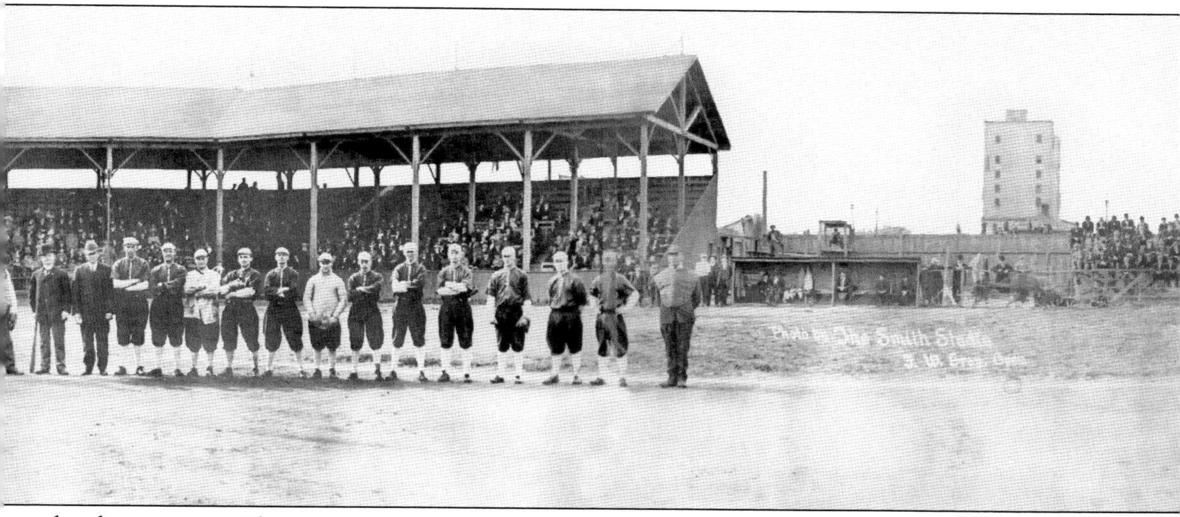

his former sport. This rare panoramic photograph of the interior of the park was taken around 1914 when the Bay City team (right) met with local rival Saginaw (left) at the park. Note the tall building of the chicory plant in the background. The park was later torn down in favor of future commercial developments that included a grocery store.

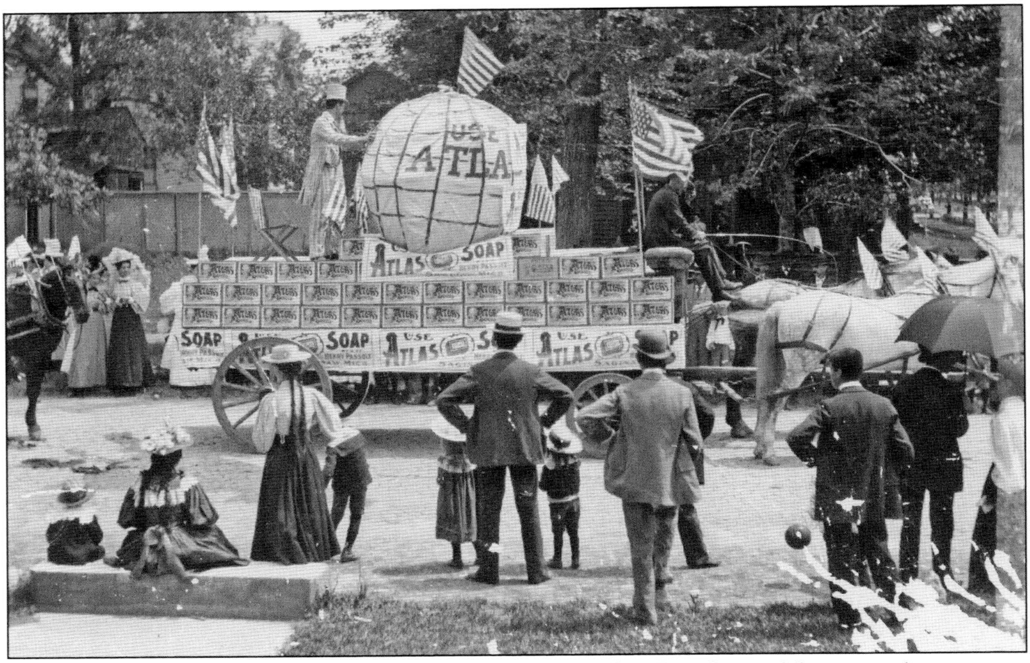

The Fourth of July has always been a patriotic time. Today, Bay City celebrates with a massive fireworks celebration, which draws people from all over the Midwest and beyond. For a while there was an organized Fourth of July parade; however, today the St. Patrick's Day parade is the only yearly organized parade on that scale. Some of the local festivals, including the Corn Fest in Auburn, still have parades, though they do not celebrate a particular holiday. In the 19th and early 20th centuries, parades were conducted fairly often. Some of the best photographs show patriotic colors on display, denoting a Fourth of July spectacle. These two photographs, from the collection of Captain Boutell, capture an 1880s Independence Day parade in Bay City.

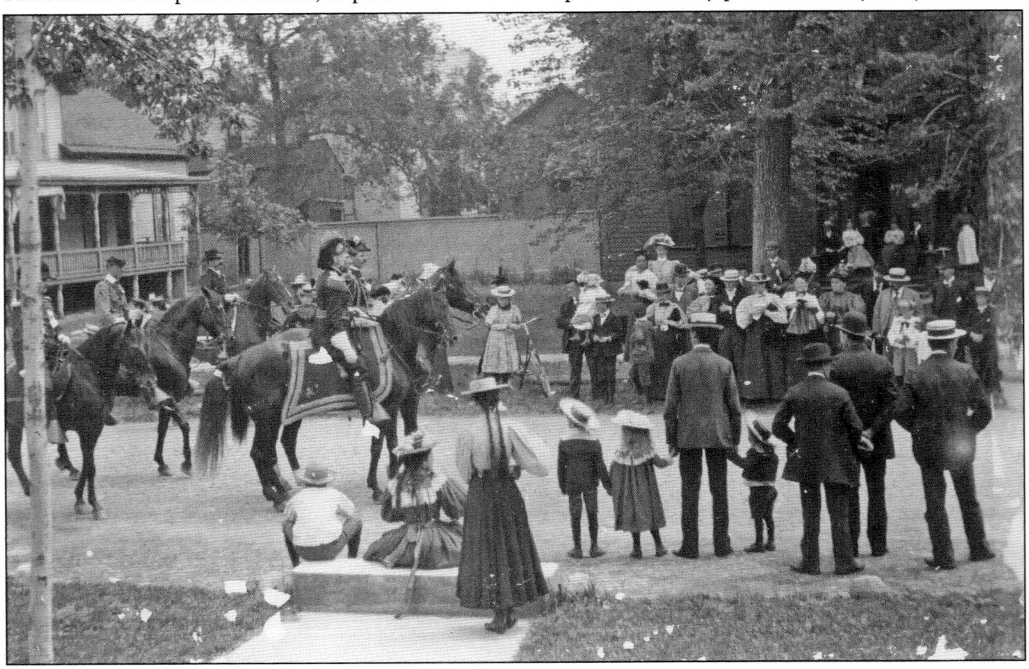

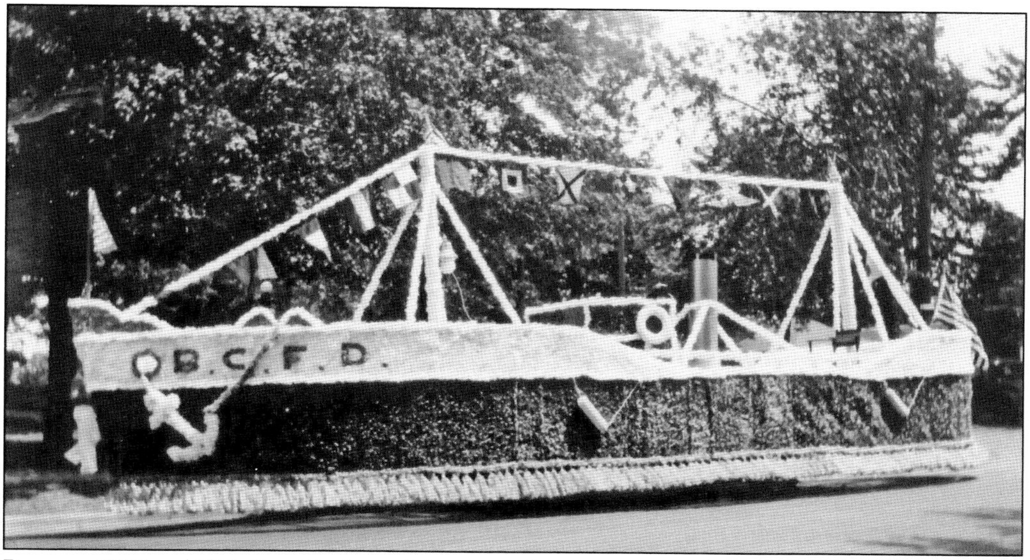

Between 1929 and 1931, Bay City hosted three grand summer spectacles called the Eastern Michigan Water Carnival. These carnivals featured a regatta, pageant, parade, sailboat and motorboat races, diving exhibitions, and many other sanctioned events related to the celebration of water. For the 1930 event, the group built a swimming pool on the riverbank at the southern end of Wenonah Park for swimming and diving competitions. Pictured is the Bay City Fire Department float featured in one of the parades.

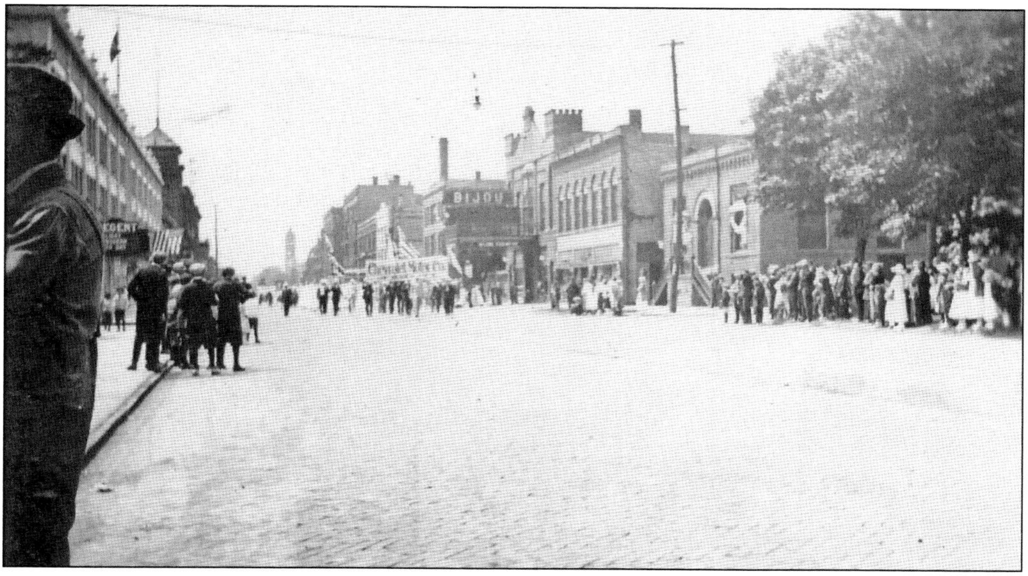

Two of Bay City's theaters, the Bijou and Regent, are visible in this parade photograph from the early 1920s. A Bay City Chevrolet banner is the parade attraction in the middle of Washington Avenue, looking south. City hall is clearly visible in the background. Several American flags are flying, so this is very likely a Memorial Day or Fourth of July parade.

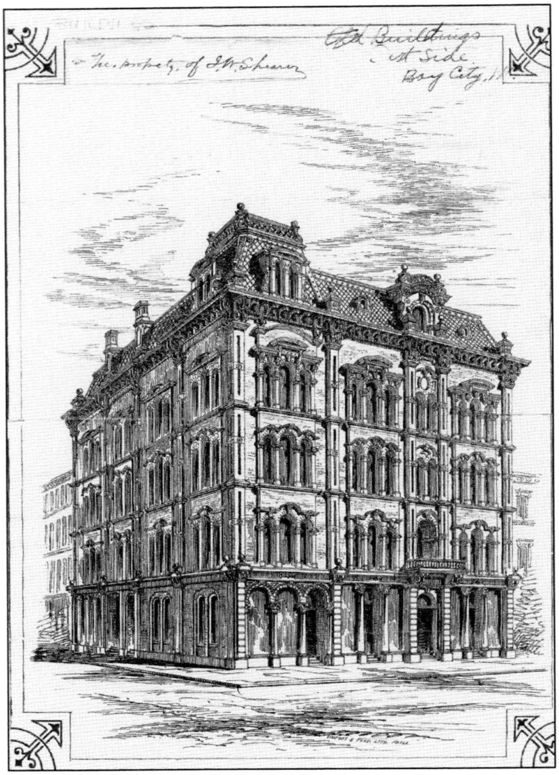

Westover's Opera House (known at the time as the Bay City Opera House) was built in 1871 on the southwest corner of Washington and Center Avenues. Designed by architects Porter and Watkins, the elaborate five-story building featured seating for 900 on the main floor and 600 in the gallery. The domed ceiling was finished with frescos of popular stage productions. Stage plays were the mainstay; however, the opera house was also host to many temperance lectures during the 1870s. The image at left is a rendering of the Westover Opera House as it looked when built. Below, the Peninsular Guard has assembled at the corner of Washington and Center Avenues for a photograph. The corner of the Westover can be seen at right, as well as the Bank and Cranage Blocks across Washington Avenue to the east.

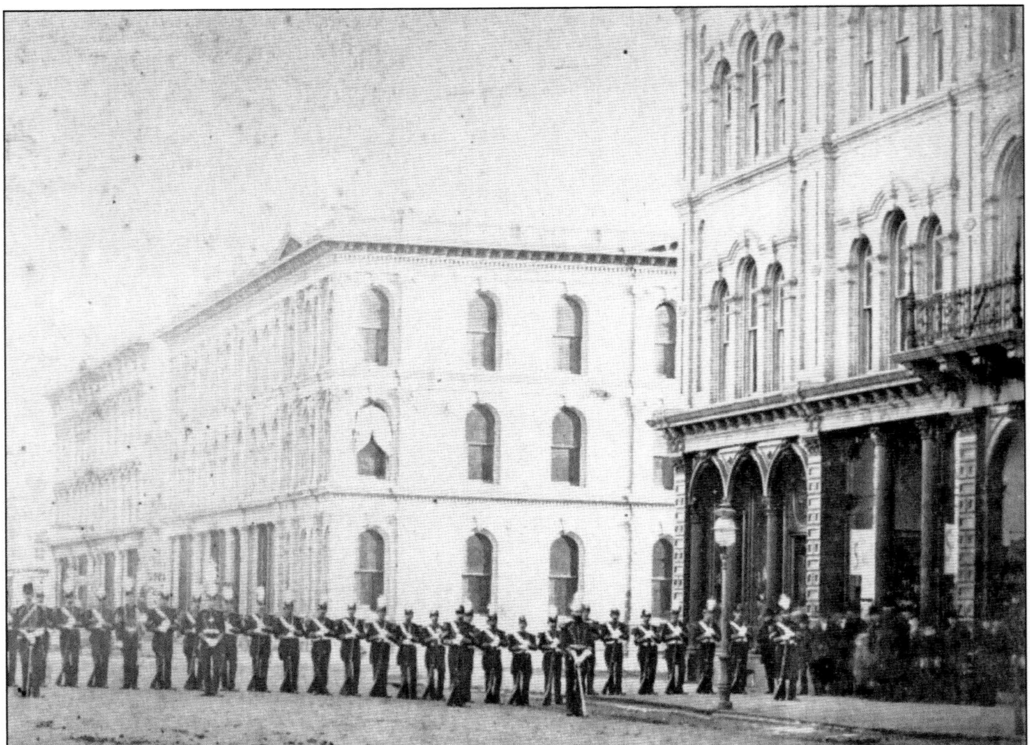

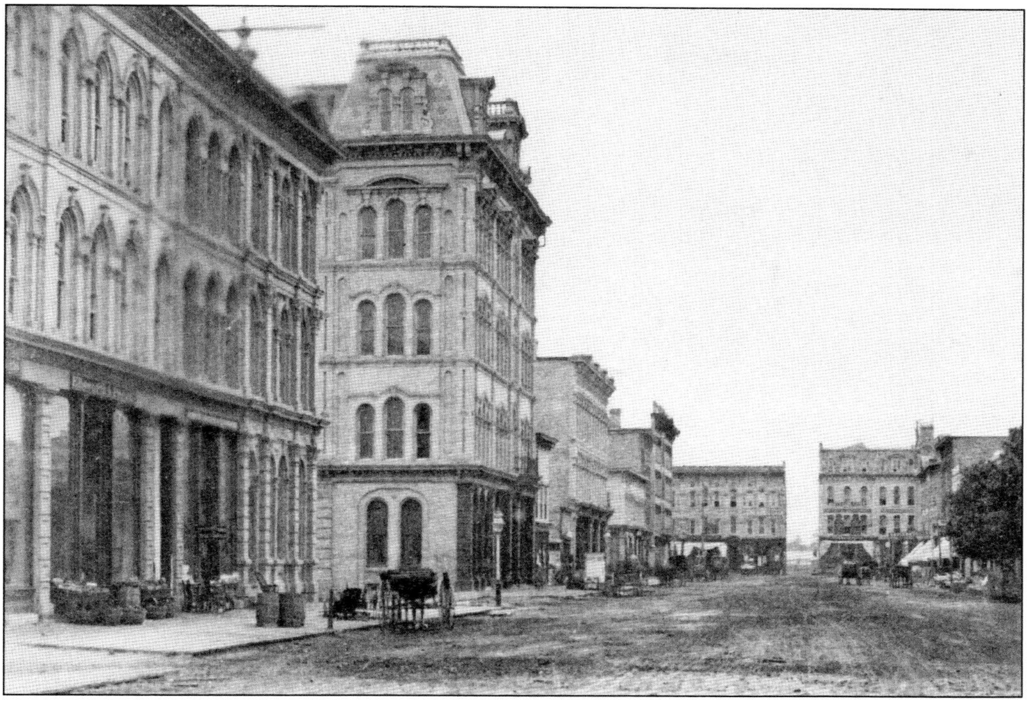

Westover's Opera House was the tallest building in Bay City. Above is a photograph of Center Avenue looking west, taken around 1875. The opera house stands proudly in the center. Westover was still the tallest building when fire broke out on a cold January evening in 1886. According to a *Tribune* writer, when plumes of black smoke "arose heavenward in the breathless air, they sent a feeling of sincere regret through all who witnessed them, for the belief that the bold structure was doomed was entertained for all." The opera house was a total loss. Prof. William Wright, who had offices in the building, was one of many who gathered to watch the fire, and he captured the conflagration on a large canvas. The painting (below) was later presented to fire department chief Harding and given to the Bay County Historical Society in 1948.

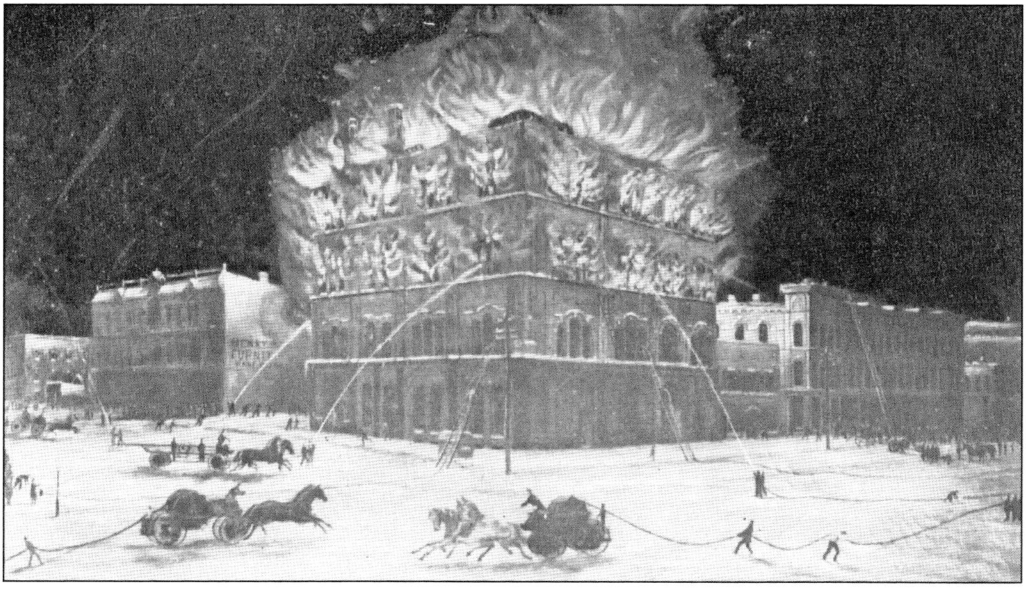

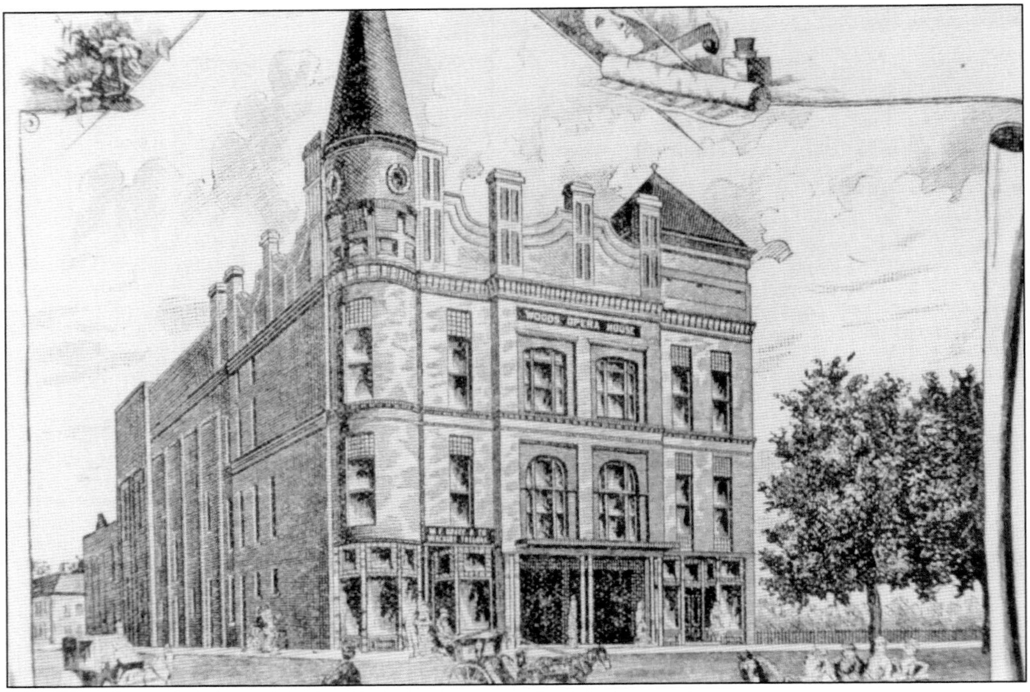

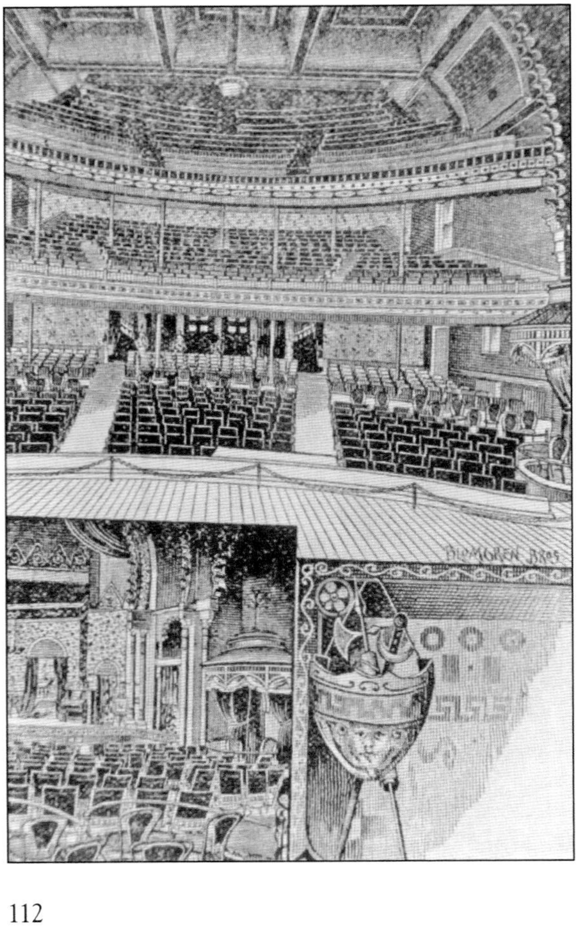

A movement to construct a new opera house in Bay City started in 1881. Several failed attempts by local businessmen and investors to raise funds by selling stocks and offering ticket subscriptions made the project questionable at best. However, Woods, the architect, offered to help fund the proposal. Construction started in January 1886, and Wood's Opera House was completed by September. The building had a Moorish theme and was said to be the finest theater north of Detroit. From the time Wood's opened through December 1899, there were over 100 performances of more than 60 different operas. *The Bohemian Girl*, *La Mascotte*, *The Chimes of Normandy*, *The Mikado*, and *Olivette* were some of the many to grace Wood's stage. In the spring of 1888, famous actor Edwin Booth (brother of John Wilkes Booth) appeared in *Julius Caesar*.

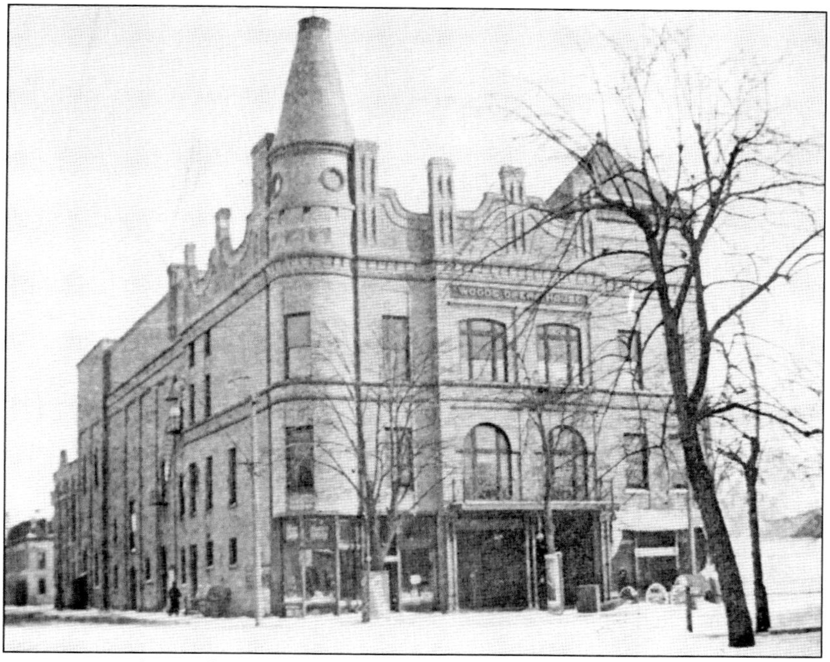

The elaborate stage of Wood's Opera House included several heavy curtains and a drop screen as seen in the T.E. Webster photograph below from around 1887. On August 29, 1902, a fire started on the stage after the actors were finished for the evening. The flammable scenery fed the flames, and soon the building was engulfed. The three-story building quickly became unstable, and firefighters were forced to fight the blaze from the outside. One man was buried under bricks as parts of the wall and roof collapsed. The building was a total loss.

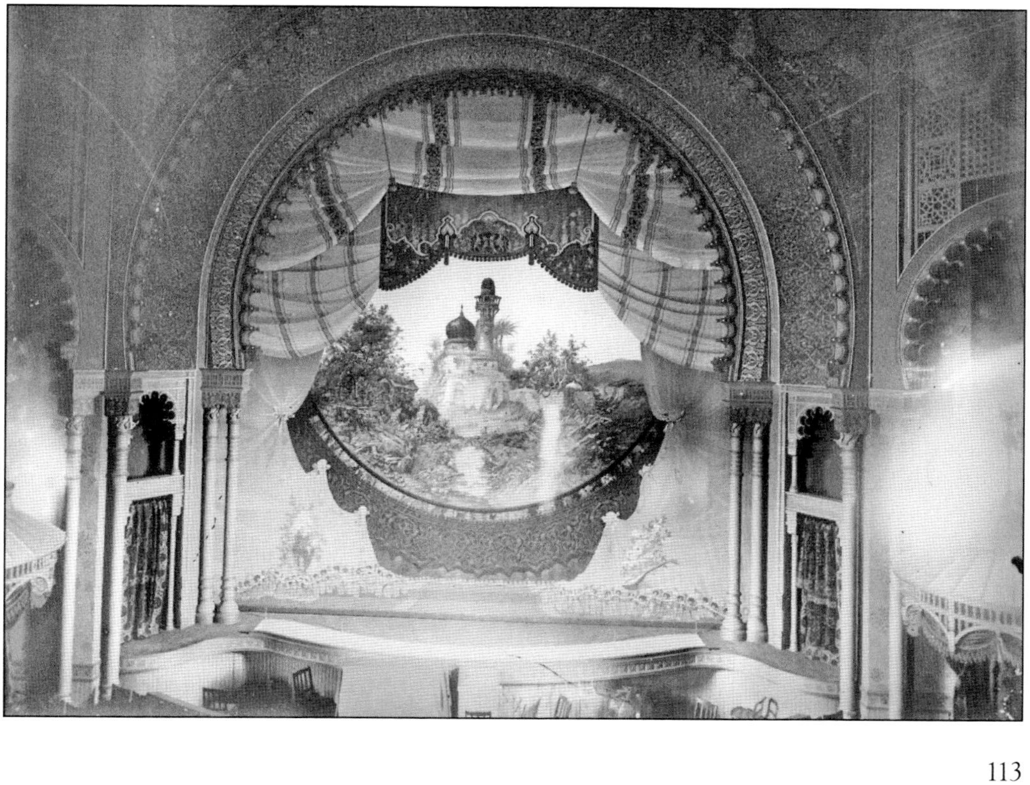

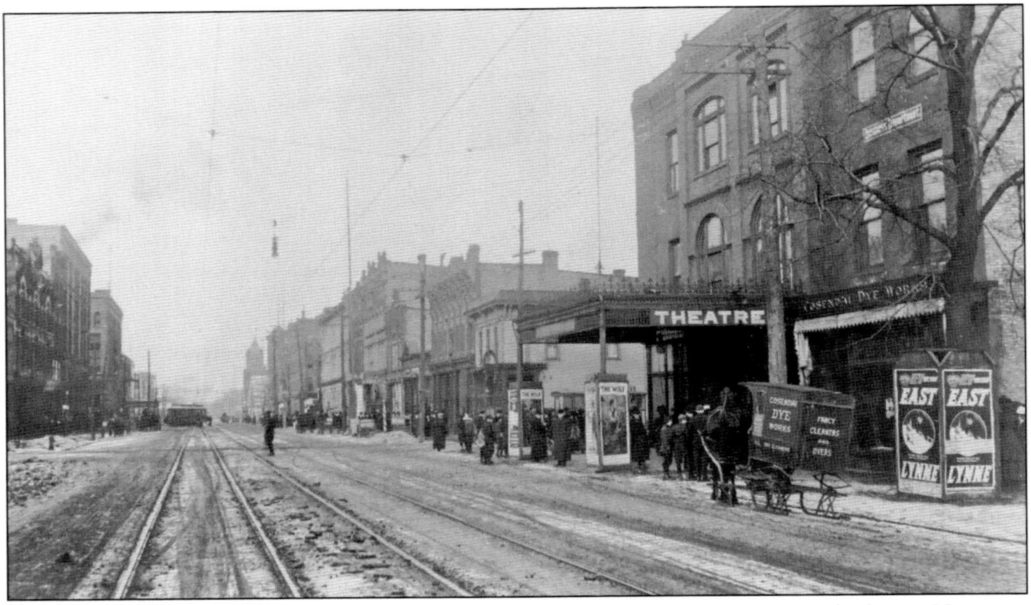

The Washington Theatre was built on the foundation of the burned-out Wood's Opera House in 1903. The above image shows Washington Avenue looking north with the theater at right, around 1905. Many popular stars graced the stage of the Washington, including Maud Adams, Eddie Foy, Marie Dressler, Ethel Barrymore, Eva Tanguay, Richard Mansfield, and Fiske O'Hara. High school graduation programs were held at the Washington, as were many local drama productions from schools and theater organizations. A projection screen made the theater a popular place to see the great movies of the day. A drop screen (below) that featured advertisements from local businesses covered the stage and projection screen when not in use. Bayview Scenic Studio of Bay City painted this screen. This photograph dates to 1926, when the Willys Knight Six Model 70 featured was released.

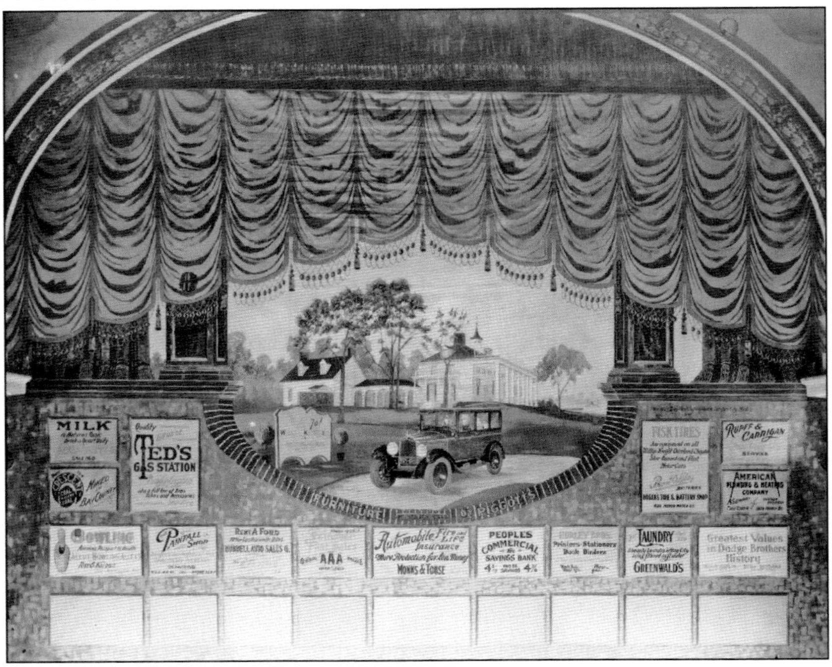

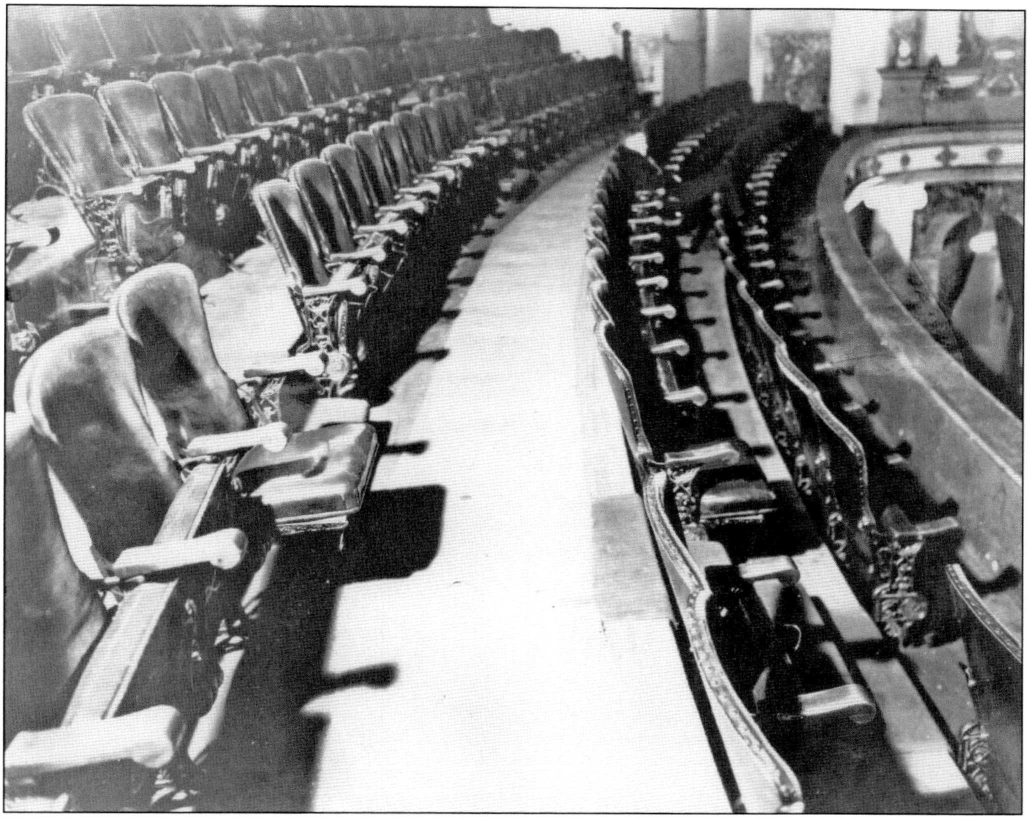

Harriet Gustin Campbell, whose father, Wilbert Gustin, was managing editor of the *Bay City Times* and its drama critic, would accompany her father to the Washington. She said of her experiences, "The Washington Theater in the Early 1900's was a good looking spacious theater with comfortable seats and wide aisles. There was a lot of red velvet in the box seats. The asbestos curtain, behind which all those wonderful and unforgettable plays and actors appear, had, as I recall, the lines from Shakespeare: 'Sermons in stones, books in running brooks, and good in everything.' Pictured on this curtain was a colorful woodland scene with a waterfall cascading over rocks. And no one could forget the hush that fell over the audience as the house lights dimmed and the footlights were turned up. Slowly the curtain rose and the play began."

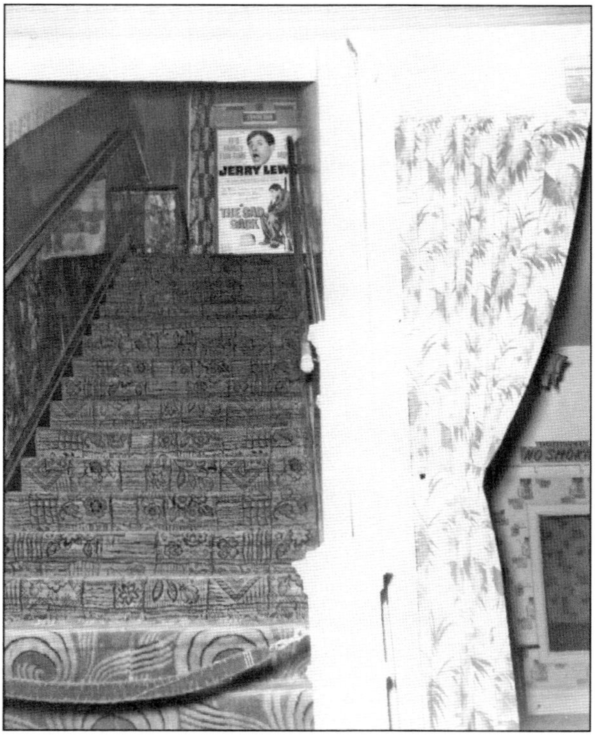

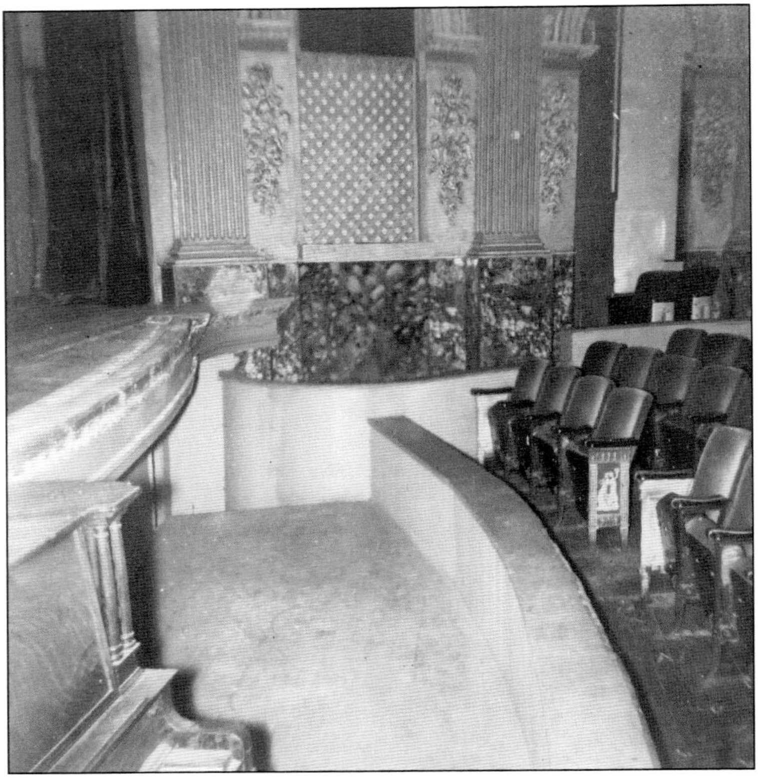

A few local musicians got their start in the orchestra pit of the Washington. Danny Ruso, Isham Jones, Ole Olsen, Gerald Marks, Arthur Amsden, and Ange Lorenzo are just a few who gained regional or national fame after their start at the Washington. This photograph, taken in the later years of the theater, shows a portion of the orchestra pit along with details of the seats and wall ornamentation.

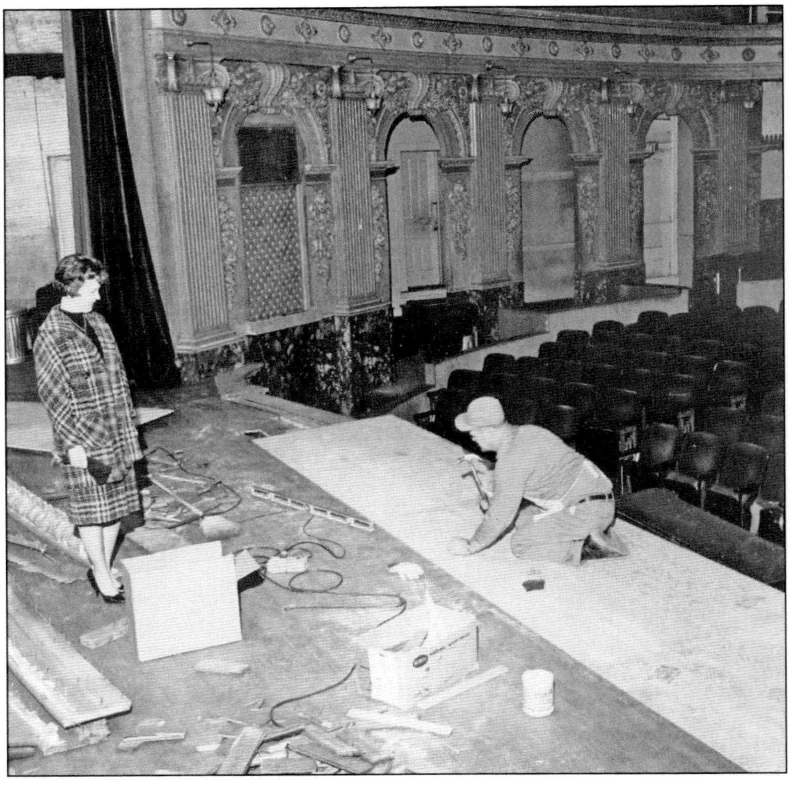

Harriet Gustin Campbell wrote of a night at the Washington: "How Eva [Tanguay] could belt out a song while she was tripping up and down in front of the footlights. Her presentation of the dance of Salome in a costume that dripped with pearls was . . . something to remember . . . walking on stage with that head of John the Baptist on a large platter. Naturally, this provided the grand finale to her show."

At right is the Washington's ticket office, complete with seating chart and a poster for the movie *Creature from the Black Lagoon*. The first moving pictures, Howe's Pictures, started a long tradition of movies at the Washington. Movie stars like Rudolph Valentino, John Barrymore, Clara Bow, Charlie Chaplin, Douglas Fairbanks, and Gloria Swanson replaced live stage personalities. As early movies gave way to the stars of the 1940s and 1950s westerns, Americans made the movie theater a staple of entertainment. The Washington, however, featured both movies and live shows until it was closed. One of the last scheduled live acts was a rendition of Shakespeare's *Twelfth Night* by the Canadian Players on March 4, 1963, only three months before the curtain dropped for the final time. The Washington was razed for a municipal parking lot later in 1963.

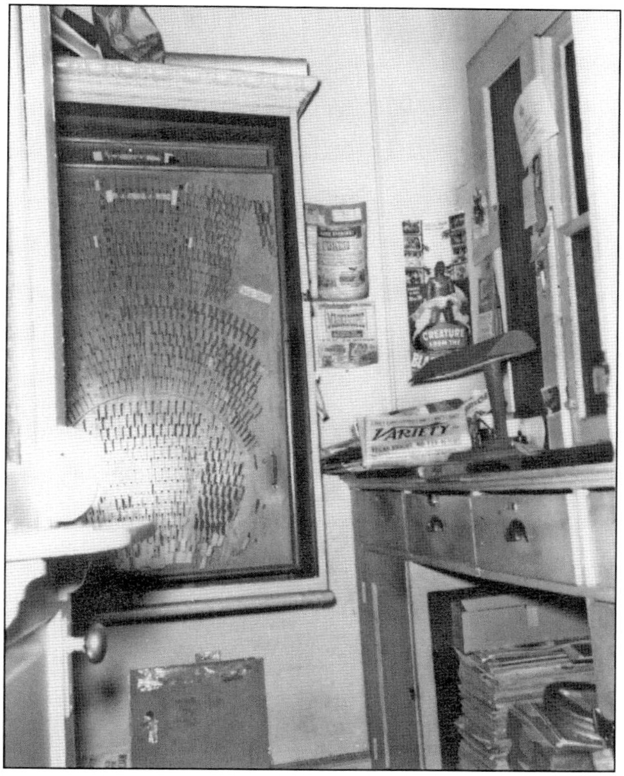

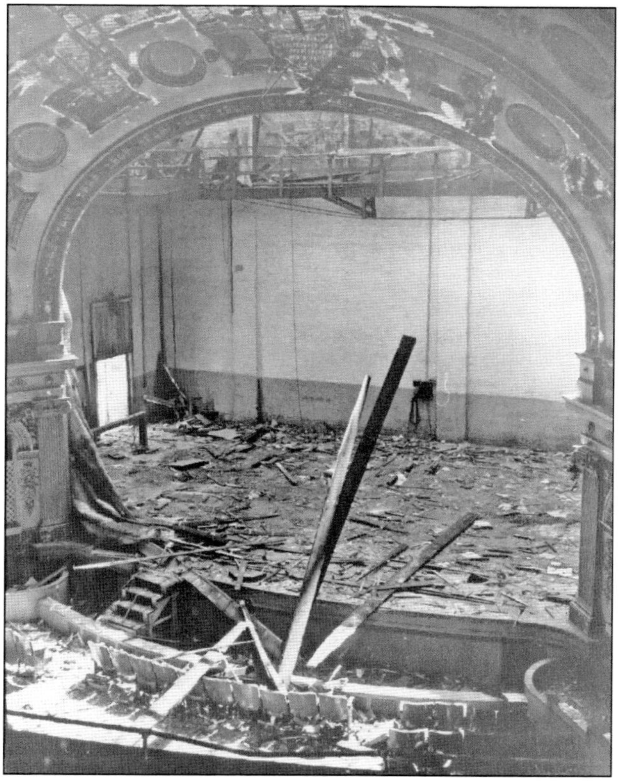

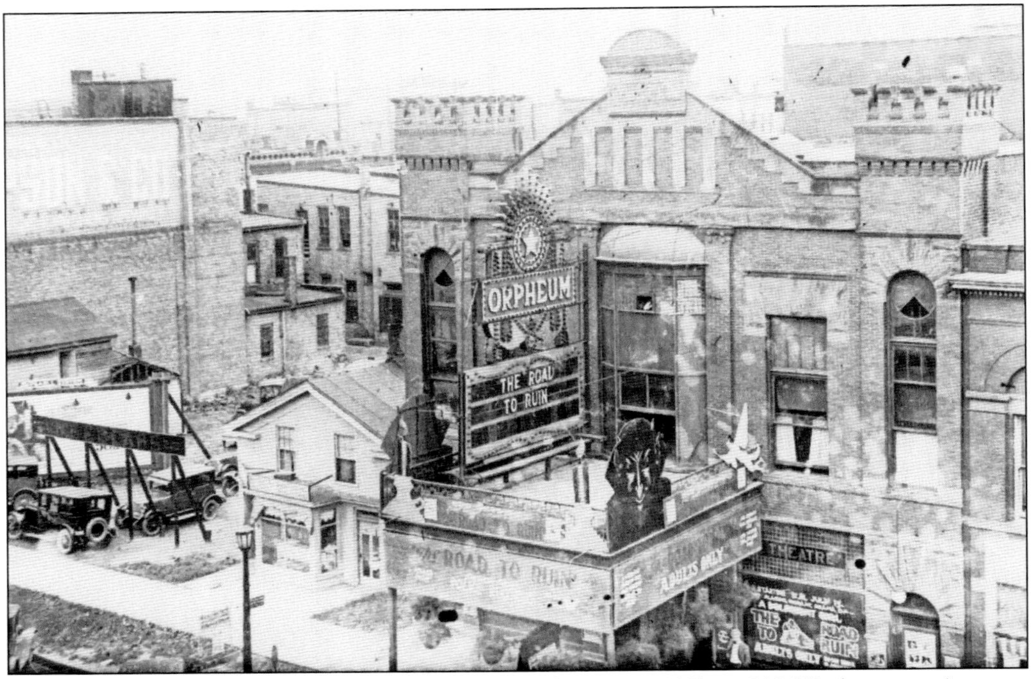

Originally opened as the Bijou Theater in 1908 (see page 109) at 913 Washington Avenue, the vaudeville house became the Orpheum briefly between 1920 and 1930. In the photograph above, the Orpheum is advertising as "adults only," which comprised the majority of the movies shown there during this time. Between June and October 1930, the theater underwent a massive renovation, with substantial changes to the exterior and interior surfaces. The new Mayan theme gave the theater a distinctive look, and it was also rechristened the Bay Theater. In October 1957, the theater became the State, a name it still carries to this day.

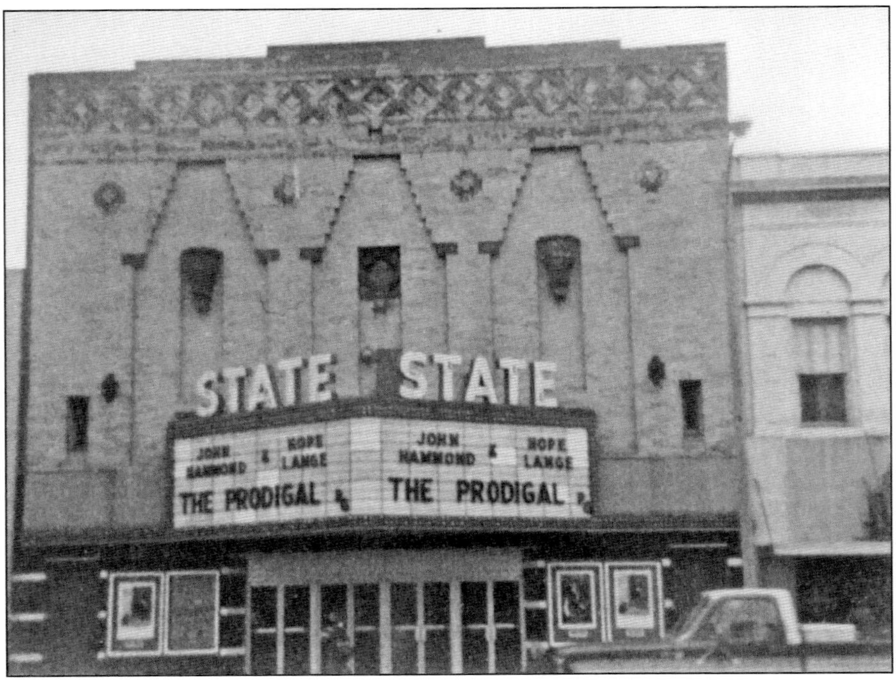

A *Times* reviewer wrote that the Regent theater in the Davidson building was said to be one of the finest, most modern, and up-to-date theaters in the state of Michigan. "Comfortable in its appointments, offering high class vaudeville and moving pictures, the Regent theater is the cream of the local theaters." Built in 1918, the 1,400-seat Regent had an eight-piece orchestra and an organist. At right, *With Byrd at the South Pole* is playing at the Regent around 1930. The Regent's stage, curtains, and drop curtain are redolent with local advertisements of the day. The Regent closed in October 1957, just as the Bay Theatre was reopening across the street after a renovation.

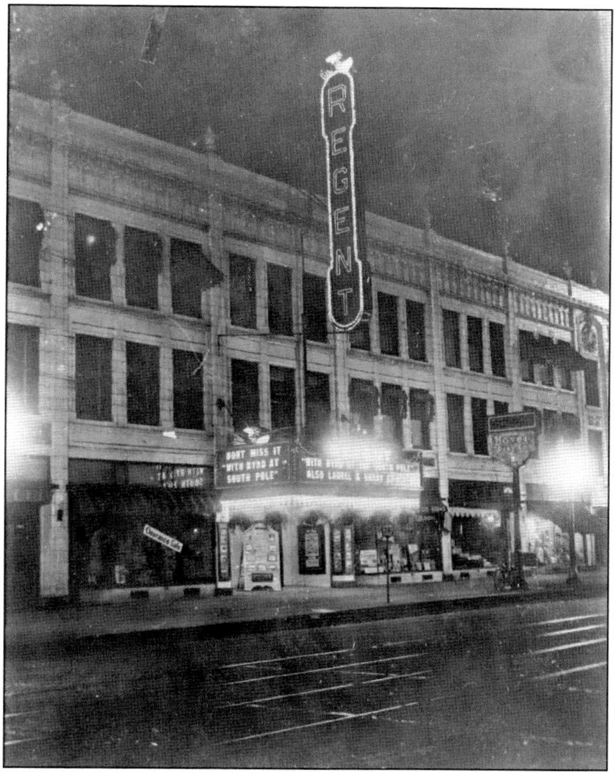

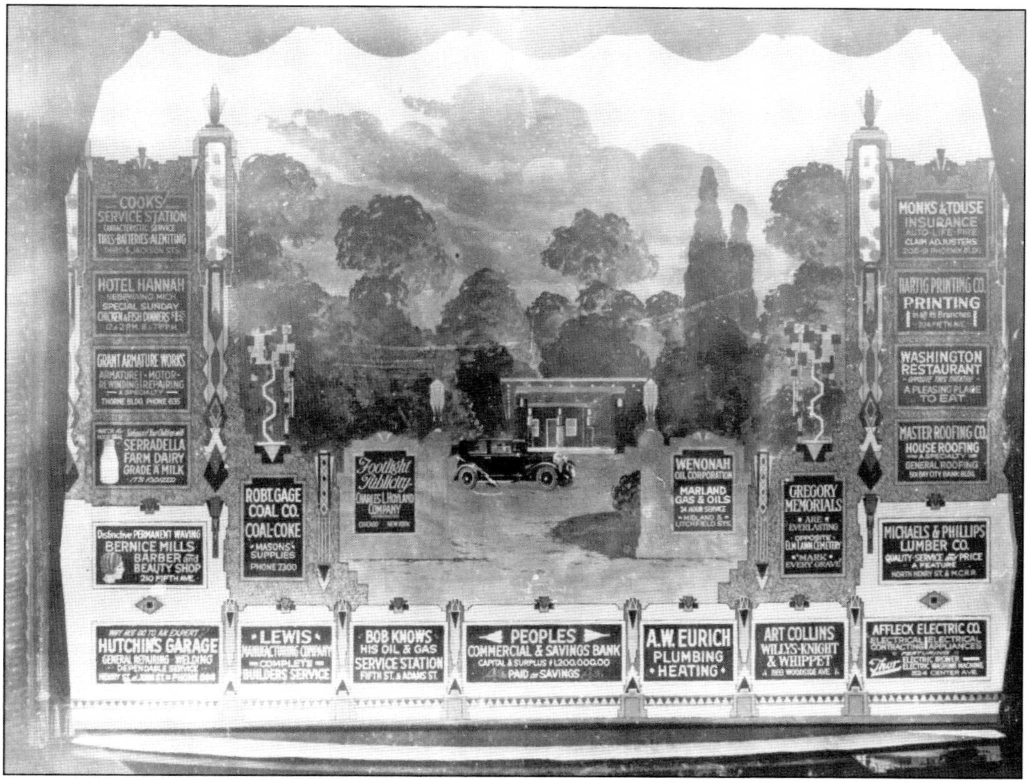

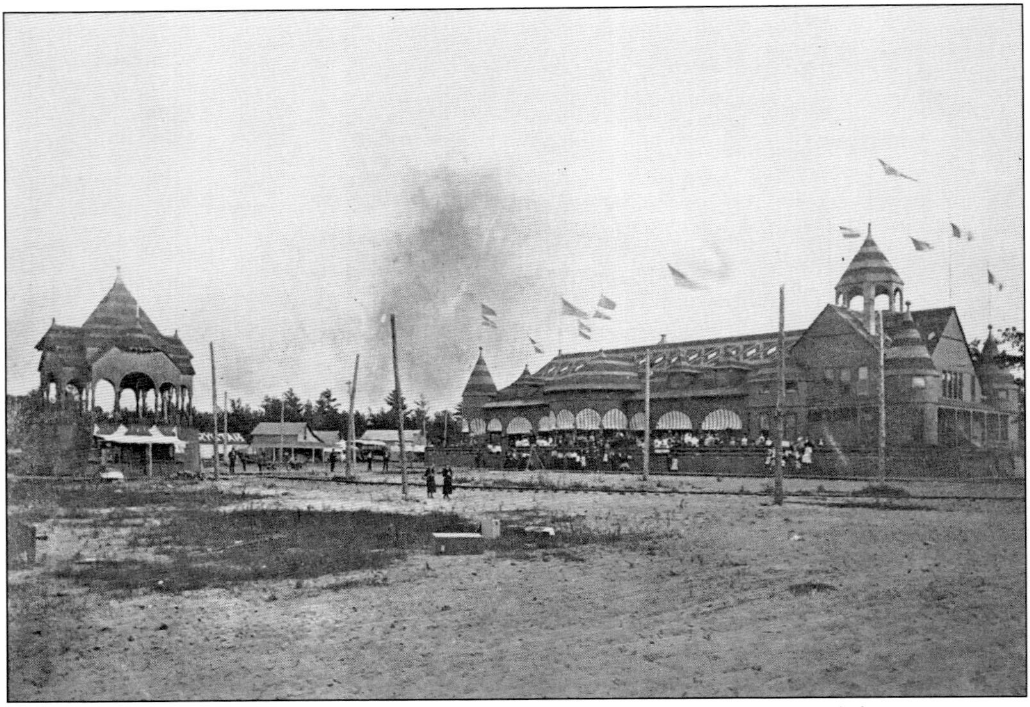

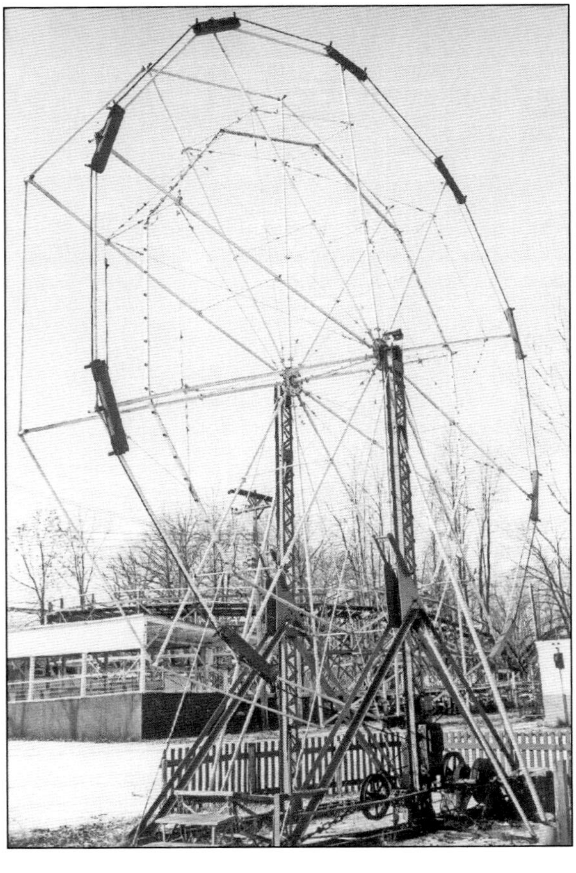

Bay City once boasted the most popular Michigan resort south of Mackinac Island. Originally called the Wenona Beach Entertainment Park, it was started in 1889 on the 50-acre site of Wenona Beach, on the shore of Saginaw Bay. The early buildings consisted of a recreation and amusement pavilion, a pier and boardwalk 200 feet into Saginaw Bay, a boat-rental facility, a swimming beach, and picnic tables.

Dwindling patronage of a park that had not seen updates for many years finally caught up with Wenona Beach. In the summer of 1965, mobile homes started occupying parts of the park. The dilapidated casino and roller rink were ordered destroyed by the Bangor Township Fire Department. The area became Wenona Beach Estates, where South Casino and North Casino Beach Streets still help to remember the area's past glory.

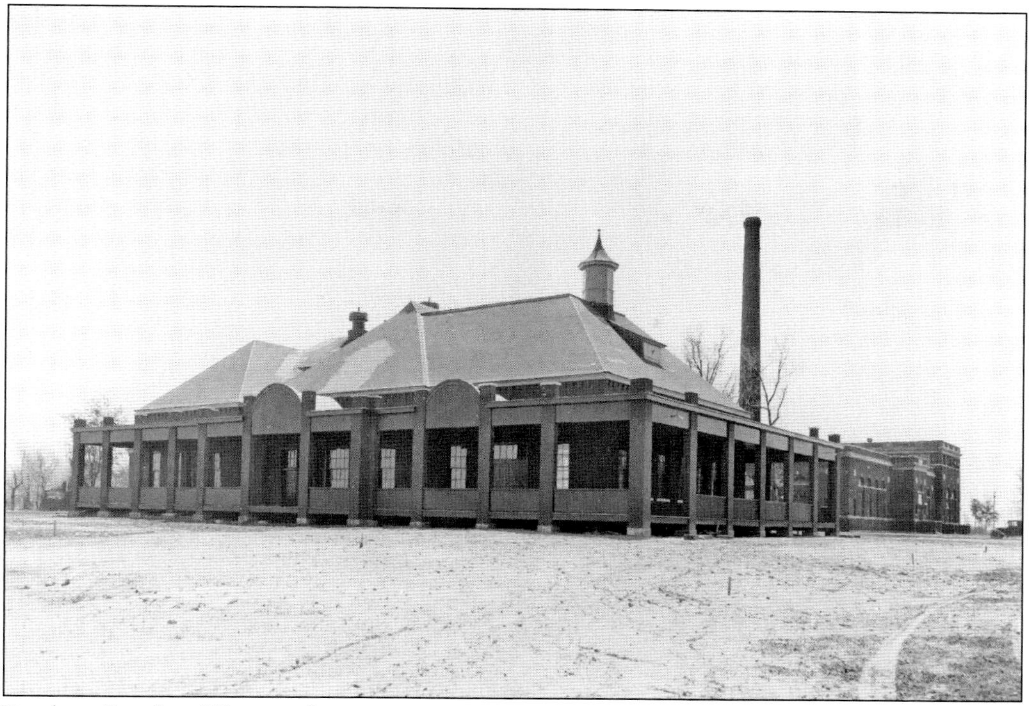

Paraleon Beach at Waterworks Park was the name given to the site at the end of State Park Drive where it meets the bay. The original waterworks building was repurposed in the 1930s as a pavilion, eventually housing a restaurant called Hi-Lo Gardens. Dancing was one of the attractions offered at the park pavilion, and the park also featured a Ferris wheel and a merry-go-round at one time.

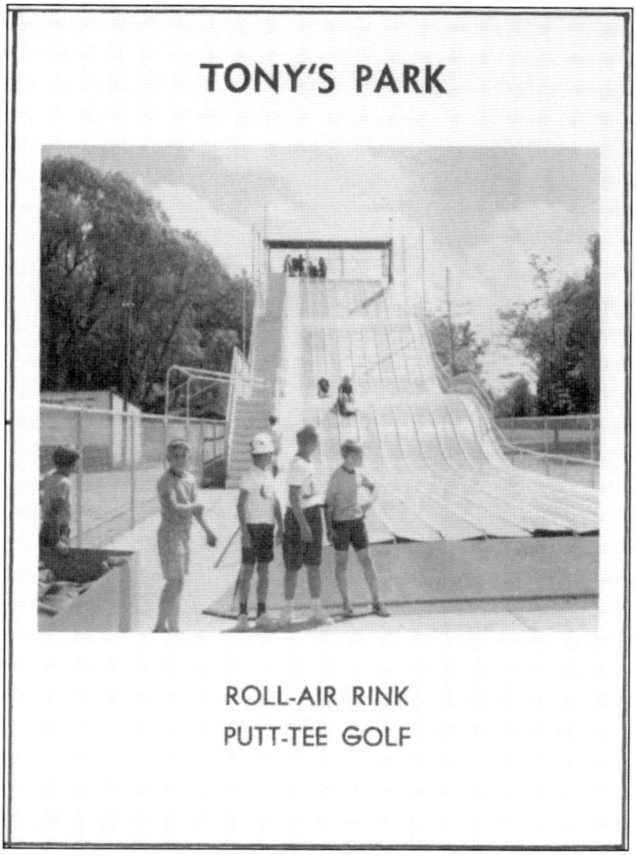

Tony's Amusement Park was started near Bay City State Park in the 1940s, and was a favorite of area children into the 1980s. The park included a boat ride, arcade, train, kiddie cars, and a large slide. The carousel, one of the focal points of the park since 1953, was restored in the early 1980s and ended up at Deer Acres when Tony's Park closed.

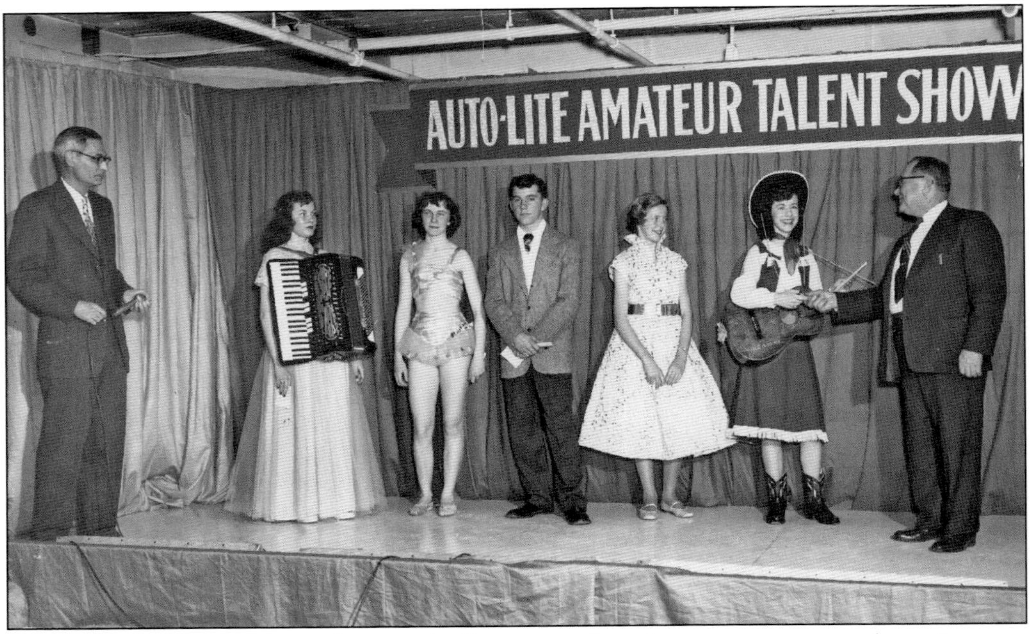

In the days before amateur videos on the Internet, talent showcases were prevalent. Amateur talent shows, similar to the earlier vaudeville art form, were essentially variety shows with a cash prize and possibility of discovery. The Electric Auto-Lite Company hosted a series of these competitions starting in 1954 as part of its salute to automobile companies. Held on a makeshift stage in its plant on Morton Street, a series of five shows was emceed by plant manager Clark F. Adams. The winner of each show competed in a live finals event that aired on WNEM TV-5. The Rockettes and Junior Rockettes of the Theatrical Arts Guild were the opening and closing acts. In 1954, the top winner was 15-year-old accordionist Tommy Miller, who also received the chance to appear on the *Spotlight on Youth* talent revue at the Washington Theatre.

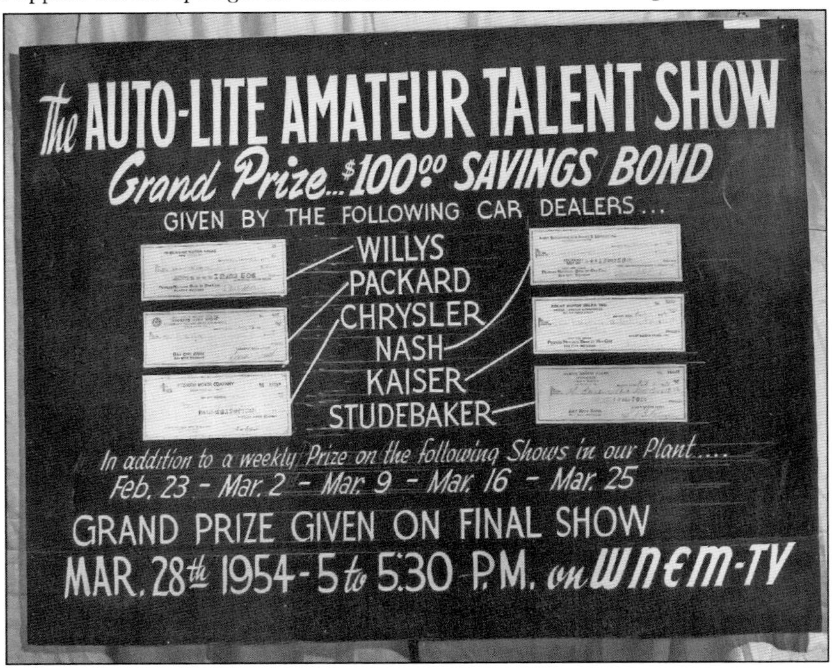

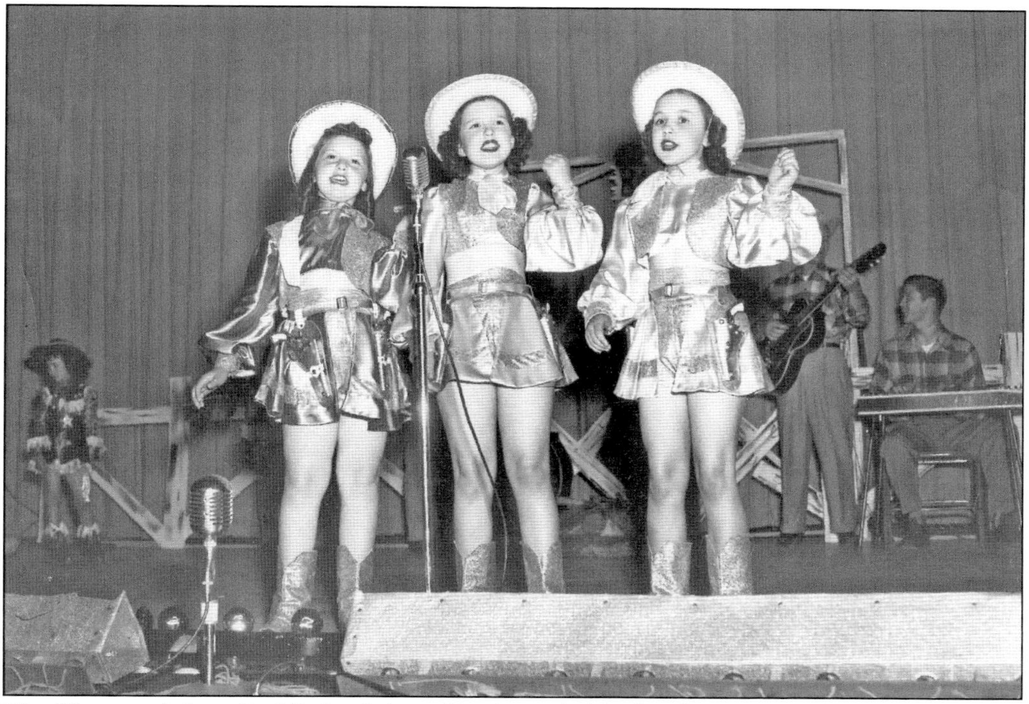

The Theatrical Arts Guild's *Spotlight on Youth* was led by local WBCM radio personality and musician Lionell "Nello" DeRemer, and routinely offered area youth a way to showcase their talents, "overcome shyness and lack of confidence," and build "poise, reliance, [and the] ability to meet others," according to a February 1947 script. Below, Shirley Koblinsky plays the part of a microphone page during a quiz segment; many of these shows were also broadcast on WBCM radio.

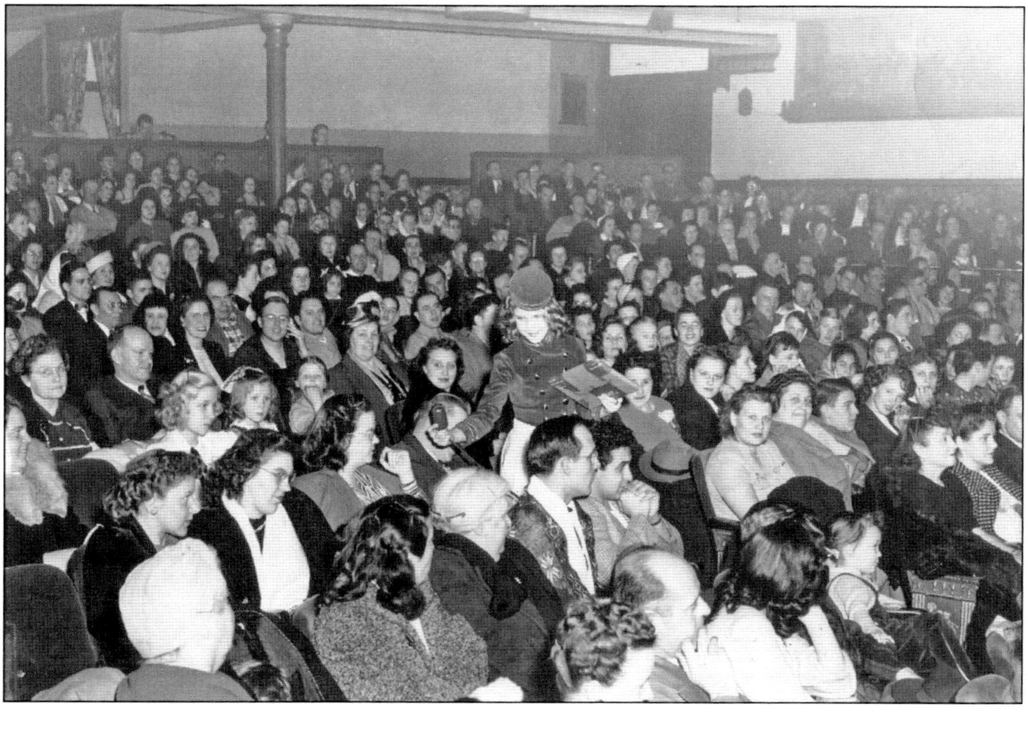

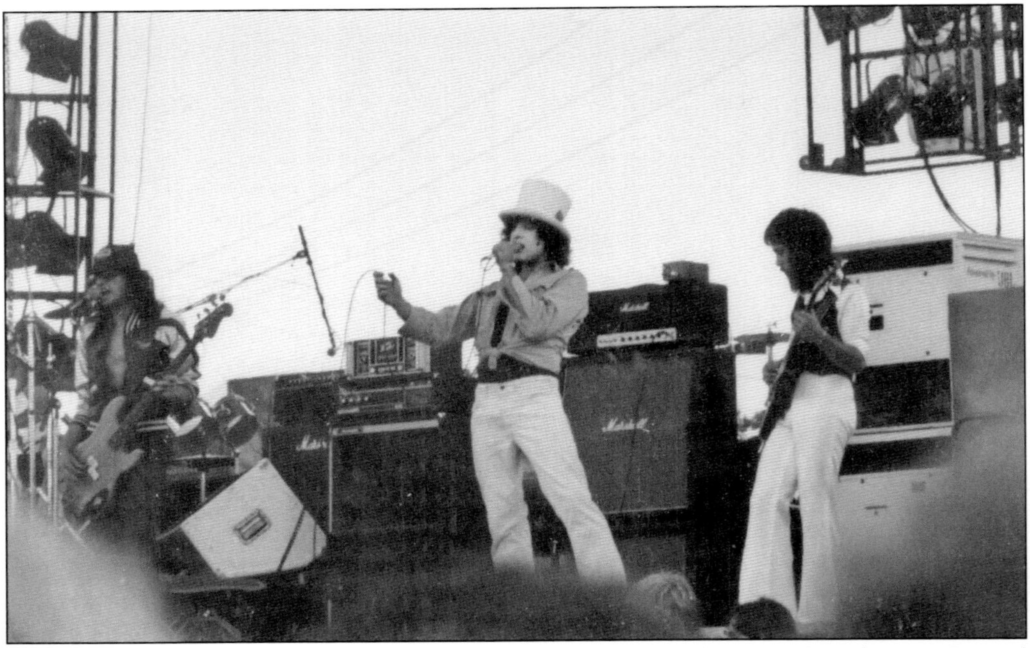

Summer Celebration was a series of four major concert events held at Engel Stadium at Central High School's campus on Columbus Avenue. The concert series was organized and sponsored by the Central High Booster Club. The first concert, held in 1977, featured bands REO Speedwagon, Brownsville Station, Firefall, and Salem Witchcraft and drew 9,000 fans. In 1978, veteran rocker and Michigan native Bob Seger (with the Silver Bullet Band) headlined the concert, supported by Van Halen, and local bands including Couture (pictured above). Attendance estimates for this 1978 concert, held on August 19, were 24,000 fans, many of whom camped the night before through a torrential rainstorm until the gates opened at 11:00 am the next day. The first of the bands did not go on until 4:00 pm. (Above, courtesy of Ray Torres; below, courtesy of Don Grischke.)

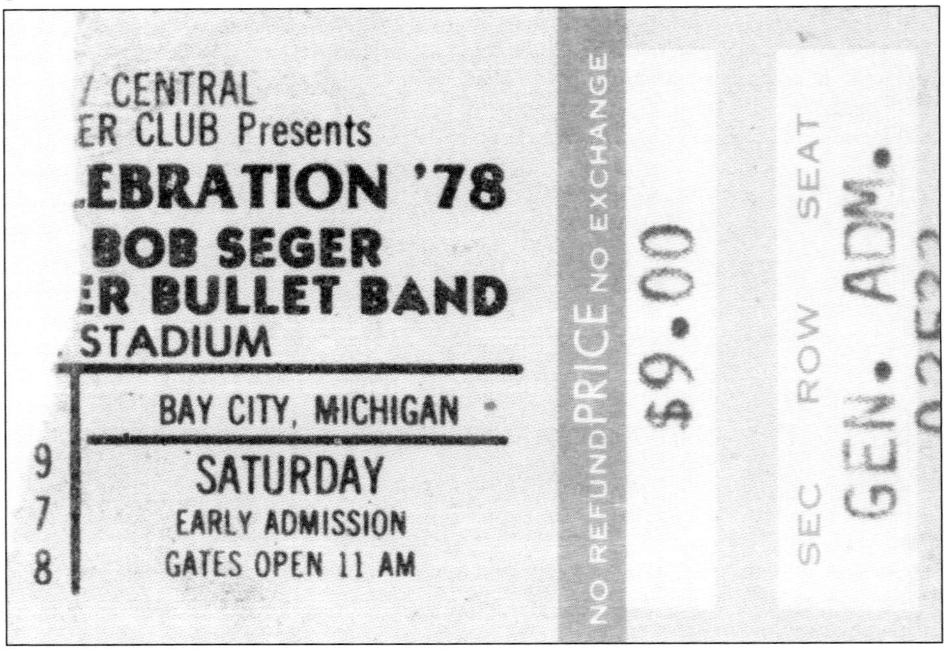

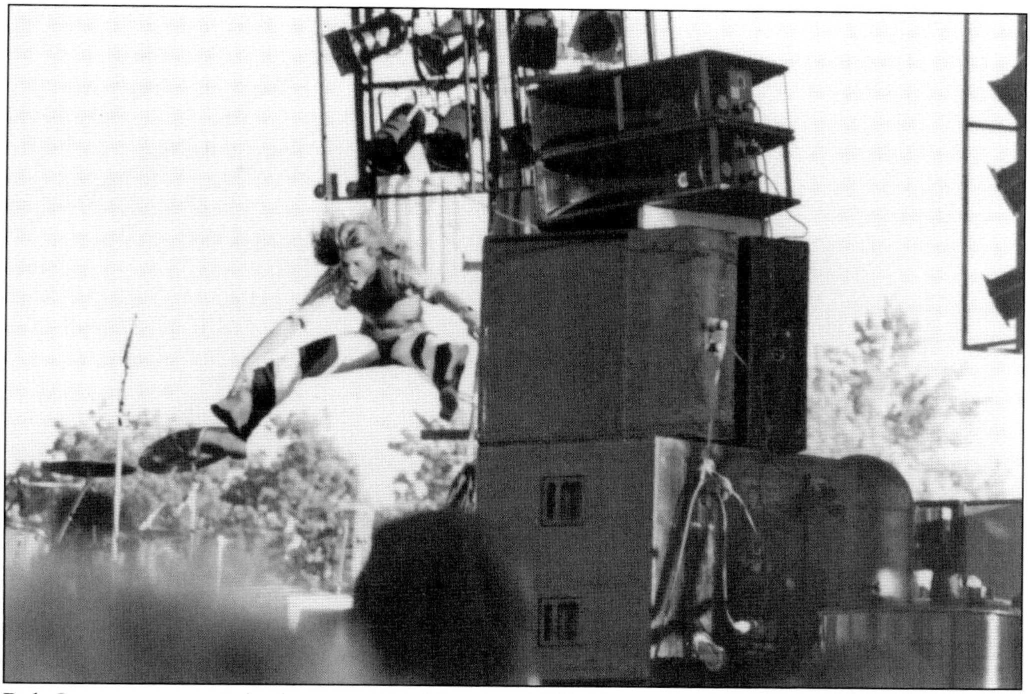

Bob Seger was certainly the star of Celebration 1978. One of his opening acts was a relatively unknown band named Van Halen. The above image captures lead singer David Lee Roth in one of his signature moves. Below, Roth, at left, is flanked by bassist Michael Anthony, guitarist Eddie Van Halen, and drummer Alex Van Halen barely visible behind the drum kit. Van Halen would go on to become one of the best-known rock bands of the 1980s. Summer Celebration continued in 1979 with Ted Nugent and the Babys playing to a crowd of 17,500. In 1980, Bob Seger was back, along with Mitch Ryder and Detroit Wheels and the Rockets. They played to a crowd of 14,500 ticketholders in what would be the final Summer Celebration concert. (Both, courtesy of Roy Torres.)

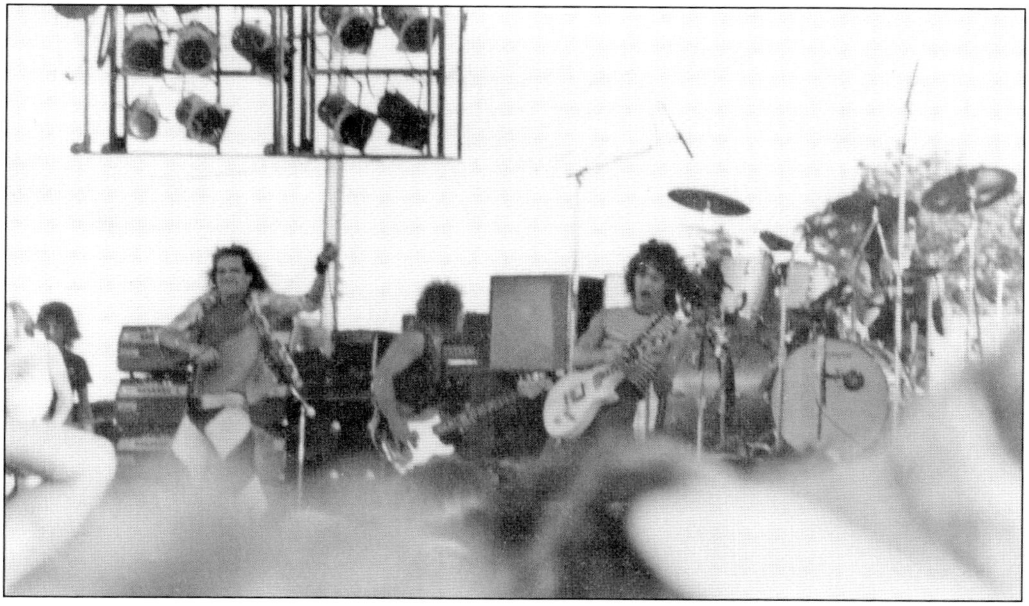

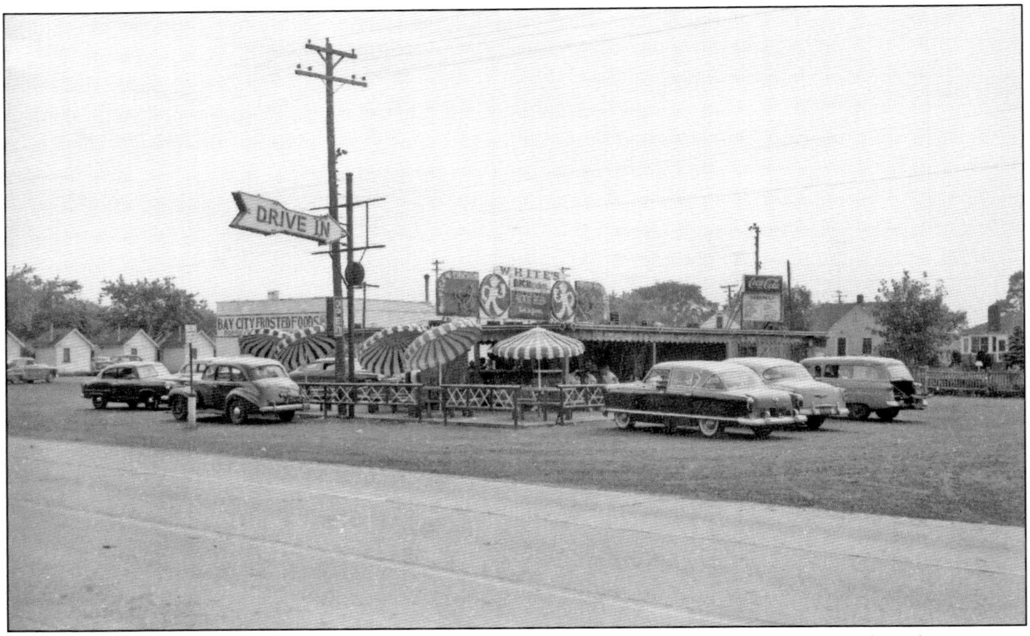

The drive-in restaurant became another icon of the automobile days of the mid-20th century. White's Restaurant was located on the west side of North Euclid Avenue, between West Ohio and West Indiana Streets. Originally started as a drive-in during the 1950s, the canopied seating area was later enclosed and the drive-in converted to a standard restaurant. White's was sold in the 1990s and has been home to several restaurants since. Richie's Drive-In was located on the east side of North Euclid Avenue, south of North Union Street. Started in 1958, it was a popular hang-out and place of employment for teenagers during the 1960s and 1970s. It later became Richie's Restaurant, a name it kept until 1980. Later known as Wolf's Restaurant, it closed in the mid-1980s and was later torn down. A gas and service station now occupies the site.

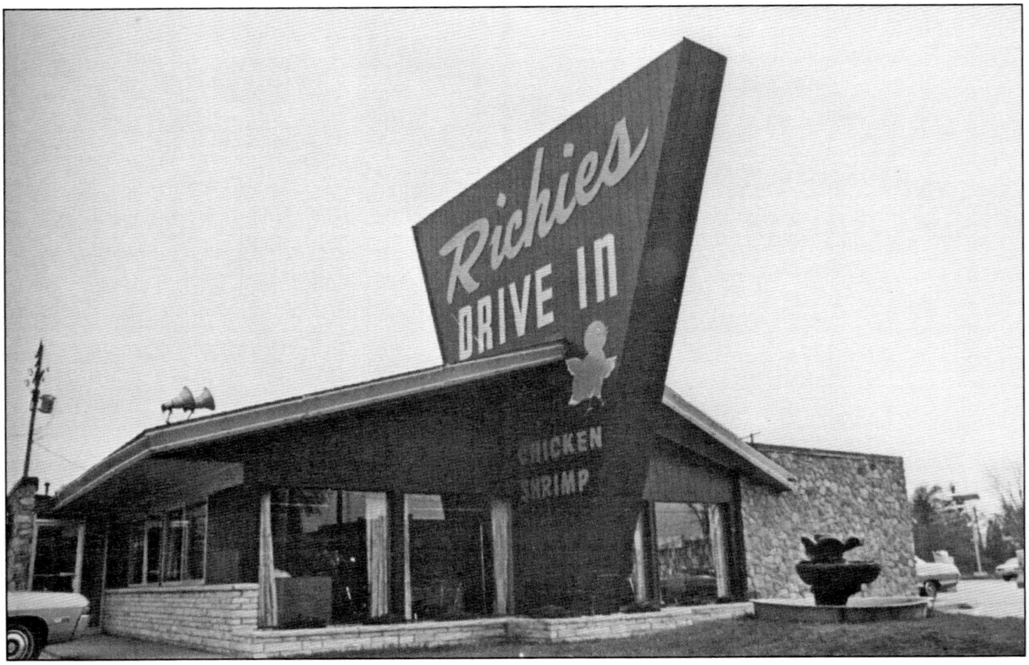

Bibliography

Bloomfield, Ron. *Maritime Bay County*. Charleston, SC: Arcadia Publishing, 2009.

————. *Legendary Locals of Bay City Michigan*. Charleston, SC: Arcadia Publishing, 2012.

Butterfield, George Ernest (ed). *Bay County Past and Present* (Centennial Edition). Bay City, MI: Bay City Board of Education, 1957.

Gansser, Augustus H. *History of Bay County, Michigan and Representative Citizens*. Chicago, IL: Richmond and Arnold, 1905.

History of Bay County Michigan. Chicago, IL: H.R. Page and Company, 1883.

Katzinger, Leon. *Bay City in Vintage Post Cards*. Charleston, SC: Arcadia Publishing, 2004.

————. *Then and Now: Bay City*. Charleston, SC: Arcadia Publishing, 2004.

Kilar, Jeremy W., and Ron Bloomfield. *Bay City Logbook, An Illustrated History*. St. Louis, MO: G. Bradley Publishing Inc., 1996.

Pediment Publishing. *Through the Lens, a Visual History of Bay County*. The Pediment Group, 2008.

Watson, James R. *Wenona Beach*. Bay City, MI: self-published, 1988.

————. *Last Chance to Wenona Beach*. Bay City, MI: self-published, 2013.

Wolicki, Dale, and the Bay County Historical Society. *The Historic Architecture of Bay City, Michigan*. Bay City, MI: Bay County Historical Society, 1998.